Sufi Rituals and Practices

Sufi Rituals and Practices

Experiences from South Asia, 1200–1450

KASHSHAF GHANI

OXFORD
UNIVERSITY PRESS

OXFORD
UNIVERSITY PRESS

Great Clarendon Street, Oxford, OX2 6DP,
United Kingdom

Oxford University Press is a department of the University of Oxford.
It furthers the University's objective of excellence in research, scholarship,
and education by publishing worldwide. Oxford is a registered trade mark of
Oxford University Press in the UK and in certain other countries

Published in the United States of America by Oxford University Press
198 Madison Avenue, New York, NY 10016, United States of America

British Library Cataloguing in Publication Data

Data available

Library of Congress Control Number: 2023943781

ISBN 978–0–19–288922–5

DOI: 10.1093/oso/9780192889225.001.0001

Acknowledgements

I remain deeply grateful to all those who, over the years, have extended their generous help and kind support. Rather than a practice, this note sincerely acknowledges their kind-heartedness in the journey towards making this book.

My academic mentor Amit Dey's relentless support and meticulous supervision made my doctoral research possible. This book draws from that foundational research expanded over the years. His invaluable suggestions, long discussions, and perceptive observations have been of great value at all times. Mere thanks can never do justice to his multifaceted contribution to my life and work.

I remain indebted to my teachers—Rajat Kanta Ray, Subhas Ranjan Chakravarty, Bhaskar Chakrabarty, Shireen Maswood, Hari Vasudevan, Madhumita Mazumdar, Suchandra Ghosh, and Bishnupriya Basak. It feels terrible that Hari could not see this finished work. I have been fortunate to receive suggestions and guidance from many professors in the course of my research—Ramakanta Chakrabarty, Akhtar Hussain, Ranjit Sen, Kazi Sufior Rahaman, Rajsekhar Basu, Abdul Gani Imaratwale and Dilip Kumar Mohanta. I have always benefitted from their experience and insight. Samita Sen—under whom I was fortunate to study during my MA, and thereafter work with on the SEPHIS e-Magazine project—has always been there like a pillar of guidance and support. The things that I have learnt from her in all these years—academic and professional—are too valuable to be thanked for. I am grateful to her for being so encouraging, understanding, and affectionate.

Bruce Lawrence and Carl Ernst have been extremely generous to extend their help and guidance whenever I approached them. They introduced me to Scott Kugle, who has always been helpful. No amount of thanks is enough for their kindness. I remain grateful to Tony Stewart and Arthur Buehler for sharing with me their experiences of researching on Sufism in South Asia. Lloyd Ridgeon has been a great friend, and his suggestions, collaboration, and generous hospitality has only benefitted my research. Years ago, as a doctoral student, I met Suleman Siddiqi in a conference. Ever since, he has always been helpful, kind, and generous, allowing me to learn from his lifelong expertise on Deccan Sufism, and unhesitatingly sharing his valuable insights and experience.

I had the opportunity of accessing many libraries both in Kolkata and beyond—National Library (Kolkata), The Asiatic Society (Kolkata), Calcutta University Central Library (Kolkata), Calcutta University Library (Alipore Campus, Kolkata), Centre for Studies in Social Sciences Calcutta (Kolkata), Ramakrishna Mission Institute of Culture (Golpark, Kolkata), Iran Society (Kolkata), Presidency College (Kolkata), Osmania University (Hyderabad), Nehru Memorial Museum and Library (New Delhi), Jawaharlal Nehru University (New Delhi), the Jamia Millia Islamia (New Delhi), Dhaka University (Dhaka), Asiatic Society (Dhaka), and BULAC (Paris). Carrying out research work in these libraries would not have been possible without the help and cooperation from their staff. Particularly Asim Mukherjee at National Library Kolkata and Shabbir Ahmed at The Asiatic Society. Without the generous hospitality of my elder brother Arshad Amin and his wife Rebecca, who as a faculty facilitated my access to the Dhaka University, the research at Dhaka would have been an uphill task.

My seniors, from college and university, have been an unending source of support, and I sincerely thank Kingshuk Chatterjee, Bodhisattwa Kar, Rohan Deb Roy, Soumen Mukherjee, and Rajarshi Ghose. Right from the days of our doctoral research, Sraman Mukherjee has been a perennial source of encouragement and delight, ever-willing to happily lend his support—in crisis and company.

My friends—Rahul Banerjee, Swastick Basu Mallick, Arka Mukherjee, Samriddhi Sankar Ray, Ritoban Das, Shahabul Islam Gazi, Jayati Mal, Moidul Islam, Lyric Banerjee, Naba Gopal Roy, Shahnaz Begum, Debraj Chakraborty, Nadeem Akhtar, Hardik Brata Biswas, Madhurima Mukherjee, Santanu Sengupta—have always extended their kind support. It is difficult to appropriately thank Atig Ghosh, who has been a close and dear friend from school days. Thanks to Sreerupa Sengupta for always being there. Pratyay Nath, a fellow medievalist on Mughal South Asia, has seen and engaged with my work closely for many years now. His observations and insights have always been of great help.

Descendants of Shaykh Nizam al-Din Awliya, Kamal Nizami and his family, and especially Kalim Nizami, have been like a family for generations, and deserve special thanks for helping me access sites and resources, but especially for the experience, that has enriched this work manifold.

This book took its final form at Nalanda University, where I joined at its inception and continue to teach. I thank the university for their support at all times, especially former Vice Chancellor Gopa Sabharwal whose unwavering support and encouragement to faculty research kept this book on track amidst many challenges. I am deeply thankful to all my colleagues who, over the years, have been generous with their ideas, observations, encouragement, and moments of laughter. I fondly recall the warm collegiality and enjoyable company of Dean Anjana Sharma, Samuel Wright (Sam), Sraman Mukherjee, Ranu Roychoudhuri, Abhishek Amar, Andrea Acri, Max Deeg, Sean Kerr, Yann Montelle, and Sumanth Paranji. From the earliest days at Nalanda, Aviram Sharma and Somnath-*da* (Bandyopadhyay) have been my lifeline, not to forget Sangeeta *boudi's* wonderful and untiring hospitality. They have been warm-hearted colleagues, adventurous companions, careful listeners, engaging discussants, yet perceptive critics—allowing me to benefit from their perspectives as thoughtful and encouraging non-specialists.

Over the years my students at Nalanda in the Sufism course have been enthusiastic participants, and a great source of questions, critical observations, and constructive discussion, many of which flowed into this work—Aditya, Anmol, Theresa, Gilani, Nupur, Oshin, Rohith, Anantha, Rajnish, Ripunjay, Sachindra, Shubham Das, Shubham Arora, Andrei, Shalini, and Shiva Madhuri. I am thankful to all of them, and others like Umang, Deepa, Annalisa, Shaashi, and Akiro for freely sharing their thoughts, in class and during the site visits.

I am thankful to the editorial team at Oxford University Press for seeing this project to its completion, through many challenges.

This book is dedicated to my parents. No gratitude is ever sufficient for the support I always had from my family—my sister and parents. Their unconditional love, laughter, life lessons, encouragement, and sacrifice, but most importantly their *duas,* make the seemingly impossible, possible.

Rajgir
28 September 2023/12 Rabi ul Awwal 1445

Contents

Figures and Map

Figures

Map

Note on Translation and Transliteration

Since this work makes use of a variety of Persian and Arabic terms, I have attempted, as far as possible, to use their transliterated forms instead of the English equivalents. Some words like sufism and sufi are anglicized. Also, words like *sama* and *zikr* are partly anglicized due to their frequent usage. Modern forms of the names of places are retained. Diacritical marks have not been used for ease of reading.

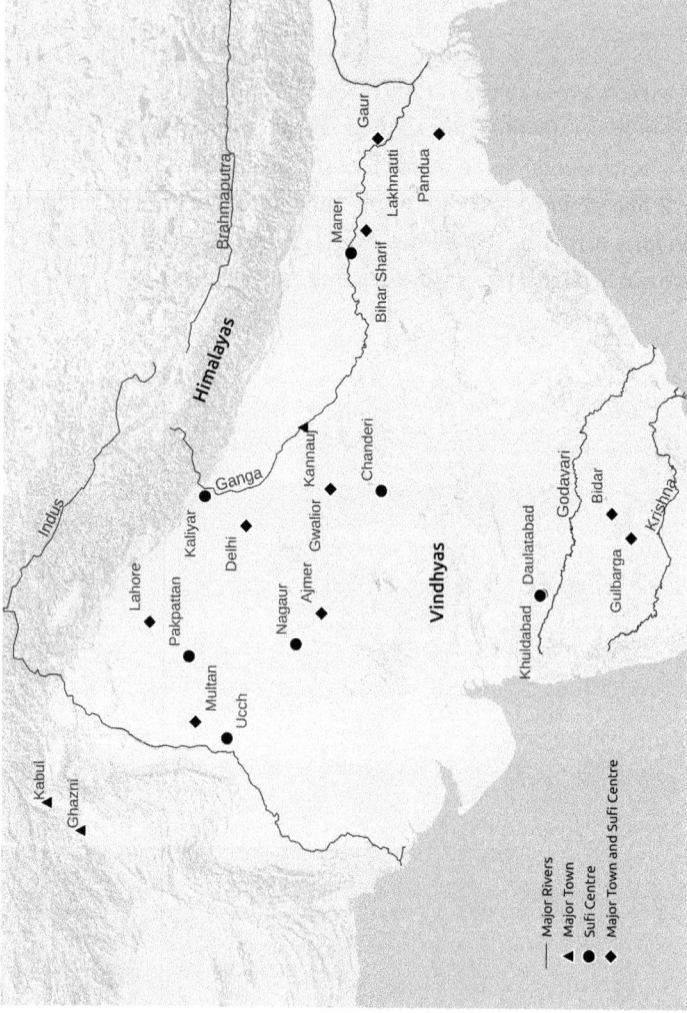

Map 1 Map of Important Sufi Centres in South Asia
Ishaan Kochhar

Introduction

What is Sama? Practice and Debate

Sufism represents the spiritual dimension of Islam in the doctrinal sense. It also signifies an individual's experience of a spiritual journey undertaken through formal initiation under a Sufi master, or being attached to a Sufi saint or his shrine as a lay follower. A seeker in the Sufi path is driven by a deep yearning and quest for spiritual salvation through intense devotion to the words of God revealed in the Quran, combined with the traditions of Prophet Muhammad as the perfect model. As a practice, the Sufi path requires an individual to advance and overcome his own *self*, towards a limitless realization of the Divine, with the ultimate aim of spiritual union with God. Sufi masters describe this as a journey where the path is uncharted, the boundaries limitless, and the goal elusive. This abstraction is one of the ways to understand the idea of Sufism.

Sufism, over its formative period, thus came to signify an interpersonal relation with God, where the disciple seeks the ultimate aim of spiritual union through rigorous practice of prayers, litanies, and meditative exercises. These are aimed towards the seeker's moral and spiritual elevation by purging his heart of insidious and materialist tendencies. Passing through long periods of austerity and spiritual rigour allowed Sufis to attain various qualities and also be socially identified as devotee (*abid*), poor (*faqir*), ascetic (*zahid*), lover (*ashiq*), gnostic (*arif*), etc. These were considered important in terms of being aware of the Divine realities, which eventually allowed the Sufi to graduate from a beginner to a *wali* (friend of God), making him the chosen one, 'honoured above the rest of His worshippers, after His messengers and Prophets.'

The current work is focused on spiritual exercises and meditative practices as integral elements of internal experience for a Sufi. These were combined with other Islamic practices, starting with an adherence to

Sufi Rituals and Practices. Kashshaf Ghani, Oxford University Press. © Kashshaf Ghani 2024.
DOI: 10.1093/oso/9780192889225.003.0001

religious law (*shariah*), along with mandatory religious practices of ritual prayer (*salat*) and fasting (*sawm*). These practices were diligently adhered to right from the early days of the Sufi tradition, whose historical reconstruction is only possible from later treatises and texts. Early Sufism was less of a structured institution, centred primarily on the life and actions of select Sufi saints, whose personal brilliance was combined with their inclination towards an inner pursuit of the Divine. The fundamental importance of spiritual authority came to be recognized through the formalization of the master-disciple relationship, where the Sufi master was considered the genius behind the rigorous training of his disciples. It was through practices of training and teaching that the path was laid for Sufism to emerge as an institutionalized form of spiritual practice, whose essence came to be understood through norms of piety, austerity, discipline, and rigour.

A gradual process of institutionalization of the Sufi tradition reached its manifest stage around the twelfth century in regions of Iran, Iraq, and parts of Central Asia, led by certain core features which could be traced to the formative period. The central among these constituted the master-disciple bond, which became formalized through elaborate rituals of initiation (*bayt*) and continued until the completion of training. The rise of the Sufi orders as spiritual brotherhoods (*silsilas*) centred around teaching and training carried out by an inspiring founder-saint, the localization of such orders through construction of numerous, often finely built, *khanqahs*, as well as the humble *jamaat khanas*, and the codification of mystical doctrines and treatises for future generations of learners.

Any historical understanding of Sufism is connected to its geographical location, rather than being seen as an unchanging universal phenomenon. The various stages in its institutionalization indicate precisely in that direction. The aim of the current work is to explore one such regional experience of Sufism—in South Asia—and within this historical context analyse forms of religious exercises and meditational practices followed by Sufis—particularly *sama* and *zikr*. Over a period of time these practices came to be recognized as intrinsic elements of Sufi spiritual training across orders. I study these rituals as a way of mystical life and also as an expression of their inner spiritual experience that is achieved only through a rigid pursuance of discipline, exuberance, etiquette, and spontaneity. Rituals and spiritual practices like *sama* and *zikr* came to be preferred by Sufi orders, who chose one over the other as their core spiritual exercise facilitating their direct experience of God. In a way, these rituals came to consolidate the spiritual position and attitude of particular orders, like the Chishti and Suhrawardi, as a voice for their spiritual ideology and practice.

Against the historical context of Sufi traditions in South Asia, the focus of this work is on the Chishti and Suhrawardi orders, the earliest to arrive in the region; the former originating in the remote village of Chisht in Afghanistan, and the latter from the seat of the Islamic Caliphate in Baghdad in Iraq. The Chishtis gradually emerged as the most popular Sufi order of the Indian subcontinent, and their early saints settled in Ajmer, Delhi, Punjab, Bengal, and Deccan. The Suhrawardi order settled in Multan and its neighbouring areas in western Punjab, currently in Pakistan, before moving further towards the east into regions like Bihar and Bengal. Along with ritual prayer and other normative religious practices, the spiritual practice of remembering God at all times through *zikr* became a key element of Sufi meditation. Inspired by the Quranic verse where God speaks to His creation, asking them directly to remember Him—*remember Me, I will remember you*—Sufis undertook various meditational practices aimed towards the act of 'remembrance'. Ritual prayer is the most common way of remembering God, along with reciting various phrases and terms addressing God, simply seeking his grace through *dua*, and eloquent invocations praising God, combined with personal and intimate prayer (*munajat*). However, the most distinctive form of Sufi remembrance came to be formalized as the *zikr*—literally meaning the exercise of 'recollection' of God's names. Over a period of time, *zikr* matured into a specialized Sufi practice, the ritual of remembrance, which came to include not only the various names of Allah, ninety-nine to be specific, but verses, praises, and long litanies that were to be repeated silently or loudly. Loud *zikr* with ecstatic behaviour became characteristic of some Sufi orders like the Rifai, who were also known as the howling dervishes. By the twelfth century, most Sufi orders accepted *zikr* as the primary spiritual practice. Although Shihab al-Din Suhrawardi of the Suhrawardi order recognized *sama* as a Sufi practice in his classic work, the *Awarif al Maarif*, Suhrawardi Sufis practiced *zikr* as their primary spiritual exercise.

Spiritual experiences were desired by Sufis of the Chishti order through their passionate practice of *sama*—listening to love poetry and mystical verses with or without accompanying musical instruments, aiming to stir an intense desire for the Divine beloved in the heart of the listener. This exercise, whose public performance later assumed the form of *qawwali*, remained the core spiritual practice of the Chishti order. However, *sama* as a practice of Sufi dervishes can be traced back to the tenth century in the *samakhanas* (lodges) of Baghdad, where dervishes would engage in ecstatic behaviour throughout the night after listening to poetry and music. *Sama*, though unique as a Sufi practice acceptable to certain Sufi communities and saints, was also at the eye of a storm that raged for a long period of time over its legality as a religious practice. The primary concerns were regarding the audition of poetry accompanied by music, both of which are contentious in the eyes of Islam. Arabic poetry, as well as Persian, invoked the image of the lover and the beloved through references to physical descriptions together with the imageries of love, wine, and intoxication. Though Sufi masters repeatedly stressed the need to employ allegorical and symbolic interpretation, the intensity of the debate on the legality of *sama* refused to settle down.

As we will see below, references in support of audition as spiritual succour are drawn from traditions of bygone Prophets, right up to the time of Muhammad, whose debatable Hadith sayings are cited in defence of audition. Some similarly debatable sayings are also referred to from the tradition of early Sufi mystics in support of the audition of pleasant sound and voice as nourishment for one's soul. However, the earliest defence of *sama* from a noted Sufi master comes from the *Kitab al Luma* of Sarraj in the tenth century, followed by generations of later Sufi scholars, many of whom were also authorities in Islamic sciences. While they were perceptive in acknowledging the dangers that may arise from *sama*, they were, at the same time, keen to defend it as a worthy Sufi practice, and hence laid down elaborate norms which could sanctify the ritual—by regulating participants, ascertaining the quality of the performers and content, and, most importantly, emphasizing the purity of intention of the entire assembly participating in the exercise.

As rituals of meditation and spiritual practice, *sama* and *zikr* were seen primarily as spiritual experiences preserved for the Sufi elite. Ways of remembering the Divine, either through verbal recollection or the audition of mystical poetry, was meant to open up the senses of the heart, thereby allowing the comprehension of Divine realities and making the heart aware of God's essences, as a gradual means of conceiving God through the heart. Such internal experiences came to be understood and expressed in Sufism through the categories of states (*hal*) and stations (*maqam*), both related to an individual's spiritual efforts and emotions of mystical love. *Hal* is described as a spontaneous descent of God's illumination on the human soul, which is manifested through one's consciousness. It is typically understood as a gift from the realm of the unseen which descends on the heart, leading to temporary experience of Divine proximity, and even union. A Sufi under such conditions makes efforts to hold on to the condition of the state that descends on the heart, unsure of whether he can relive the experience again. On the other hand, *maqam* comprises an individual's conscious efforts, whereby the heart strives to attain the superior inner qualities of God. This is undertaken by following the spiritual path (*tariqa*) under the guidance of a Sufi mentor. Attaining each *maqam* requires the individual to practice and interiorize certain qualities in order to achieve a particular station and standing in front of God. Repentance (*tawba*), asceticism (*zuhd*), poverty (*faqr*), patience (*sabr*), trust in God (*tawakkul*), and satisfaction (*rida*) are some of the important stations in which Sufis train themselves under the supervision of a spiritual guide.

As spiritual experiences, both *sama* and *zikr* are recognized by Sufis as connected to the categories of *hal* and *maqam*. There is a difference of opinion among Sufis themselves with regard to the number of stations and the various types of states, which became complex over a period of time, and came to be expressed through a range of vocabularies. Being a process of listening, *sama* is believed to induce a variety of states depending on the psychological and emotional maturity of the listener. Sufi participants in *sama*, as discussed later, require proper training in the complexities of the spiritual path in order to benefit from the assembly of audition. Sufis agree that the descent of Divine manifestation in *sama* may not happen due to multiple reasons, untrained and inattentive participants being one of them. However, whenever a state descends on participants in *sama*, it is advised not to restrain them from expressing that state in front of the assembly. Incidents have been recorded where Sufi novices, warned against expressing their state by displaying ecstatic behaviour, have died from exhaustion caused by forced suppression of emotions. At the same time, Sufis also warn that *sama* is more suitable as a spiritual aid, rather than being the goal in itself. Thus, as Sufis attain higher stations in the course of their spiritual training, *sama* as a spiritual aid also loses its relevance, to the point where poetry and music sound no better than the 'croaking of ravens'. Individuals are strongly discouraged from engaging in *sama* when they outgrow its usefulness as a means of spiritual advancement.

In South Asia, the Chishtis were not oblivious to the antecedents of *sama*—the controversy, debate on its legality, and its unique appeal as a Sufi spiritual exercise. And yet their deep engagement with this practice as well as its defence as their core spiritual exercise makes the study of *sama* historically relevant and fascinating at a juncture when the Chishti order was spreading its roots in India. It is this historical narrative that the book is concerned with. How Chishti Sufis defended *sama* as a religious exercise is best observed through the oral teachings of their individual masters, which from the time of Nizam al-Din Awliya came to be preserved in textual form beginning with the *Fawaid al Fuad*—the teachings of the Chishti saint compiled by his disciple and poet Amir Hasan Sijzi. Thereafter, *malfuzat* records of subsequent Chishti Sufis, collected in Delhi and in the Deccan, came to constitute the primary corpus of oral discourses which carried the teachings of the particular master. These came to be supplemented by biographical works on the lives of early Chishtis Sufis, the most reliable being the *Siyar al Awliya* of Sayyid Muhammad Mubarak Kirmani 'Mir Khwurd'. It is from these records that the opinion of individual Chishti masters on a variety of issues—historical as well as from their own times—can be gleaned as we study these texts today. The issue of *sama* comes forth repeatedly in these teachings, as well as in response to questions posed to the saint by disciples and lay devotees—discussed with reference to early Sufi masters, the strict guidelines and etiquettes on *sama* as laid down in Sufi treatises like the *Kitab al Luma* and the *Kashf al Mahjub*, observations on and rules framed around *sama* by living Chishti saints, criticisms levelled against the practice, the opinion of the contemporary *ulama* on *sama*, the religious climate of the Delhi Sultanate, where audition of poetry and music was often seen as an un-Islamic practice, and the defence of *sama* by Chishti Sufis on various occasions, among other factors. These constitute the issues covered in Chapters 1 and 3. Standalone treatises in defence of *sama* arising from the Chishti circle are rare, though not altogether absent. One such brief, discussed and translated in Chapter 2, was prepared by the disciple of Nizam al-Din Awliya when the saint was summoned to the court of Sultan Ghiyas al-Din Tughluq to defend *sama* in an arbitration assembly (*mahzar*). Maulana Fakhr al-Din Zarradi's *Usul al Sama* allows us to understand the Chishti emphasis on Hadith traditions when defending *sama*, as well as the inherent differences among Islamic legal traditions with regard to *sama* as a permissible exercise.

We tend to imagine, although mistakenly, that Sufi orders are closed social groups at variance to one another, engaged in strong competition within the larger arena of Islamic religious practice, and our approach ignores complementarity in favour of noticeable differences. So, Chishti and Suhrawardi orders are seen to be different from each other on many issues, like the practice of *sama*. Challenging such an exclusivist approach with regard to Sufi rituals, Chapter 4 argues that spiritual practices are not patented to individual Sufi orders. Rather this needs to be understood more as a spiritual preference and attachment. The chapter explores Suhrawardi attitudes towards *sama*, as well as the Chishti approach to *zikr*, as beneficial religious exercises which need to be pursued for specific spiritual gains.

Among the early generations of Sufi masters, whose teachings were more personal and informal, as well as among the later generations when a formalized structure of teaching and training became essential, the instruction was to choose one's company depending on conduct and etiquette (*adab*). Seekers of the spiritual path were strictly instructed, across generations, by masters like Abu al-Husayn al-Nuri and Abu Said ibn Abi al-Khayr to avoid individuals who lacked social etiquette, and at the same time train a novice in proper *adab*. Lists of rules were recorded in almost all important Sufi treatises on the issue of *adab*, along with its centrality to spiritual training. Hence this quality also became an element of one's behaviour within the communal life of the *khanqah*, as well as during specific religious congregations. Chapter 5 elaborates on this quality, considered a prerequisite among Sufis. Regulation of one's conduct was not limited only to occasions of meditational exercises, but rather considered as an overall conditioning of oneself—internally as well as externally, with relation to God as well as the spiritual guide.

As we now turn towards the early debates on the legality of *sama*, the practice of *adab* continues to remain the thread that runs throughout the ensuing discussion, at times discreetly, connecting our understanding of how *sama* came to be understood by early generations of Sufis to the history of Sufi rituals as they eventually unfolded in South Asia.

The word *sama* is understood both literally and technically. It is a compound word originating from a number of sources. Some read it as a primitive noun, derived not from a particular word, nor can any word be made out of it. It is generally agreed that the meaning of *sama* is connected to the act of 'audition', which also signifies hearing. It is derived from the root word *sa-am*, which means 'that which is been heard'. Therefore, *sama* denotes both the 'exercise' of audition, as well as the 'content' heard—poetry that is recited or music that is played.[1]

As a Sufi ritual, *sama* (literally 'audition') usually constitutes an assembly of Sufis and dervishes united through a common goal of contemplating the Divine by listening to poetry and couplets of mystical orientation, recited by a good melodious voice. Such an assembly of *sama*, occasionally ecstatic in its outward demeanour, may or may not be accompanied by musical instruments. Though the permissibility of listening to music as a spiritual aid is debated in the eyes of Islamic law (*shariah*), it is generally believed that a good voice is a gift from God. He bestows such qualities on whomsoever He pleases.[2] Therefore listening to a melodious voice is considered a pious deed as it makes the heart wake up to the remembrance of God. Prophet Muhammad is believed to have said as part of Hadith traditions that God did not send any prophet but with a melodious voice,[3] so that His sermons and revelations may be preached in a voice that sounded sweet to the common masses, pleasing their hearts. Listening to that sweet voice therefore created a sense of gratitude towards God in the heart of the listener. This sense of gratitude towards God for his benefaction (*niamat*) in turn attracted blessings from the Unseen.

[1] Amnon Shiloah, *Music in the World of Islam: A Socio-Cultural Study* (Detroit: Wayne State University Press, 1995), 31.
[2] Quran 35:1.
[3] Shiloah, *Music in the World of Islam*, 33.

The Quran places importance on a melodious voice, urging believers to *give good tidings to my servants who listen to al-qawl and follow the fairest of it.*[4] At the same time the Quran also condemns improper actions, like engaging in false conversations or indulging in dancing girls and drinking wine, even if they are triggered by a sweet voice or melodious music. Censure of music and singing thus arises out of the actions with which it becomes associated, in particular contexts. The following verse of the Quran is of relevance here: *And of the people is he who buys the amusement of speech to mislead (others) from the way of Allah without knowledge and who takes it in ridicule.*[5] The above verse is argued to have been revealed in a particular context when Nazr bin Harith, a non-believer in Islam, recited to his fellow Arab friends of the Quraysh tribe the wonders of Persia through the heroic legends of Rustam and Isfandiyar. The aim was to lead these men away from the path of Islam, preached by Muhammad, through music and singing, which was greatly attractive to Arabs. It is in this context that recitation and singing in a sweet voice with the aim of leading people astray from the path of religious faith was condemned. The verse *And when our verses are recited to him, he turns away arrogantly as if he had not heard them, as if there was in his ears deafness* can be read in continuation of the previous one.[6] Scholars interpreted 'takes it in ridicule' to refer to those men who made fun of the Prophet Muhammad when he began preaching among the Arab tribes, and in the same breath displayed arrogance towards the doctrines of the Quran. They refused to pay heed to the warnings of the Day of Judgement, feigning deafness, and continued to indulge in immoral acts of music and seeking pleasure with dancing girls. It is in this particular context that the Quran prohibits singing of sweet melodies, together with recitation of sensual poetry.[7]

Of all the voices in creation, the one of the donkey is recognized in the Quran to be the harshest.[8] While among all the Prophets mentioned

---

[4] Quran 39:17–18.
[5] Quran 31:6.
[6] Quran 31:7.
[7] M. L. Roy Choudhury, 'Music in Islam', *Journal of Royal Asiatic Society: Letters*, 23/2 (1957), 58–63.
[8] Quran 31:19.

in the Quran, Daud is particularly singled out for having a rich and melodious voice, and his beauty was no less than a miracle contained in a human body. It is said that when Prophet Daud read the *Zabur* in seventy different intonations, humans, birds, and wild animals gathered around him to listen, completely enchanted and tamed under the mesmerizing impact of his voice.[9] It is narrated that on one occasion after Daud completed one of his recitation assemblies, 400 biers had to be carried out having gone into a state of complete rapture, ultimately giving up their lives while listening to the melodious recitation of the Prophet. Even if we consider such traditions to be largely hyperbolic, the underlying emphasis on the benefits of a melodious voice, in an assembly of audition, remains undeniable.

The quality of a melodious voice, as much as it is recognized for Prophets, is also valued among ordinary beings, particularly on occasions of reciting the Quran, an act which is considered the preserve of the sweetest voice in the assembly. The praise of God and His benefactions upon mankind are best appreciated when heard from a beautiful voice. Such a voice is believed to be beyond any human achievement and can be possessed only through the benefaction of the Lord.

Permissibility for *sama*, outside the Sufi context and not as a spiritual practice, is also drawn from the Quran, where God urges mankind to listen to all that exalts the essence of the Lord. Listening to the names and attributes of God—which also double up as His praise—from a sweet voice is believed to be the purest, and hence best, of all exercises undertaken by any individual. Being a revelation from the Unseen, these names and attributes are uncreated and unmediated by human agency. Their recitation brings happiness to the heart and calms the soul of the listener. In doing so it turns the heart and mind of the listener towards God, and His remembrance. In the context of such injunctions, listening to a melodious voice is considered to be the purest and best of all exercises permissible for humans.

It can be argued that the non-permissibility of listening to sweet voices arises from circumstances where the listener is not led towards remembering God and His attributes. Advocates of *shariah* thus censure *sama*, keeping in mind occasions where both the content—vulgar and sensual

[9] Shiloah, *Music in the World of Islam*, 33.

poetry—and the outcome—desires of the flesh, leading to immoral conduct, adultery, and sin—can distract the individual away from the path
of the Divine. Since such distraction often results from listening to music
and poetry, it does not come as a surprise when legists (*faqih*) from the
four legal schools of Islam condemn the act of listening to music as 'unworthy', if not 'unlawful', for a religious-minded Muslim.[10]

It is believed that human beings are naturally attuned to appreciate
all that is melodious and invoke the praise of God and His Prophets.
However, scholars of Islamic law argue that in most instances it is difficult
to maintain moral discipline in an audition assembly. On many occasions
the assembly tends to lapse into an exercise where immoral conduct,
chaos, and vulgarity ensue, sparked by the recitation of sensual poetry
and verses. Keeping such behaviour in mind, legists label *sama* as forbidden since it excites the heart towards improper actions. Individuals
overwhelmed by the power of music end up losing control over their behaviour, thereby participating in *sama* to seek worldly pleasure. We can
argue, then, that *sama* is permissible only under circumstances where it
is recited by a melodious voice, and heard with a pure heart and noble intention, attracting blessings from God.

That poetry in itself can be beneficial is established through a tradition
pertaining to Prophet Muhammad where it is narrated that he used to
ask one of his companions, Hassan bin Sabith, to recite poetry, which
the latter did when he attended any assembly of the Prophet. It is also related to the tradition of the Prophet where he once remarked that anyone
singing a good verse in a melodious voice will be assisted by Archangel
Gabriel in his efforts. As a result, this tradition is taken as an attestation
of the beneficial qualities of poetry. Poetry becomes harmful in instances
when it leads to derogatory actions forbidden in the eyes of the *shariah*.
However, if poetry is read in a melodious voice containing elements of
deep spiritual knowledge and hidden wisdom, then the exercise is permissible. Such an exercise then turns the heart and thoughts of the individual towards the Almighty, adding to his good deeds. Through this,
participation in *sama* and listening to the poetry becomes a commend-
able exercise.

[10] Henry George Farmer, 'The Religious Music of Islam', *Journal of the Royal Asiatic Society*,
84/1–2 (April 1952), 60–65.

In another tradition of the Prophet it is said that he instructed individuals to read and recite the Quran in a melodious voice, since reciting the Quran in such a manner attracts greater blessings from the Unseen. Any individual who listens to such a recitation of the Quran in silence, immersed in contemplation, experiences a deep impact on his heart and mind. Conversing during a recitation of the Quran creates distractions and breaks the rhythmic continuity within the assembly. It also interrupts the natural flow of blessings that descend from the Unseen. Also, it is forbidden to wail on hearing any recitation of the Quran.

It is incorrect to argue that *sama* is forbidden based on the authority of the *hadith*, since the tradition of Prophets having a good voice, along with Prophet Muhammad encouraging the recitation of poetry and playing of musical instruments on certain occasions, has been taken as ample proof for permissibility of listening to good poetry in a melodious voice. Based on such precedents, proponents of *sama*, like the Sufis, have argued that this exercise has been recognized as permissible in the eyes of the law.

For many Sufi saints trained in the mystical path, listening to *sama*, with or without music, constitutes an inseparable part of spiritual training. Participation in *sama* is aimed at creating a deep sense of love and remembrance for God within the Sufi saint. It purifies the heart of the listener to an extent which is not achievable through any degree of outward austerity, stirring within it an intense love for God, and often leading to ecstatic behaviour. As a result of being practiced as an esoteric Sufi ritual, *sama* attracted harsh criticism from legists and *ulama*, who accused Sufis of transgressing limits of religious and moral etiquette. Sufis in turn upheld the legality of the exercise of *sama* by arguing that it comprised an inseparable part of their spiritual training, helping them in the worship of God and to 'experience religious feelings to a higher and more effective degree'.[11] Not all Sufi orders practiced the exercise of *sama* at all times, and many Sufi orders did not encourage such a spiritual exercise. However, it is interesting to note that views on *sama*, as an act of listening, began to emerge long before Sufism had institutionalized itself through the formation of individual orders (*silsilas*). It is towards some of

---

[11] Amnon Shiloah, 'Music and Religion in Islam', *Acta Musicologica*, 69/Fasc. 2, (Jul.–Dec. 1997), 144, 148.

these earliest interpretations of *sama* from the early Sufi masters that we now turn.

Dhun Nun al-Misri (d. 861), known for his knowledge of the 'inner science' of hearts, argued that 'listening (*sama*) is a power that creates a feeling of intense love for the Divine and stirs the heart to seek God. Sufis who listen to it spiritually (*ba-haq*) attain unto God (*tahaqqaqa*) and those among the common folk who listen to it sensually (*ba-nafs*) fall into heresy (*tazandaqa*)'.[12] What Dhun Nun probably indicated through the above was that Sufis should not listen to the mere sound of words, but the spiritual reality that lay hidden behind them. Only through such deep realization does Divine beneficence descend into the heart of the Sufi, stirring it up. Those who are trained to decipher the true meaning of the verses experience a sense of ecstasy within their heart. Others who listen to the mere words and its sound are veiled from the mystical experience. Since a melodious voice is a gift from God, it is mandatory for all men and women to listen to it as a permissible action. However, permissibility depended on the end for which it was put to use, according to the nature, intention, and intellectual ability of the listener—permitted when used for spiritual progress, and forbidden when desired only for worldly pleasures. Therefore, while listening to *sama* individuals were required to be careful regarding the intention with which they were participating in the exercise. Those who believed in *sama* as a proof of God (*haqq*) participated in it with the right emotions. Others who took *sama* to be a pleasurable act distracted themselves from the true goal of the exercise.

When queried about the qualities of *sama*, the famous Sufi master Abu Bakr al Shibli (d. 946), a contemporary of Hallaj, through a similar statement chose to distinguish between the exterior (*zahir*) and interior (*batin*) qualities. For him, *sama* meant discord and disruption when experienced with external senses. But for Sufis trained in the emotions of the interior, *sama* was a practice with the promise of great spiritual reward. Those trained to understand its intricacies benefit from the spiritual state to which it leads, while the uninitiated end up creating great unrest and tribulation within their hearts. For gnostics, *sama* proved to

[12] Ibid., 149; Uthman al-Hujwiri, *Kashf al Mahjub*, trans. R. A. Nicholson, *The Kashf al Mahjub: The Oldest Persian Treatise on Sufism* (Leyden: E. J. Brill, 1911), 404. Henceforth *Kashf al Mahjub*.

be a succour, creating within their hearts a deep sense of love and longing for the Divine.

Sarraj, Qushayri, and Ghazali mention in their accounts that once during prayer in the month of Ramadan, Shibli was thrown into a state of ecstasy upon hearing a phrase repeated by the Imam—'With such words do lovers converse!'. The fact that Shibli cried out and turned pale in the face points to the impact of *sama* not only through formal congregations, but even through chance hearing of phrases.

Taking a rather cautious position on *sama*, Abu Sulaiman al-Darrani (d. 820) emphasized that 'music does not produce in the heart what is not in it; hence it should be forbidden for those who are subject to mere intoxication'.[13] The above statement can be taken to imply that the heart is the storehouse of all spiritual qualities. However, hardened by feelings of the material world, the human heart is seldom receptive to such spiritual subtleties. Music in this case does not create afresh within the heart what it does not originally contain—mystical feelings. But for a heart trained in the nuances of spiritual knowledge, poetry and music act as catalysts. It helps bring forth the latent feelings of yearning in an individual's heart, turning it towards God. A necessary precondition, it can be argued, for attending such audition assemblies lies in the ability of the heart to realize the meaning hidden in the verses recited. Otherwise, to an individual listener, steeped in worldly feelings and emotions, it can bring forth disastrous consequences. As a result, *sama* is forbidden for those who are given to desires of the flesh, to whom music is nothing but a means to induce a feeling of worldly intoxication.

One of the earliest Sufis from the tenth century, Abu Talib al-Makki, wrote in his treatise *Qut ul-Qulub* (Food of Hearts) that 'the (singing) voice is an instrument said to carry and communicate meaningful ideas; when the listener perceives the meaning of the message without being distracted by the melody, his *sama* is lawful; otherwise, and when the content expresses physical love, simple desire and simple futilities, the *sama* is pure diversion and must be banished'.[14] In the above statement, the emphasis on listening rests more on understanding the language of poetry. Makki argues that music is primarily a vehicle for conveying

---

[13] Shiloah, 'Music and Religion in Islam', 149.
[14] Ibid.

Divine realities to the Sufi. Hence it is incumbent on the Sufi to interpret the content of audition along spiritual parameters, without diverting into any form of material interpretation. This again is possible only if the listener concentrates exclusively on the content of the audition, rather than being distracted by the melody that accompanies it. It is only under such conditions that *sama* is deemed lawful; otherwise, if the content of the assembly expresses physical love, material desire, and intoxication, *sama* does not benefit the listener spiritually, and hence acts as poison, rather than an elixir.

In the garb of cautioning participants in assemblies of *sama,* early mystics subtly pushed the idea that *sama* as a spiritual exercise is not meant for all. An act aimed at arousing the heart to Divine realities, understanding the benefits of *sama* requires sufficient training in the Sufi path. Those untrained by the Sufi master (*murshid*) on the intricacies of audition become trapped in desires of the flesh, doing more harm than good to their spiritual progress. Rather, it is meant for the ones committed to the path of gnosis (*irfan*), who are thereby sufficiently trained to participate in *sama* in the right state of the heart. This entail an ability to interpret poetry along spiritual parameters, whereby its understanding leads to spiritual states, exhibited many times through external sobriety or ecstatic behaviour.

The earliest defence for *sama* drawn from the traditions of Prophets was later picked up by the famous Sufi master Abu Nasr al-Sarraj (d. 988). Sarraj, in his treatise *Kitab al-luma fi al-tasawwuf* (Book of Glimmerings on Sufism)—the oldest Arabic work on the principles of Sufism—built up his brief in support of *sama* along Prophetic traditions, with evidence drawn from the *Hadith*,[15]

ما بعث الله نبيا الا حسن الصوت
Ma ba'ash allahu nabiyyan illa husn al saut
God has not sent any Prophet but with a melodious voice

زينوا القران باصواتكم
Zayn ul Quran bi aswatikum
Beautify the Quran with your voices

[15] Abu Nasr al-Sarraj, *Kitab al Luma fi'l Tasawwuf*, ed. R. A. Nicholson (Leyden: E. J. Brill, 1914), 268.

ما اذن الله تعلنا لشي كما اذن النبي حسن الصوت

Ma asan Allahu ta'ala lishayyin, kama asana al-nabi husn al-suat
God has not given permission so strongly for anything as He has
given permission to the Prophets for melody

Sarraj continued his argument that Muhammad listened to music with
his companions for pleasure on days of Eid, and other occasions of happiness. At the same time, the Prophet also stressed the worth of a melodious
voice capable of rhythmic recitations of verses and couplets.[16] Sarraj cited
anecdotes from the life of the Prophet to establish the above arguments
supporting the audition of music. For example, one day two young girls
in the house of the Prophet were singing a popular song celebrating the
day of the Battle of Bu'ath.[17] When Abu Bakr entered the house and saw
the girls playing the tambourine and singing, he rebuked them for their
improper actions. He described the instrument as the *mazamir-i shaitan*
(reed pipe of Satan). At this the Prophet, who was lying down, sat up and
allowed the girls to play, as that was a day of happiness for their tribe.[18]

Sarraj's account of *sama* builds on the argument that for those who
are trained to participate in the exercise, *sama* leads to various degrees
of spiritual achievement. He backs his argument on spiritual training by
listing three categories of participants in *sama*: beginners (*mubtadiyan*)
and disciples (*muridin*); advanced (*mutawassitin*) and purists (*siddiqin*);
and, lastly, the gnostics (*arifin*).[19] The spiritual maturity of each category differs from the other. Nonetheless, all are recognized as the elect
(*khwass*), as opposed to those who listen to *sama* with a worldly frame
of mind.

Together with the above categories, Sarraj goes on to categorize *sama*
into different types.[20] First is that which is heard through the normal

---

[16] al-Sarraj, *Kitab al Luma*, 275.
[17] The Battle of Bu'ath was fought in 615 between the rival tribes of the Aws and the Khajraz.
The Aws were supported by the two Jewish tribes, Banu Nadir and Banu Qurayza, allowing them
to secure a narrow victory. The state of continuous warfare between tribes and clans made the
situation in Medina extremely unstable. It was against this background that these tribes decided
to invite Muhammad to be their arbiter in order to work out a formal peace arrangement. See
Irving M. Zeitling, *The Historical Muhammad* (Massachusetts: Polity Press, 2007).
[18] Shiloah, *Music in the World of Islam*, 32–33; Choudhury, 'Music in Islam', 67–68.
[19] al-Sarraj, *Kitab al- Luma*, 277.
[20] Ibid., 278.

instincts (*tab*) of an individual. Listeners in this category consist of the common folk who participate in *sama* with the aim of deriving certain spiritual benefits. However, their hearts are hardened to such an extent through worldly affairs that not much of the real essence of the exercise reaches the heart. As a result, *sama* for such individuals gives rise to nothing but worldly thoughts and desires. The second type of *sama* involves individuals who, though not fully trained in the way of a Sufi, can, nonetheless, realize some mystical emotions within their hearts. In a way the individual realizes, albeit partially, the worth of participating in *sama*. Hence he is receptive to the blessings that descend upon him from the Unseen and influence his spiritual state (*hal*). For Sarraj the last type of *sama*, recognized as the best of the three, is that where the Sufi hears through God (*haqq*). Naturally such a type of *sama* is reserved only for Sufis of the highest merit. They are the ones said to have acquired the ability to witness the attributes of God on hearing them during *sama*. It is said that such Sufis listen to the Divine Truth through the ear of their heart. Their hearts are cleansed of the darkness of the material world to such an extent that they are illumined by the light of Truth. As a result of Divine beneficence, the inner hearts of Sufis at this advanced stage take a form similar to a mirror reflecting the image of God in whichever direction the Sufi turns. In such a state, the heart of the Sufi hears through God only that which God wishes him to hear.

For Sarraj, then, the categories of *sama* correspond to the level of the participants. Beginners and disciples strive to emerge out of their involvement in worldly affairs, and thus participate in *sama* through material instincts. The spiritually advanced and purists approach *sama* with a degree of spiritual awareness within their hearts. Finally, the gnostics are the most advanced in the spiritual path, and *sama* for them is the best exercise.

In the period between the inspiring careers of Sarraj and Ghazzali stands another renowned Sufi master—Abdul Qarim bin Hawazin al-Qushayri (d. 1072). His *Risala al-Qushayriya fi ilm al-tasawwuf* stands out as the foremost encyclopaedic work originating from the early Sufi tradition, and it has continued to be one of the most frequently referenced manuals on Sufi ethics and practices.[21] Qushayri was born in northern

---

[21] Abul Qasim al-Qushayri, *Al Risala al qushayriyya fi ilm al-tasawwuf*, trans. Alexander Knysh, *Al Qushayri's Epistle on Sufism* (Reading: Garnet Publishing Limited, 2007).

Khurasan, but was trained in Nishapur under the tutelage of the great Sufi master of the Baghdad school, Abu Ali al Hasan al Daqqaq (d. 1015), who was in turn connected to the spiritual genealogy of Junaid. Qushayri's most famous work, the *Risala*, was written with the intention of portraying Sufism as compatible with the Islamic sciences and law (*shariah*), with the larger aim of creating a harmonious coexistence. With that end in mind, Qushayri is critical of the beliefs and practices in Sufism that do not comply with *shariah* traditions, and hence stand out in contradiction to the opinions of Sunni legal scholars. He is also critical of the imitators who attempt to malign the Sufi tradition without sufficient training in and knowledge of its intricacies.

On the issue of training in the Sufi path, Qushayri's *Risala* addresses a vast number of subjects on mystical training and spiritual stages that need to be properly adhered to for the most rewarding spiritual experience, for both novices and Sufi masters. One such stage that he particularly emphasizes concerns the concert of *sama* for spiritual benefit. In this section Qushayri returns to the Quranic injunctions when he argues that 'listening to music' is permissible when the content is sweet and melodious, but more importantly when the listener accepts the exercise not as mere amusement. Rather he is able to rise above his worldly passions to decipher the spiritual merit of the exercise. In an assembly of *sama*, Qushayri continues, the Sufi listener must be engaged in complete remembrance of God and His highest attributes. It is in such a state that a Sufi attracts Divine beneficence from the Unseen that not only allows him to progress on the spiritual path, but more importantly is also admissible in the eyes of the law.[22]

Qushayri refers to scholars from the Islamic legal tradition, like Imam Shafi, who did not prohibit listening to music, but cautioned against its ill-effects on the inexperienced listener who saw *sama* only as entertainment. Qushayri immediately follows this up with a defence in favour of Sufis, recognizing them as spiritually adept. Therefore Sufis do not approach *sama* negligently, as an 'entertaining' musical session, nor do they listen to *sama* immersed in worldly thoughts.

Qushayri's master al-Daqqaq, however, was strictly against the participation of common folks in *sama*, as they may end up listening to it

---

[22] Ibid., 342.

under the influence of their lower self. It was permitted only for ascetics and Sufis, since they have sufficiently conditioned their hearts not to be distracted by worldly thoughts during *sama*. These mystics receive the Truth only through the verses of *sama*, which excite their heart for the Divine Beloved, so that mercy descends upon them. Qushayri continues on the authority of Daqqaq, dividing the participants in *sama* into three categories: those who aspire to listen (*mutasammi*), those who listen (*mustami*), and the 'real' listeners (*sami*). The first type listens according to his mystical moment (*waqt*), the second one listens according to his overall spiritual state (*hal*), while the third listens in truth (*bi haqq*). *Sama* is therefore a permissible exercise for a Sufi who has attached himself to God.[23]

Sama is also a facilitator for those who strive against their lower self by eliminating all worldly attachments, thereby purifying oneself in the quest for the Divine mysteries. It is during such moments of Divine unveiling that a Sufi is overwhelmed and gripped by ecstasy (*wajd*), which either leads towards calmness, or agitated limb movements that overcome him.[24]

On the issue of physical ecstasy, Qushayri recounts an anecdote from an earlier Sufi master who discouraged extreme outward manifestations of ecstasy like shrieking and rending of clothes. Once when Prophet Moses was delivering his sermon amongst his followers, one of the listeners tore up his shirt in ecstasy. At that point Moses received a revelation, 'Tell him, tear up your heart. Not your clothing, for Me!'. In another incident, the proverbially sober Junaid once warned his young companion not to utter a shriek when he heard God's name in remembrance (*zikr*). Bound by obedience to his master's instruction, the young companion started controlling himself to an extent that his body turned pale, with sweat dripping from his hair and body. At last, one day, unable to bear this exhaustion, he gave a cry and passed away. Calmness through concentration attests to the inner strength of great Sufi masters in the face of Divine manifestation (*tajalli*). No matter how overwhelming the emotion may be, an adept Sufi master can remain in complete control of his limbs and senses.

[23] Ibid., 356.
[24] Ibid., 343, 347–348.

Abu Hamid al Ghazzali (d. 1111) recognized Sufis as the chosen ones of God. Their pleasure and sorrow, desire and longing, hearing and listening revolve around the remembrance of God, and His will. One of the ways in which the heart of the Sufi experiences strong attachment with the Divine is through a feeling of intense love emanating from the audition of His names, attributes, and praise. For Ghazzali, it is through *sama* that such emotions are extracted from within the depths of the heart.

Ghazzali, in the *Ihya Ulum al Din* (Revival of the Religious Sciences), begins the discussion with a range of traditions that elaborate the rules concerning audition. He goes on to emphasize that *sama* reveals the beauty and hidden treasures of the human heart, stirring it in remembrance of the Divine. This section of the *Ihya* begins with statements from Imam Shafi, the founder of the Shafi school of Islamic law, who labels singing as 'a sport which is disliked and which resembles what is false; he who meddles much with it is light of understanding, you shall reject his testimony'.[25] Similar is the opinion of Malik bin Anas, who forbade singing, either in an assembly or by a slave girl bought for that purpose. According to Ghazzali, such is also the opinion of Abu Hanifa, along with the rest of the scholars from that generation.

Ghazzali then picks Abu Talib al Makki as an exception in this regard, since the latter agrees to the permissibility of singing and music drawing from the traditions of the first generation of believers in Islam, the first generation of Companions of Muhammad, and their followers. He follows this with other traditions from scholars and ascetics alike who agree to listening to music and poetry in whatever form it may be performed. However, one warning coming from a Sufi shaykh on music and audition is that it 'is slipperiness itself; only the feet of the learned stand firm upon it'. This statement could be taken to be in agreement with what later generation of Sufis would emphasize as being a practical danger when participating in *sama*. Listeners need to be well trained in the Sufi path to be able to withstand, emotionally as well as physically, the state (*hal*) that descend on such assemblies.[26]

[25] Duncan MacDonald, 'Emotional Religion in Islam as Affected by Music and Singing', translation of 'Ihya Ulum al-Din of al-Ghazzali', *Journal of the Royal Asiatic Society of Great Britain and Ireland* (Apr. 1901), 201.
[26] Ibid., 205.

Hujwiri, however, rightly pointed out in his treatise, the *Kashf-al Mahjub*, that it may not be possible, every time, to regulate participants in *sama*, as some young initiates in the Sufi path take this exercise to be more of a norm than an exception, diluting its spiritual worth. Perhaps as preemptive of such a situation, Ghazzali narrates a tradition from Mimshad Dinawari, who was once instructed by the Prophet in a dream not to forbid *sama*; rather he was asked to 'say to them that they open before it with the Quran and close after it with the Quran.'[27] This was to secure the sanctity of *sama* as a spiritual exercise, not amusement, seeking grace from the Unseen. Ghazzali also refers to Junaid, who once stated that in a gathering of Sufis, God's grace descends on three occasions: at the time of eating, at the time of conversation, and when listening to music and singing. In all these actions Sufis follow the way of the righteous, so that while listening to music they strive to hear the hidden truth in the verses.[28] Later generations of Sufis in South Asia followed such traditions in justifying as well as securing the legitimacy of *sama*, as we shall see in the following chapters.

In the *Ihya*, Ghazzali approaches the issue of legality of audition connected to the spiritual exercise of *sama* through a combination of legal injunctions and acceptable examples of the practice drawn from reputed authorities, which ultimately allows him to establish the permissibility of music and audition. The first step in ascertaining the permissibility of listening is the pleasantness and beauty of the voice that comes to the listener. Only thereafter does the listener attempt to unravel the message and wisdom hidden in those pleasant sounds that may originate from animals, birds, and musical instruments, as well as the human voice.[29]

Ghazzali is clear that musical instruments such as the pipe and stringed instruments, including the *ud*, *sanj*, *rabab*, and *barbat*, should be termed unlawful for audition as they are associated with intoxicating practices like wine drinking. Thus, if sound and music are pleasing to the ear, yet they lead the mind towards unlawful things, these should be forbidden.[30]

Speaking on the lawfulness of poetry and music, Ghazzali considers these two components independently, arguing that if lawful poetry,

[27] Ibid., 206.
[28] Ibid., 206–207.
[29] Ibid., 209–210.
[30] Ibid., 214.

understood through proper interpretation of meaning, is combined with music emanating from permitted instruments or sources, then 'the compound, when they are joined together, is allowable'. Thus for him it is not music alone that makes *sama* unlawful or lawful, but a combination of good poetry with pleasant music. The final exercise therefore should not be considered forbidden.[31]

The permissibility of listening to and reciting poetry is argued by Ghazzali not from the doctrinal and legal sources of Islam, but from reports from the life of Muhammad on the authority of his wife, Ayesha, when the Prophet listened to his Companions reciting poetry and recited poetry himself on multiple occasions. On one such occasion he is said to have remarked that 'from poetry is wisdom'. Thus Ghazzali argues that the acceptance of poetry by earlier authorities starting from the Prophet proves its legality.[32]

One can possibly argue that *sama*, in certain situations, can also bring out dark elements present within a human heart, if not undertaken with the right intention. Ghazzali classifies *sama* as an act undertaken as a sport (*lahw*) that leads to delight (*lazzat*), and finally as a permissible (*mubah*) exercise. *Sama* as a frivolous exercise is unlawful because it creates disturbance within the heart, leading it astray from the spiritual path. *Sama* is a delight when it brings joy to the heart of the listener by helping the Sufi move ahead on the spiritual path towards the Divine beloved. Ghazzali finally attests to the permissibility of the ritual based on traditions from Prophet Muhammad. He draws certain conclusions based on his analysis of *sama*:

1. It is good to enjoy music sometimes.
2. *Sama* can be undertaken near a mosque.
3. Going by the tradition of the Prophet allowing his wife Ayesha to participate in music, women and children may be allowed to draw happiness from it.
4. It was approved by the Prophet himself on multiple occasions.[33]

---

[31] Ibid., 215.
[32] Ibid., 215–217.
[33] Shiloah, *Music in the World of Islam*, 43–44.

Ghazzali argues that it is not possible to measure the impression made by music and poetry in general, since such impact varies from one individual to another, depending on the circumstances under which he hears them. The impact also depends on the condition of an individual's heart, as Abu Sulayman al Darrani once remarked that 'music and singing do not produce in the heart that which is not in it, but they stir up what is in it.'[34]

Based on this, Ghazzali identifies seven occasions during which poetry and music can be performed for a purpose:

1. Singing of pilgrims, thereby inviting others to pilgrimage

Before setting out for hajj, pilgrims sing praises, with poetry and musical instruments, of the holy sites and rites, so that it may rouse desire in the hearts of others to visit the house of God. Since invitation to such acts of piety is permissible in the eyes of law, Ghazzali argues that the use of poetry and melody only facilitates in arousing a sense of longing for pilgrimage.

2. As a war cry

The use of poetry and melody to inspire warriors for battle is different from the use meant for pilgrims. Such encouragement to bravery in the battlefield and hostility towards enemies is meant only for those for whom warfare is permitted.

3. To encourage the army during a battle

Such verses, which praise acts of courage and bravery, are meant to impact the mind in preparing for unavoidable circumstances of warfare. Its usage among warriors is intended to uphold courage and energy in the battlefield, and to avoid homesickness and softening of the heart.

[34] MacDonald, 'Emotional Religion', 220.

4. To evoke lamentation and sorrow

Ghazzali divides verses of poetry used on occasions of grief into two kinds. The first one, which he considers blameworthy, arouses grief from the passing away of a dear one, and is seen by Ghazzali to reflect feelings of 'anger with the decree of God Most High and . . . that which cannot be repaired'. Thus such a lamentation is ideally prohibited. The praiseworthy form of lamentation is considered to be the one in which an individual grieves over his own shortcomings of faith and his sins. Such a lamentation is accepted as praiseworthy 'for it arouses energy in amending' the moral lapses faced by an individual.

5. Music and singing to express joy

Singing with the use of music should be done only on occasions that are fit to be celebrated, and hence for Ghazzali arouse emotions of happiness and pleasure among participants. Such acts are 'allowable if the joy is allowable, as singing on the days of festival and at a marriage and on the occasion of the arrival of one who has been away and on the occasion of a wedding feast and the first head-shaving and at the birth of a child and his circumcision and when his learning of the Mighty Quran is complete'. Ghazzali, while listing proof 'that singing and dancing are not forbidden', cites a number of traditions from the era of the Prophet, which refer to celebrations through singing, music, and recitation in the presence of the Prophet.

6. Music and poetry when expressing love and longing for a beloved

A Sufi saint on the spiritual path longs for the Divine beloved while forgetting his own self. For Ghazzali, music and poetry can facilitate in arousing a sense of pleasure when beholding the Beloved, and, when separated, a sense of longing in desire for the Beloved. While the experience of Divine manifestation (*tajalli*) is recognized to be the highest spiritual achievement, separation from the Beloved also carries within it a strong hope for reunion. Therefore, *sama* for the Sufis is considered beneficial by Ghazzali for arousing love, creating a sense of longing, and the pleasurable feeling of hope, all centred around the experience of union with the

Divine. However, music and singing for *sama* is contingent on the goal, and considered allowable 'if union with the object of longing is allowable'. If audition of music and singing leads to fantasy and imagination rather than towards the reality of union, then it needs to be condemned as unlawful, and hence forbidden.

7. For love of God

Music and singing, for Ghazzali, is permitted for those who are immersed in the love of God and behold Him in all creation. No sound reaches the ear of such individuals that does not praise the perfection of the Lord. So complete is their love for God that all forms of music and singing only convey to them the beauty of the Divine, leading towards states of rapture and ecstasy. Such states can only be attained when music and poetry light up the fire of love within the heart of the Sufi, purifying it of all worldly taints, leading towards the highest spiritual experience for any seeker of the path through manifestation of the Divine.

The Sufi who is overcome by the love of God relates all that he hears in *sama*, or outside it, to the Lord—while verses on black tresses remind him of 'the darkness of unbelief', fair cheeks of the beloved remind him 'of the light of Faith', joy of union arouses hopes of 'meeting God Most High', and referring to parting leads to despair 'of the separation from God Most High in the company of the rejected'. What the Sufi listener connects with the Lord on hearing the verses may not be necessarily what the reciter (*qawwal*) intended to convey while reciting. But it is in the power of imagination and understanding of the Sufi being 'consumed in the love of God' that he goes beyond the apparent literal meaning of the verses to connect what he hears with what his spiritual training requires him to do—remain immersed constantly in the contemplation of God and His attributes.

Such subtle states of the heart are available only to the most adept Sufis and travellers in the spiritual path, who are granted the knowledge of seeking pleasure from remembering the Beloved, triggered by whatever reaches their ear—music, poetry, or a chance hearing. Ghazzali argues that the immature and the perverted wonder at such qualities of a Sufi, and mistake the pleasure Sufis derive from music and poetry as being accessible to all. Unlike Sufis, lay individuals lack the power of perception, and approach music and singing through their material senses, rather than the heart.[35]

Sufis tread in the spiritual path drawn by the love of God (*mahabba*) that only increases with their spiritual progress. Ghazzali calls this passion (*ishq*), similar to what Arabs saw in Muhammad as he retired for long periods of meditation and contemplation. Such passion for the Lord on beholding His beauty (*jamal*) can only be perceived by the heart, since, for Ghazzali, it is not the external beauty of form, but that of God's inner essence that is unveiled to the spiritual seeker.[36] This passion is aroused through music and singing in *sama*, where on certain occasions mere audition of the qualities of God, without manifestation of them, can have a severe effect on the heart of the listener, where in a state of ecstasy he can even lose his life.

Having largely established the legality of music and singing through the spiritual practice of *sama*, and hence ascertaining its permissibility and encouragement on certain occasions, Ghazzali also elaborates on conditions that render the practice of music and singing (*sama*) unlawful. He identifies five circumstances:

1. *Sama* is prohibited when produced by women

Ghazzali states that music and singing, even the recitation of the Quran, by women and beardless youths should be avoided in all circumstances for the 'fear of temptation'. And one should avoid looking at them, during such practices, for the same reason. He thereafter analyses whether such an injunction is applicable in all situations involving women and beardless youths, or in certain circumstances where temptation is a possibility. From the perspective of law, this can be approached in two ways. First, temptation is usually attached to the presence of women. Therefore, being alone with a woman beyond permissible limits of modesty is prohibited, in all circumstances. However, being in the presence of beardless youths is permissible as long as no element of temptation is involved. Hence in such circumstances they need not veil their faces. Second,

---

[35] Ibid., 220–230.
[36] Ibid., 231.

temptation and lust are aroused primarily through vision, rather than audition, both for women and young men. At the same time, it is not the voice that is forbidden—for women conversed freely with men right from the time of the Prophet—but the action performed through that voice, like singing and recitation, which, combined with the face of a woman, triggered temptation. Thus, according to Ghazzali, the legal prohibition depends how individuals interact with women and young men in particular circumstances.

2. *Sama* must not be accompanied by musical instruments

Certain musical instruments that excite lust and are associated with drinking and amusement should not be used in *sama*. Three are listed: 'pipes and stringed instruments and the *kuba*-drum'. Other instruments which are allowable as accompaniments for *sama* include the *duff*, 'and the *tabl* and the *shahin* and beating with the *qadib*'.

3. The content of *sama* must be compatible with the devotional spirit of the assembly

Ghazzali clearly states that the content of *sama* should not contain anything that is obscene, like detailed physical description of any particular woman, a satire poem, or anything that speaks falsely against God and His attributes, His Prophet, and Companions of the Prophet. Drawing from the tradition of the Prophet, Ghazzali argues that satire poems on unbelievers are allowable, as is love poetry containing praise of a woman's features, only if the latter is applied by the listener to a particular woman who is dear to him, and not to all and unknown. Should the latter occur, then audition should be forbidden.

4. Listeners of *sama* must not be led by lust or by selfish desires of the heart

Ghazzali is clear in arguing that youths who are easily overcome by worldly desires should not participate in audition of music and singing, irrespective of whether they attribute what they hear to a particular individual or not. Ghazzali refuses to believe that men, young in age, maturity of mind, and spiritual conditioning, can resist the arousing lust that rises within their hearts upon listening to poetry and music. For their hearts are overcome by worldly desires, and require conditioning before they can join assemblies of music and singing.

5. Listeners of *sama* must not be commoners

For Ghazzali, *sama* is permissible only for individuals who are driven by love and longing towards God. For others, music and singing is dear to them as amusement, so that lust controls their hearts, rather than spiritual rigour. *Sama* is permitted only when the occasion demands it, never as a regular exercise of music and singing—precisely what commoners believe *sama* to be. Thus, no matter on how many occasions they participate in *sama*, for Ghazzali their hearts are never content, nor do they gain any spiritual benefits from this. Ghazzali argues that since tradition attests to the permissibility of *sama* in the life of the Prophet, commoners are not forbidden from it initially. But they should not turn it into a regular habit, and start drawing pleasure from it.

Sama is permissible only when Sufis use it to quieten their hearts, thus serving as a medicine rather than a habit. They also support *sama* with other regular religious exercises like *zikr*, prayer, and recitation of the Quran. For Ghazzali, *sama* loses its beauty and efficacy when done in abundance, since no permissible thing should be done in excess. And only Sufis know the right means to regulate such an exercise in order to maximize the spiritual gain coming forth from it. Hence it is forbidden for the common masses.[37]

Ghazzali concludes this section by reaffirming the permissibility of music and singing (*sama*) as a legal exercise, elaborated from the traditions of the Prophet. However, he also admits there may arise certain circumstances external to it, also mentioned above, for which he uses the term 'accidents', whereby listening (*sama*) to music and singing can be harmful for those who undertake it. Certain regulations, as detailed above, are thus prescribed by Ghazzali in order to ensure the legality of the practice, as well as to stop individuals from harming themselves by foolishly indulging in it.

[37] Ibid., 235–241.

For Ghazzali, if careful attention is not paid, then a lawful exercise could become unlawful due to its attachment to certain 'accidents' that arise externally. Thus for *sama* it is a lawful exercise as long as certain permissible criteria, like a measured voice and proper company, are adhered to. It becomes unlawful only when certain unwanted excesses are committed while participating in the exercise. From the authority of Imam Shafi, it is known that music and singing are permissible as long as they do not lapse into a source of employment, amusement, and sport. If the latter are not indulged in, then such practice is worthy and permitted. Ghazzali elaborates in great detail, however, on the various conditions raised by Shafi while arguing for music and singing as prohibited or permissible.[38]

Though discussed above, it may be repeated that one of the primary 'accidents' that turn *sama* into an unlawful assembly in the opinion of Ghazzali is the music and singing by slave girls associated with drinking. Ghazzali replies to critics of *sama* by arguing on this position that music and singing by unknown women in the presence of unknown men leads to temptation and hence must always be considered unlawful. However, if the slave girl practices music and singing for her master, it cannot be called unlawful as the feeling of temptation is missing in such situations. This was vindicated by the singing of the two slave girls in the house of Ayesha, the wife of the Prophet, 'and the singing of the women who sang at his arrival'. Therefore, for Ghazzali, singing that moves the heart towards joy and longing, during festivals and other occasions of celebration or for the Divine, is permissible, while that which excites the heart towards lust and temptation for the immodest company of women should be forbidden.[39]

With Ghazzali, we find a comprehensive exposition on the permissibility of *sama*, both with regard to the nature of the participants and the particular occasions when *sama* can be undertaken as a lawful exercise, as well as situations when it needs to be prohibited as unlawful. Being a scholar himself, Ghazzali successfully takes the debate deeper into the field of Islamic legal scholarship before turning towards the path of Sufism. His engagement with *sama* in the doctrinal sense brings out his position of strong defence for the practice, through well-crafted

[38] Ibid., 243.
[39] Ibid., 244–252.

arguments, against a comprehensive theoretical framework. Not only does he collate previous traditions on the subject, but at the same time he puts forwards his own arguments and instructions with compelling originality.

Abu Hamid Ghazzali's towering intellectual personality quite understandably eclipsed the contributions of his younger brother, Ahmad Ghazzali (d. 1126), who is remembered for his remarkable spiritual attainment as a Sufi shaykh and a spiritual mentor, together with being a seminal figure in early Persian Sufi literature alongside personalities like Usman al-Hujwiri. Ahmad Ghazzali's engagement with the subject of music as a Sufi practice is primarily connected to the text *Bawariq al-ilma fir radd ala man yuharrimus sama bi al-ijma* (Glimmers of Allusion in Response to Those Who Forbid Sufi Music), which scholars have since proven to be incorrectly attributed to him. Contrary to his elder brother, the topic of *sama* as a Sufi practice does not find mention in the writings of Ahmad Ghazzali, though other sources, like the *Tamhidat* of Hamadani and the *Lisan al-mizan* of al-Asqalani, attest the practice of *sama* by Ahmad Ghazzali himself. They even carry detailed descriptions of Ahmad Ghazzali's ecstatic behaviour in *sama* assemblies, indicative of the widespread nature of the practice together with its acceptability among Sufis of this period.[40]

Another Sufi scholar whose insight on and engagement with the exercise of *sama* matches up to Ghazzali's exposition was Usman al-Hujwiri (d. 1077). Hujwiri was born and brought up in Jullab and Hujwir, the two suburbs of Ghazna. He trained himself in the spiritual path under the guidance of Abul al-Fazl al-Khatli, spending the remaining days of his life in Lahore, a city that rightfully served as the gateway into the heartland of Hindustan. His work, the *Kashf-al Mahjub* (Unveiling of the Veiled), written during the last years of his life in Lahore, is a response to a set of questions posed to Hujwiri by a fellow Sufi from his hometown, named Abu Said al-Hujwiri. The work remains the earliest and one of the most authoritative Sufi instructional treatises in Persian, at a time when Arabic was in much use.[41]

---

[40] Joseph Lumbard, *Ahmad Al -Ghazali: Remembrance, and the Metaphysics of Love* (Albany: State University of New York Press, 2016), 9, 19–21, 102–103.

[41] *Kashf-al Mahjub* is not an ordinary Sufi treatise, but an invaluable work on the lives and doctrines of Sufis. The work is still recognized as one of the best compilations on the Sufi path. See Carl Ernst, *Revealing the Mystery (Kashf al-Mahjub)*, trans. R. A. Nicholson (New York: Pir Press, 1999), 'Foreword'.

Hujwiri closes his work with a detailed discussion on the last veil that he terms as audition (*sama*). The section on *sama* opens with an argument from Hujwiri, a well-accepted idea, that of all the senses possessed by human beings, the sense of audition is the most important, and superior to other sensory activities like seeing, tasting, smelling, and touching.[42] Hujwiri, acknowledging the debate on the lawfulness and unlawfulness of *sama*, elaborates this point by arguing that if the subject of recitation concerns unlawful things related to 'backbiting and calumny and foul abuse and blame of any person, and utterance of infidelity'—then it is unlawful irrespective of the medium it is expressed in—prose or poetry. However, if the content of audition concerns lawful topics like 'morality and exhortations and inferences drawn from the signs of God and contemplation of the evidences of the Truth', then it is lawful irrespective of the medium it is expressed in.[43] For Hujwiri, lawful things do not require any particular medium for expression. Their character and essence remain unaltered whether they are conveyed in prose or poetry. Therefore, audition of poetry is completely lawful, depending on the interpretation the listener arrives at.

Hujwiri divides the participants in *sama* into two classes. First are those who hear the spiritual essence of the verse and are on the path of truth (*haqq*). Their hearts and minds are engaged in the remembrance of God, and they see none other than the Lord Himself, through their contemplation. This is lawful among all types of audition, and those who participate in such *sama* maintain the spirit of religious sanctity. The essence of *sama*, for Hujwiri, lay in the hearing of everything in 'quality and predicament', rather than going simply by the superficial meaning of the verse. Second are those who interest themselves more with the material meaning of *sama*, rather than its inner qualities. As a result, such individuals find themselves lost in worldly distractions, where listening to the sweet sound produces nothing but a sense of falseness in their heart. In this way, the entire exercise of audition results in nothing but distraction. A strong word of caution is issued by Hujwiri to those who participate in *sama* lured by worldliness. Sufis argue that such an audition is carried out

---

[42] *Kashf al Mahjub*, 393.
[43] Ibid., 398.

through one's outer senses that lead to heresy (*tazandaqa*) on the part of the listener.

Hujwiri argues that *sama* affects participants differently in consonance with their spiritual development. He goes on to mention three classes of listeners: beginner (*mubtadiyan*), intermediate (*mutawassitan*), and adept (*kamilan*), while elaborating on the effect *sama* has on individuals belonging to each category.[44] Hujwiri closes his discussion on *sama* by proposing a set of rules and regulations one needs to adhere to in order to participate in the assembly of audition. *Sama* is a blessing from the Unseen. Hence, for Hujwiri, Sufis should take part in the exercise only when they feel an urge for it and when a strong desire for audition arises.

The earliest Sufi master to pen an exclusive treatise on *sama* in the period following Hujwiri and Ghazzali was Abd-al-Rahman al-Sulami (d. 1201). His *Kitab al-Sama* was the first treatise to be written exclusively on the subject of *sama*, both as a defence of the practice and also as a commentary on the ritual's principles and etiquettes. Understandably, it became the model for later works on the subject.

Sulami was born in Nishapur in a prestigious Sufi family, and was trained in the Malamati tradition that allowed him to connect through his forefathers to the ideologies of the early generation of Sufi masters. However, at a time when Sulami himself matured to a venerated Sufi master, the institution had undergone certain advances, the most primary of which was the incorporation of Islamic scholars into Sufi fraternities. Abu Hamid Ghazzali, discussed above, represents the earliest individual example of a Sufi scholar in this tradition. While Sufism gained formal recognition, its rituals, like *sama*, came under criticism from religious scholars who did not hesitate to label these practices as innovations (*bidat*) within the Islamic tradition. *Kitab al-Sama* was written precisely as a response to such criticisms.

Sulami based his treatise on Hadith traditions, Quranic verses, accounts from the Companions of the Prophet, founders of the four legal schools, and early Sufi masters. He agreed with critics that *sama* for the lay individual is no better than a frivolous pastime, which attracts blame and hence necessitates repentance on the part of the listener. However, Sulami also identifies *sama* as a spiritual practice for Sufis that leads to

---

[44] Ibid., 407.

varying degrees of experience contingent on the spiritual state of the listener. For Sufi initiates (*muridin*) and ascetics (*zuhud*), *sama* makes them aware of their misdeeds and worldly actions. While *sama* gives rise to emotions of love and fear for God in the heart of the Sufi, it also provides them with hope and the compassion to be patient on the spiritual path. For gnostics belonging to higher spiritual stations, *sama* makes them realize the Divine reality, stirring them into a state of ecstasy drawing from initial external agitation. For Sulami, it is the state of the listener that decides the impact of *sama* on him. Those who experience *sama* from a higher spiritual state are relieved from the ills of their lower self (*nafs*), thereby moving closer towards the Divine.

Sulami reinforces this argument from the tradition of Junaid of Baghdad, who emphasized that *sama* was directly related to the state of the listener. It may so happen that one listener may remain unmoved after hearing the Quran, while another can draw spiritual succour even by listening to simple verses of poetry. Sulami argues that those who receive Divine grace (*al-muhaqqiqin*) rest at a station where *sama* for them is beyond any falsehood. *Sama* for Sulami is a 'laudable practice (*yastahibbu*) for the people of realized knowledge, permitted (*yubahu*) for the pious people of scruples and ritual worship, and reprehensible (*yukrahu*) for those who listen as entertainment'.[45]

Issues concerning primary preconditions for participating in *sama* range from the spiritual maturity of the listener to the content of recitation. As elaborated above, the two are much intertwined. Scholars like al-Maqdisi in the thirteenth century chose to focus on the latter. He categorized *sama* into forbidden, permitted, estimable, and laudable. According to Maqdisi, 'the effect of melodies is comparable to a container, if the drink is pure it confers delicacy and transparency on the container; if muddy, the container will look opaque and ugly'.[46] The spiritual worth, and success, of *sama* is, therefore, primarily ascertained through the quality of the verses recited. Al-Maqdisi advised *sama* only for those well trained in the Sufi path, while keeping away the inexperienced, lest their hearts become distracted by thoughts of lust and sensuousness. The

[45] N. Purjawadi, *Kitab al-sama* (Tehran: Markaz-i Nashr-i Danishgah, 1990–1993), 14–18, in Kenneth Honerkamp, 'Abu Abd al-Rahman al-Sulami (d. 412/1201) on Sama, Ecstasy and Dance', *Journal of the History of Sufism*, 4 (2003), 1–13.

[46] Shiloah, 'Music and Religion in Islam', 149–150.

latter are allowed to attend the ceremonial proceedings but should not 'actively' take part in them. Thus it can be argued that Maqdisi emphasized the content of *sama*, without ignoring the maturity of the listener.

Ibn al-Arabi (d. 1240), the Andalusian Sufi-scholar from the thirteenth century, moves away from the focus on *content*, and returns to a *quality-of-the-listener* argument. He distinguishes between the participants in *sama* based on those who listen through the intellect (*aql*) and those who listen through the lower self (*nafs*). For Arabi, someone listening with *aql* 'hears everything, from everything and through everything'. Only such a listener is in complete control of his emotions and attains greater proximity (*qurbat*) to God. A Sufi's control over his external emotions is reflected through his 'silent amazement and physical motionless'. Such composure, for Arabi, stands out in stark contrast to those who engage through their lower self and 'hear only through melodies and sweet, yearning voices'.[47]

We can argue that Ibn al-Arabi favoured participation in *sama* under circumstances where the external composure of the listener remains unaltered. Such a state of external behaviour is possible when the Sufi remains deeply absorbed in the spiritual ambience of the assembly. He achieves a spiritual state where his heart is unveiled to Divine beneficence. This experience of witnessing results in physical manifestation in a Sufi—complete calmness to ecstatic bodily movements. Ibn al-Arabi evidently supported the former behaviour in an assembly of *sama*. It can hence be argued that a Sufi who has achieved spiritual maturity, yet is an ecstatic participant in *sama*, ends up exhibiting their emotion through limb movements.

Ibn al-Arabi categorizes *sama* into two fundamental types—the *mutlaq* (soundless) and the *muqayyad* (accompanied by music)—bringing into focus the involvement of musical instruments in the exercise. The latter is again divided into the *ilahi* (divine), the *ruhani* (spiritual), and the *tabi'i* (physical/sensual). Spiritually advanced Sufis who reach the stage of *ilahi* speak to God and listen through God's divine essence. Audition in the *ruhani* consists of listening to praises of God, on how the entire creation sings the glory of the Creator. For al-Arabi, what Sufis normally

---

[47] Ibn al-Arabi, *Kitab al-tadbirat al-ilahiyya fi islah al-mamlaka al-insaniyya*, 223–224, cited in Arthur Gribets, 'The Sama Controversy: Sufi vs. Legalist', *Studia Islamica*, 74 (1991), 51.

practice as *sama* is the *tabi'i*. This is *sama* accompanied by music. Very few Sufis achieve the stage of soundless *sama*—an audition through the ear of the heart carried out mainly through contemplation with intense concentration.

Following in the footsteps of Ibn al-Arabi, al-Uskudari (d. 1628) categorizes *sama* into the natural and spiritual, of which the latter he identifies as soundless *sama* where the accompaniment of music is not required. This, according to him, is achieved only by those who attain the highest degree of spiritual perfection.[48] Once again we find the distinction of audition (*sama*) being made on the basis of the spiritual adeptness of the listener. It is natural for individuals listening with a worldly approach to interpret verses of *sama* materially, as seen in many instances above. However, those who are aware of its mystical content interpret it in the light of the attributes of God. They are the ones equipped to benefit from such assemblies, being in possession of the knowledge that allows them to gain maximum benefits from such esoteric spiritual exercises.

Ikhwan us Safa (Brethren of Purity), an encyclopaedic work, contains over fifty tractates on important arguments related to audition (*sama*). This work borrows its concept from the Greek idea of sound whereby it primarily connects to the soul and not to the body. However, when sound is rendered to rhythm it establishes a connection between the soul and the body resulting in the creation of music. This exercise then becomes *sama*. Like all other senses, audition too is a gift of God, and in the eyes of God the use of such a gift by all human beings is perfectly justified, albeit done in a rightful way.[49]

In some Sufi circles the use of tambourine (*duff*), flute (*shabbaba*), handclapping, and dancing (*raqs*) invite severe criticism from scholars and legists who label such fraternities as 'bands of disgrace'. One such scholar, Ibn Taimiyyah (d. 1328), is recognized as one of the strongest critics of Sufi practices that challenge the limits of *shariah*. Ibn Taimiyyah differentiates between permissible and non-permissible Sufi rituals. Within the former he includes the ritual of *zikr*, an exercise involving the repetition of the names and attributes of God over and over again, as a means of remembering Him spiritually. However, when participants enter a state of

---

[48] Shiloah, 'Music and Religion in Islam', 150; Gribets, 'The Sama Controversy', 51.
[49] Choudhury, 'Music in Islam', 94–95.

physical ecstasy, losing control over themselves, they fail to comply with the limits laid down by the great teachers of Islamic law (*kharij shurut al-mashaikh*). The *sama* of Sufis, according to Ibn Taimiyyah, results in intoxicating effects that suspend rational thinking. Hence the assembly turns into a congregation (*sama al-mushrikun*) of quasi-Sufis (*fuqara*), infidels, and polytheists, who perform actions that are strictly prohibited (*al-muharrama*), leading to ecstasy. Ibn Taimiyyah thus rests his case somewhere between the two extremes of total prohibition of music and poetry, and the legality of chanting a permissible set of hymns.

Scholars like Ibn Radjab (d. 1392), in the generations following Ibn Taimiyyah, chose to refrain from such an extreme position, in favour of a more moderate approach. In his work *Nuzhat al-Asma,* he recognizes *sama* both as permissible and also as a pastime, depending on the contents of the assembly. If the verses recited are of a quality that takes the listener towards frivolity and sensual desires, it should be termed *ghina* (secular song) and, hence, immediately forbidden. However, if the recitations are serious in content, embedded with mystical ideas, it should be recognized as harmless. With regard to musical instruments, however, Ibn Radjab considers all as non-permissible, irrespective of their nature.[50]

Sama as a central practice among Sufis from the tenth century received extensive attention by the early saints, as well as in the treatises that came to be written later in the form of Sufi manuals for guiding subsequent generations of disciples on various issues. The issue concerning the practice of *sama* came to be based on certain important conclusions, which included *sama* being a permissible Sufi practice only when a melodious voice is combined with a pure heart with noble intention, the listener or participant should not be a beginner, and must have undergone rigorous spiritual training to condition his heart to be affected by music, and a strong hierarchy among participants, was advocated by important Sufi saints, depending on their level of training. Finally, *sama* had to be organized in an assembly where like-minded seekers of the spiritual path congregated, recalling the saying by the Sufi master Junaid, who emphasized three conditions for audition assemblies: proper time (*zaman*), a suitable place (*makan*), and compassionate brothers (*ikhwan*).

---

[50] Shiloah, *Music in the World of Islam*, 35.

1

In the Shadow of the Sultanate

Sama in North India

Beginning from the eleventh century, the territorial spread of Sufism across Central Asia and Iran, followed by the crystallization of Sufi orders (*silsilas*) over the twelfth and thirteenth centuries, led to a simultaneous dissemination of rituals like *sama*. In South Asia, Sufis began to arrive from the thirteenth century, one wave after another, creating a process that over the next few centuries turned this region into a rich hub of Sufi activities. Since most of the first-generation Sufi masters who arrived and settled in north India, and as far as Bengal had their spiritual training in Central Asia, Iraq, and Iran, it is of little surprise that they carried their spiritual practices into this new habitation. Subtle variations that arose later within Sufi practices may have occurred under the influence of the immediate social environment. Even though some of these teachings and spiritual practices, like *sama,* had been the focus of controversy, it did not discourage Sufi masters from continuing to practice such exercises in their new social and cultural environment.

In South Asia, *sama* was championed by the Chishtis—one of the earliest Sufi orders of this region. Tracing their roots to the small village of Chisht near Herat in modern-day Afghanistan, Chishti Sufis were trained in important Sufi centres spread across Central Asia, Iran, Iraq, Nishapur, and Khurasan. They considered *sama* to be an intrinsic part of their spiritual practice, a way of union with God that must be combined with strict self-discipline and austerity.[1] In India no Sufi order matched the Chishtis in their vehement support for *sama.*

The rise of Chisht can be traced to the tenth century when the region in and around Central Asia was undergoing a phase of Islamization leading

---

[1] Carl Ernst, *Eternal Garden: Mysticism, History, and Politics at a South Asian Sufi Center* (New Delhi: Oxford University Press, 1992), 147.

Sufi Rituals and Practices. Kashshaf Ghani, Oxford University Press. © Kashshaf Ghani 2024.
DOI: 10.1093/oso/9780192889225.003.0002

to the emergence of important towns like Herat, Chisht, and Jam. These towns in turn became important centres of Sufi activities in the following centuries. Sufi saints and their establishments received support from the successive Muslim sultanates who consolidated their power and authority in the region. Foremost among these patrons were the Ghurid sultans from the Shansabanid clan, who emerged as rulers of this region after defeating their Ghaznavid overlords in the twelfth century. The arrival of Chishti Sufis in north India coincided with the military expeditions of the Ghurid army seeking territorial control and political authority in north India, which ultimately led to the establishment of the Sultanate of Delhi in the early thirteenth century.

Sufis of the Chishti order trace their descent from their founder Abu Ishaq Shami (d. 940), who left Syria and settled in Chisht never to return again. The spiritual genealogy of Shami, though debated among scholars, connects him to Prophet Muhammad through Mimshad al-Dinawari, Hasan Basri, and Ibrahim ibn Adham. Traditions narrate that when Abu Ishaq approached Khwaja Mimshad in Baghdad for discipleship, the latter is said to have remarked 'From today onwards we will call you Abu Ishaque Chishti, and whosoever enters your fold till the Day of Resurrection will be likewise called Chishti'.[2] The creation of a sacred geography with the spiritual centre of Chisht at its core can be ascribed to this statement of Khwaja Mimshad. Henceforth, saints of this order began to connect their spiritual origin to the region of Chisht, rather than to any other spiritual centre.

After Abu Ishaq Shami, the spiritual mantle was picked up by Abu Ahmad Chishti (d. 965/6), who passed it on to his son, Abu Muhammad, and thereafter to the latter's son, Khwaja Abu Yusuf. After the death of Khwaja Yusuf in 1066–1067, his son Khwaja Qutb al-Din Maudud succeeded him. When Khwaja Maudud died in 1181/2, his son Khwaja Ahmad succeeded him. Following a parallel chain of succession, something that would later become common among Chishtis in north India, Khwaja Hajji Sharif, the disciple of Khwaja Maudud, took Khwaja Usman from Harwan, near Nishapur, as his disciple. It is from this parallel line

[2] Zahurul Hassan Sharib, *The Sufi Saints of the Indian Subcontinent* (Delhi: Munshiram Manoharlal Publishers, 2006), 2.

of Khwaja Usman 'Harwani' that Chishti saints in South Asia trace their descent.[3]

The death of Khwaja Maudud and the lifetime of Khwaja Usman Harwani saw the rise of the Ghurids in their remotely located patrimony of Ghur, in modern-day Afghanistan. This was also the period that witnessed the decline of Ghazna, the famous capital city of Sultan Mahmud's sultanate by the same name. This shift in the balance of power resulted in continuous power struggles among different factions of Turks. Eventually the Ghurids, under Ghiyas al-Din Muhammad, emerged victorious. He ruled as the Sultan of Ghur from 1163 to 1203, controlling the western provinces until Nishapur. His younger brother, Muiz al-Din Muhammad, expanded the Ghurid domains eastward, particularly towards north India. He ruled from Ghazna and Lahore, between 1173 and 1206, the latter being the last notable garrison town of the erstwhile Ghaznavids, and their gateway into the vast plains of north India. This continuous struggle for political supremacy had made the environment unsustainable for Sufi activities. As a result, Khwaja Usman Harwani moved west towards Nishapur. It is here that his most famous disciple and founder of the Chishti order in India, Muin al-Din Hasan Sanjari, trained himself.

When Muin al-Din arrived in north India, he chose to settle in the town of Ajmer, the stronghold of the Tomar Chauhans. Though we lack historical records on the career of Muin al-Din before his arrival in India, and even after, legends and hagiographical accounts tirelessly repeat fantastic tales of possible confrontations that occurred between the Sufi master and the Tomar king Prithviraja Chauhan, also known as Rai Pithaura. The victory of Muin al-Din over his adversary, primarily through the blessings of his spiritual master, is supposed to have been foretold when the saint once remarked, 'We have seized Pithaura alive and handed him over to the army of Islam'.[4]

Though the historicity of this apocryphal statement needs to be ascertained, it is nonetheless interesting to read it in the context of the political situation in north India in the twelfth century. It clearly indicates the defeat of Prithviraja not through spiritual confrontation, but in the hands

---

[3] S. A. A. Rizvi, *A History of Sufism in India*, vol. 1 (Delhi: Munshiram Manoharlal Publishers, 1978), 114–115.

[4] Sayyid Muhammad Mubarak al-Kirmani, *Siyar al-awliya*, ed. Chiranji Lal (Delhi: Matba-i Muhibb-i Hind, 1885), 45–47. Henceforth *Siyar al-awliya*.

of the invading Ghurid army. The Ghurid army is also understood as a foreign power, the *army of Islam*, which is sanctified by a resident Sufi. Nationalist historiography on many occasions sought to project Ghurid invasions through the lens of religious confrontation, whereby an 'alien and hostile' Islam overran and defeated the indigenous, peace-loving, and necessarily 'weak' Hindu civilization by overpowering its last hero in the person of Prithviraja Chauhan. Since then it has been a story of *foreign* cultural and political domination over the *indigenous* Indian civilization. However, popular hagiography claims that the Chauhan ruler was captured alive by the Ghurid army after his defeat. Such a convenient narrative, originating understandably from a much later period, not only seeks to add historicity to the supposed prophecy of the Sufi saint, but at the same time marks the beginning of an important tradition in South Asia whereby temporal authority came to rest on the blessings of important Sufi masters. These Sufi saints, believed to be possessing guardianship over God's earthly domain, leased out worldly authority from time to time to Sultans as rulers of vast territories, through prophecy as a form of blessing and sanctification.

Given the above context, it is of little surprise that Muin al-Din Chishti has been elevated to the position of the patron saint of Hindustan, whose authority rests above all other Sufi saints who followed him into this land. The coming of Islam and its long period of dominance in South Asia is popularly ascribed to his blessings, and more importantly to the physical presence, in the region, of his shrine complex (*dargah*). Visits to his shrine (*ziyarat*) by powerful rulers of South Asia, once or more during their lifetime, reinforces this idea of a sacred geography created for perpetuity through the physical remains of this early Sufi saint. Their *ziyarat* can be seen in the sense of seeking to renew, for generations to come, the lease of political authority that they believe to have received from him. Even the mighty Mughals at the height of their power and political authority could not afford to overlook this critical element of spiritual legitimacy that connected them to the shrine and cult of Muin al-Din Chishti, until the last days of their rule.[5]

---

[5] Simon Digby, 'Early Pilgrimages to the Graves of Mu'in ad-din Sijzi and Other Indian Chishti Shaykhs', in M. Israel and N. K. Wagle, eds, *Islamic Society and Culture* (New Delhi: Manohar, 1983), 95–100; Bruce Lawrence, 'Veiled Opposition to Sufis in Muslim South Asia: Manipulation of Mystical Brotherhoods by the Great Mughal', in Frederick De Jong and Bernd Radke, eds,

Figure 1.1 Dargah of Khwaja Muin al-Din Chishti, Ajmer

Along with establishing the Chishti order in South Asia, Muin al-Din is believed to have also introduced some of the core spiritual practices of the order that continued through his successors. Primary among them was the practice of *sama* among his disciples. The Sufi master used to frequently participate in *sama* with such passion that all those who attended the assembly, in and around Ajmer, sought to immerse themselves in the ecstatic spirit that prevailed in the gathering.[6] This tradition remains unaltered even to this day, when during the *urs* of the saint the most important ritual at the shrine is the performance of *sama*, held at the designated chamber (*samakhana*) after evening prayers.[7]

Islamic Mysticism Contested: Thirteen Centuries of Controversies and Polemics (Leiden: E. J. Brill, 1999), 436–451; Kashshaf Ghani, 'The Gunpowder Empires: Mughals', in Lloyd Ridgeon, ed., *The Routledge Handbook of Sufism* (London: Routledge, 2020), 387–393; Pratyay Nath, 'Pilgrimage, Performance, and Peripatetic Kingship: Akbar's Journeys to Ajmer and the Formation of the Mughal Empire', *Journal of the Royal Asiatic Society*, Series 3 (2022), 1–26.

[6] P. M. Currie, *The Shrine and Cult of Muin al-din Chishti of Ajmer* (New Delhi: Oxford University Press, 1989), 69.
[7] Ibid., 126.

The tradition of losing oneself in divine contemplation through audition assemblies (*mehfil-i sama*) goes back to the progenitors of the Chishti order, long before Muin al-Din initiated himself as one of their disciples.

Abu Ishaq Shami Chishti was also very fond of *sama*. It is said that such was the strength of his personality that scholars, legists, and the *ulama* could not voice their protest against Abu Ishaq's practice of *sama*. Rather many were attracted to the exercise of audition (*sama*). Every individual who had the good fortune to attend *sama* in the company of the shaykh became enraptured in its ambience. *Sama* being a communal exercise, mystics were more inclined to assemble and contemplate as a group so that blessings bestowed on one would benefit others in the assembly. Therefore, whenever Khwaja Abu Ishaq was in a mood to engage in *sama*, he would gather his compatriots, and the *qawwal* was informed well beforehand so that he could prepare himself in the spirit of the assembly, rather than be unprepared and incur the displeasure of the Sufi saints.[8]

The usefulness of *sama* in enhancing the spiritual qualities within a mystic is well illustrated in an incident involving the Chishti Sufi Khwaja Maudud Chishti. Once, it is said, while the Khwaja was lost in *sama*, he was no longer visible to the rest of the assembly. On being asked, the Khwaja later replied that the assembly of *sama* is an exercise where the ones who are truly lost in the act of spiritual contemplation find themselves elevated to the realm of Divine proximity.[9] Under such circumstances they no longer remain visible to those who are yet to gain sufficient knowledge in the inner (*batin*) affairs of spirituality. It is impossible for the human eye to perceive such truths unless one's inner vision is fully acquired.

Relations between Sufi saints and political authorities were also determined in the context of *sama*. An anecdotal record concerning *sama* narrates an interaction between Khwaja Usman Haruni and Caliph. The latter had once sent a messenger to the saint asking him to give up on the practice of participating in *sama*. In support, the Caliph, who was close to the Suhrawardi order, cited from the tradition of Junaid, who, while advising one of his disciples on *sama*, had remarked 'If you wish to keep your religion safe and maintain your patience, do not indulge in the

---

[8] Ibid., 143.
[9] Ibid., 142.

audition which the Sufis practice; and when you grow old do not let your-self to be the cause of guilt in others'.[10] This advice by Junaid on absten-tion from *sama* was taken as a pretext by the Caliph to convince Khwaja Usman Haruni to restrain from participating in such frivolous practices. The Caliph went so far as to issue an order in the sense that any individual found participating in *sama* should be hanged and all *qawwals* be killed, lest common people were to become depraved by this heinous practice.[11]

Khwaja Usman Haruni, in turn, replied that *sama* represented a se-cret covenant that existed between God and His seeker. Its essence cannot be apprehended by minds regulated by worldly reason and material thoughts.[12] The shaykh further stressed that, being a Chishti Sufi, it was impossible for him to go against the tradition of his masters who for years had kept themselves engaged in this ritual, deriving spiritual benefits from it. Yet he decided to visit the royal court and settle the issue in the presence of the *ulama*. The Caliph allowed the *ulama* to hold an arbitra-tion council (*mahzar*) on the matter, to determine the legality of *sama*.

As the day arrived, on witnessing the spiritual charisma of Khwaja Usman Haruni the *ulama* fell at his feet and sought mercy, repeatedly conforming to his saintly status, and admitting that for a Sufi of his stature *sama* is fully permissible. Usman Haruni in his defence further elaborated that at a time when Junaid himself abstained from the prac-tice of *sama*, it was his own decision. He never intended to impose it on those who were adept in *sama*. Junaid's warning was intended for novices who ran the risk of losing their way early in their spiritual journey, while participating in *sama*. Thus, it was not incumbent upon the Chishti saint to follow the regulation of Junaid on the issue of *sama*. Khwaja Usman Haruni is believed to have remarked that had Junaid come in contact with the saints of the Chishti order, he would have certainly changed his stance on the practice of *sama*, because of the emphatic enthusiasm of the Chishtis for the ritual.

When the details of the proceedings reached the ears of the Caliph, he immediately permitted Khwaja Usman Haruni to continue his practice of *sama*. Ignoring the discontent of his courtiers, the Caliph declared *sama*

[10] *Kashf al Mahjub*, 412.
[11] Sayyid Muhammad Husayni Gisu Daraz, *Khatima: Tarjuma adab al muridin*, Urdu trans. Sayyid Yasin Ali Nizami (Delhi: Adabi Dunya, 2007), 140–141. Henceforth *Khatima*.
[12] Ibid., 141.

as legal only for the shaykh, and likewise ordered *qawwals* to perform in the audition assemblies of the shaykh. He also arranged for their emoluments from the royal treasury.

The above sequence of events, though historically questionable, illustrates the passion of Chishti Sufis regarding the practice of *sama*, received from their *ajami* predecessors. Therefore the strong inclination of Muin al-Din and his successors to uphold *sama* as a spiritual exercise par excellence cannot be read in isolation. Neither does the oft-repeated argument hold ground that the questionable ritual of *sama* was followed by Chishti Sufis in order to appeal to the music-loving, largely non-Muslim, Indian population with the aim of securing their position in an unknown sociocultural environment, and furthering the cause of conversion.[13]

For Chishti Sufis in South Asia, *sama* remained the core exercise for spiritual contemplation representing both the ontological and epistemological *sine qua non* of Islamic mysticism.[14] Participation in such an intense spiritual exercise helped Chishti Sufis in their spiritual advancement, facilitating their journey towards union with the Beloved. Thus Chishtis viewed *sama* as an exercise limitless in scope, which if applied in the right spirit of the assembly could transfer the entire proceedings into the realm of Divine experience. Hence benefits accrued from the practice of *sama* were considered unique and irreplaceable by any other form of spiritual exercise.[15]

Sama however remained an essentially elite practice, restricted to initiates of the Chishti order and strictly distanced from common masses. For Chishtis, such a highly organized spiritual practice, if accessed by all, could lead to an inevitable vulgarization that needed to be avoided. While we find limited participation of masses in the ritual of *sama*, Chishti treatises describe *sama* as the highest form of spiritual exercise, to be organized and participated under strict conditions. This demanded both psychological and intellectual training for Sufis who participated in it, together with elaborate rules of etiquette to regulate the practice.

---

[13] K. A. Nizami, *Some Aspects of Religion and Politics during the 13th Century* (New Delhi: Oxford University Press, 2002), 191; Ernst, *Eternal Garden*, 147.

[14] Bruce Lawrence, 'The Early Chishti Approach to Sama', in Israel and Wagle, eds, *Islamic Society and Culture*, 70–71.

[15] Ibid., 74.

An analysis of the Chishti approach to *sama* thus helps understand this unique ritual observed by one of the earliest Sufi orders of South Asia.

Rise of Chishti Sufism

Though the geographical origins of the Chishti order can be traced to the remote village of Chisht in Afghanistan, it matured and flourished in the Indian subcontinent. It is not an exaggeration when the Chishti order is identified as an Indian Sufi order, whose social appeal, over centuries, has cut across communities who inhabit this region.[16] The first Chishti Sufi in India, Muin al-Din Chishti, was born and brought up in Sijistan and Khurasan respectively. He eventually became the disciple of Khwaja Usman Haruni, who resided in Harwan, adjacent to Nishapur. After completing his training under Khwaja Usman Haruni and receiving the robe of discipleship, Muin al-Din set out to visit Baghdad, Hamadan, and Tabriz, where he met important Sufi masters like Najim al-Din Kubra, Abdul Qadir Jilani, Yusuf Hamadani, and Jalal al-Din Tabrizi. He remained in that region for few years before moving eastward to Ghazna, Lahore, and finally to Delhi, where the Ghurid Turks under the command of Muiz al-Din Muhammad had recently registered their victory against the last ruler, Prithviraja Chauhan.[17]

Another tradition, largely drawn from the hagiography woven around the saint, narrates that when Muin al-Din reached Medina after receiving the robe of discipleship (*khilafat*), he engaged himself in deep contemplation in the mosque of the Prophet. It was here that he was supposedly commanded by Prophet Muhammad in a dream to move towards Hindustan, and settle in Ajmer where darkness prevailed, and which could only be eliminated through the light of Islam:

> O Muin al-Din! You are a helper of my religion. I entrust to you the country of Hindustan. There prevails darkness. Proceed to Ajmer and spread there the Gospel of Truth.[18]

---

[16] Carl Ernst and Bruce B. Lawrence, *Sufi Martyrs of Love: The Chishti Order in South Asia and Beyond* (London: Palgrave Macmillan, 2002), Introduction.

[17] Rizvi, *History of Sufism*, 121–122.

[18] Sharib, *The Sufi Saints*, 8.

One may read into this narrative as a later concoction of popular Chishti hagiography in an attempt to connect the arrival of Muin al-Din Chishti to Hindustan with the direct guidance he received from the Prophet. Such a charged narrative centring on the act of direct bestowal of spiritual authority from the Prophet himself to Muin al-Din helped elevate Chishti Sufis as spiritual protectors of the Delhi Sultanate and their supposed pre-dominance over contemporary Sufi orders as torchbearers of mystical Islam in the region.

Bothered by the heightened political activity in Delhi following the collapse of the Tomar regime, Muin al-Din decided to move away to a quieter place for which he chose Ajmer, the seat of power of the erstwhile Chauhana rulers. Even as his number of disciples swelled, many from the Ghurid army who aspired independent areas of authority for themselves, Muin al-Din carefully avoided all luring to power, authority, and wealth, choosing to lead an ascetic life. Perhaps the foundational principles of the Chishti order for the coming generations of Sufi masters were laid in the very manner in which Muin al-Din spent the remaining years of his life in Ajmer—as a simple and pious Sufi saint devoted to God, with no attach-ments whatsoever to rulers, nobles, men of wealth, power, or authority. His idea of closeness to God was manifested through a deep compassion for the masses who experienced the saint's 'river like generosity, sun like affection and earth like hospitality'.[19]

The most able disciple of Muin al-Din to carry forward his spiritual legacy could have been none other than the young Hamid al-Din. He be-came the disciple of Muin al-Din at Ajmer and later accompanied him to Delhi. Such was the austerity and rigour practiced by Hamid al-Din that he was once said to have remarked that he desired nothing that went against Divine will. This impressed his master greatly, who bestowed upon Hamid al-Din the title of *Sultan al-tarikin* (King of Hermits).[20] Following a deeply ascetic lifestyle far from the chaos of urban life, Hamid al-Din took up residence in Suwali, near Nagaur in Rajasthan. He had a cow to provide him with milk, and a small farmland of one bigha which he cultivated for food grains. His mother and wife, who were women of

---

[19] *Siyar al-awliya*, 46–47.
[20] Abdul Haq Muhaddith Dehlawi, *Akhbar al-akhyar* (Delhi: Mujtabai Press, 1913), 29–30.

great piety and merit, supported the household by spinning yarn and cooking.[21]

Given the above, it is not surprising that Muin al-Din once asked his disciples to record the conditions required to live like an ascetic:

1. One should not earn money.
2. One should not borrow money from anyone.
3. One should not reveal to anyone nor seek help from anyone if one has eaten nothing, even for seven days.
4. If one gains plenty of food, money, grain, or clothing, one should not keep anything until the following day.
5. One should not curse anyone; if anyone is very hurt, one should pray to God to guide one's enemy towards the right path.
6. If one performs a virtuous deed, one should consider that the source of the virtue is either due to the kindness of his pir, to the intercession of Prophet Muhammad on one's behalf, or to divine mercy.
7. If one performs one evil deed one should consider oneself responsible for the action and try to protect oneself from such deeds.
8. Out of fear of God one should be careful to avoid actions which may involve him again in evil.
9. Having fulfilled all the above conditions, one should regularly fast during the day and spend the night in prayer.
10. One should remain quiet and speak only when it is imperative to do so. The *shariah* makes it unlawful both to talk incessantly and to keep totally silent. One should utter only such words as those which please God.[22]

While Hamid al-Din chose to settle in rural north India, Qutb al-Din Bakhtiyar Kaki, the other celebrated disciple of Khwaja Muin al-Din, chose Delhi to settle down and carry out his spiritual activities. He was born in Aus, an important centre of activity for Sufis following the Hallaj tradition, in the province of Jaxartes. As he grew older, Qutb al-Din moved

[21] *Siyar al-awliya*, 156–157; *Sarur us Sudur*, 9–10, 14, 43, in Nizami, *Some Aspects of Religion*, 185–186.
[22] *Sarur us Sudur*, 51–52, in Rizvi, *History of Sufism*, 123–124.

to Baghdad, the most famous centre for Sufi activities in the twelfth century. There he met Khwaja Muin al-Din in the mosque of Imam Abul Lais Samarqandi and immediately took to his discipleship, ignoring eminent Sufis like Abdul Qadir Jilani, Shihab al-Din Suhrawardi, and Auhad al-Din Kirmani. After his training in Baghdad, when Khwaja Muin al-Din left for India, Qutb al-Din travelled further through Khurasan and Multan, before making his way into India out of a deep desire to meet his master.[23]

When Qutb al-Din was travelling through Central Asia and Iran towards Lahore and Delhi, the entire region was torn apart by political instability. Immediately after the demise of Ghiyas al-Din Muhammad, the western domains of the Ghurid Sultanate fell into the hands of the Khwarazm Empire, who were steadily advancing eastwards. Threatened by the formidable Khwarazm Sultan, Muiz al-Din Muhammad left his possessions in India in the hands of his trusted slave General Qutb al-Din Aibak and hastened towards Ghazna. He was assassinated in Damyak, and the entire Ghurid kingdom in Afghanistan came under the control of the Khwarazm Shah. However, the latter soon faced the fury of the Mongols from the north, who wreaked havoc across West Asia. Under the command of Chingiz Khan, the Mongols not only razed the Khwarazm Sultanate to the ground, but the last Khwarazm Shah, Jalal al-Din Mangabarni, suffered an inglorious defeat at the hands of the Mongols in 1221. Pressing political situations in the west required the attention of Chingiz Khan, which fortunately spared Delhi from the wrath of the Mongols, allowing Sultan Iltutmish to consolidate his realm further by gradually eliminating his opponents in the Punjab region.[24]

It was in such political turmoil that Qutb al-Din Bakhtiyar Kaki arrived in north India. While passing through the Punjab he stopped at Multan in 1214, when Nasir al-Din Qubacha was the governor. Qutb al-Din renewed his acquaintance with Baha al-Din Zakariyya, the Suhrawardi Sufi master. During the course of his stay the Mongols attacked the region, possibly pursuing the Khwarazm Shah. Nasir al-Din Qubacha, fearing defeat in the hands of Mongols, approached the Chishti saint for help, who gave the governor an arrow and instructed him to shoot it at

---

[23] *Siyar al-awliya*, 48–49; Fazlullah Jamali, *Siyar-al-arifin*, 16–19, in Rizvi, *History of Sufism*, 123–124; Nizami, *Some Aspects of Religion*, 188.
[24] Rizvi, *History of Sufism*, 133–134; Nizami, *Some Aspects of Religion*, 31–33.

Figure 1.2 Dargah of Qutb al-Din Bakhtiyar Kaki, Delhi

the direction of the Mongol camp after evening prayers. Nasir al-Din Qubacha did as instructed, and the next morning the Mongols were said to have retreated from the region.[25]

Though the Mongols retreated purely for political reasons, the fame of Qutb al-Din as a powerful saint spread phenomenally. Multan was already under the spiritual authority (*wilaya*) of the Suhrawardi saint Baha al-Din Zakariyya. Once Qutb al-Din had expressed his desire to settle there, he was given a cup of milk by Baha al-Din, which was filled to the brim. This was a gentle message that the region had no place for another Sufi saint, and that the Chishti master needed to move on and look for a fresh territory in which to settle down. After this clear message, Qutb al-Din had to turn down repeated requests from Nasir al-Din Qubacha to settle in the region, and moved further east until he reached Delhi sometime after 1221. In Delhi he was warmly welcomed by Sultan Iltutmish, who was visibly happy to receive the Chishti saint in his capital, away from the domain of his political rival Qubacha.

---

[25] Rizvi, *History of Sufism*, 134–135; Sharib, *The Sufi Saints*, 28.

The presence of Qutb al-Din Bakhtiyar Kaki in Delhi helped to legit-imize the nascent authority of Iltutmish as the Sultan, who was yet to es-tablish his complete control over his rivals. In the history of the Delhi Sultanate, this remains one of the earliest instances of a Sultan seeking legitimacy from the presence of an eminent Sufi saint within his realm. Many more instances would follow. But for Iltutmish, aspiring to be in the position of unquestioned authority within the Delhi Sultanate, securing the blessings of the disciple of the revered Muin al-Din Chishti was a great support to his rule, which was being challenged by the same governor of Multan who had tried to retain Qutb al-Din within his own domain, though without success.

Keeping with the tradition of his master in Ajmer, Qutb al-Din chose to settle in Kilokhri near the Yamuna, away from the imperial centre. However, after repeated requests from Sultan Iltutmish, the saint moved to Mehrauli. He was regularly visited by eminent personalities and other shaykhs, including the Sultan himself. Though he distanced himself from the affairs of the court, Qutb al-Din supported public works undertaken by the government, the most notable of which was the construction of the water tank *Hauz-i Shamsi*.

However, separation from his master pained Qutb al-Din greatly. On more than one occasion, he sought permission from Muin al-Din to visit him at Ajmer. In one such instance Muin al-Din replied, 'Apparently you are at a distance from me, but inwardly you are close to me. Remain where you are'.[26] Perhaps Muin al-Din realized the responsibility he had bestowed on the shoulders of his disciple, which required the presence of the latter in the capital amongst the common people to address their wor-ries and grievances, along with spreading the message of Chishti order at a time when many eminent Sufi saints from the western lands had assem-bled in Delhi, which was being seen by immigrants as the capital of the eastern Islamic world.

Shortly before his arrival in north India, when Qutb al-Din Bakhtiyar Kaki was residing in Multan for a brief period, he came across a young boy who had come down to the city for further studies in the seminary of Maulana Minhaj al-Din Tirmizi. He was deeply given to ascetic life and continuous meditation, largely due to the influence of his pious mother,

[26] Nizami, *Some Aspects of Religion*, 189; Sharib, *The Sufi Saints*, 23.

who introduced him to prayers and practices of meditation. The boy was named Farid al-Din. On meeting Qutb al-Din, young Farid presented himself to become the disciple of the saint. He was initiated into the Chishti order, but was strictly advised to complete his education before taking up the spiritual path. And it was only after Farid al-Din completed his education that he left for Delhi to join the hallowed company of other spiritual initiates in the *khanqah* of Qutb al-Din.[27]

Of all the Chishti masters, Farid al-Din is acclaimed for his deep asceticism and severe penitence. Not only his master, Qutb al-Din, but the legendary Khwaja Muin al-Din, while visiting his disciple in Delhi on one occasion, was also impressed by the ascetic rigor of the young Farid. Thereafter, Muin al-Din invited Qutb al-Din to join him in prayer to seek an honourable future for Farid al-Din. This incident remains the only instance in early Chishti history of a young disciple being blessed not only by his immediate master, but by the master of his master, none other than the founder of the Chishti order in South Asia. It was during his discipleship under Qutb al-Din that Farid al-Din undertook the extremely difficult and rare meditative exercise of the inverted chilla (*chilla-i makus*), which required the individual to tie a rope around his feet and remain suspended upside down in a well for forty nights, while continuing with his spiritual exercises and fasting. He would be pulled out only at daybreak.[28]

After completing his spiritual training in Delhi, Farid al-Din left for Hansi in Hissar district. However, he finally settled in Ajodhan, a remote village on the bank of the river Sutlej in the Punjab, which was chosen by the saint so that he could withdraw himself completely from worldly affairs and immerse himself in spiritual exercises. So severe was his ascetic life that he remained under continuous fasting, while meditating at the same time. At times when he did not receive any *futuh* to break his fast, it would be prolonged, and on rare occasions hunger would get the better of his spiritual determination. In order to calm his pangs of hunger, Farid al-Din would gnaw on a piece of wood carved in the shape of a flatbread (*chapatti*), and also pick up pebbles from the ground and put them inside his mouth. Such was the purity of his inner self that those pebbles, it is

---

[27] Rizvi, *History of Sufism*, 138–139; Ernst and Lawrence, *Sufi Martyrs of Love*, 155.
[28] *Siyar al-awliya*, 68–69.

said, would immediately turn to cubes of sugar. Initially he thought it to be a trick by the devil. However, when this miracle happened thrice he was convinced of its source from the Unseen. This led him to being revered as *Ganj-i Shakr*, or 'storehouse of sugar', an epithet which stuck with him thereafter. He popularly came to be revered as Farid al-Din Ganj-i Shakr, or simply Baba Farid.[29]

Although the population of the surrounding region, consisting of tribes and other communities, was initially hostile towards the saint, resulting somewhat from his lonely and ascetic lifestyle, with the spread of his fame as a spiritual master people started visiting his *khanqah* in huge numbers, which at times created discomfort for the saint. Nonetheless it is noteworthy that many of the tribes and clans in Punjab claim their initiation into Islam through the hands of Baba Farid. Ray Siyal, the founder of the Siyal clan of Jhang district, claimed to have been converted to Islam in the thirteenth century by Baba Farid, after which all subsequent generations of Siyals were Muslims.[30] A number of Jat and Rajput clans who became Muslims in the medieval period attribute their conversion to Baba Farid and his Suhrawardi contemporary, Baha al-Din Zakariyya. These include clans such as the Bhatti, Chhina, Dhudhi, and Dogar, among others.[31] It is probable, however, that many of these clans were not present in Ajodhan during the lifetime of Baba Farid, in which case gradual conversions must have taken place in the generations after Baba Farid, through the presence of his imposing shrine complex in Ajodhan, which by the sixteenth century came to be known as Pakpattan (the holy ferry). The integration of these tribes and clans within the socio-religious sphere of shrine activities facilitated their gradual conversion to Islam.[32]

The spread of the Chishti order in South Asia can be attributed to Baba Farid, who ensured that his disciples settled in different regions of the country to preach the ideals of Sufism among the masses, thereby expanding the Chishti legacy far and wide. Of his many disciples,

---

[29] Ibid., 67–68.
[30] Richard Eaton, 'The Political and Religious Authority of the Shrine of Baba Farid', in Barbara Daly Metcalf, ed., *Moral Conduct and Authority: The Place of Adab in South Asian Islam* (Berkeley: University of California Press, 1984), 352.
[31] Ibid., 345–346.
[32] Ibid.

Jamal al-Din Hansawi was the dear and loved one for whom the saint used to remark, 'Jamal is our *jamal* (beauty)'. But the most celebrated disciple of Baba Farid, who later went on to become the greatest Sufi master of the fourteenth century, was none other than Muhammad ibn Ahmad ibn Ali al-Bukhari, popularly known as Nizam al-Din Awliya. He was born in Badaun, where his family had settled after migrating from Bukhara. The shaykh lost his father in childhood. However, much like his master, he too was initially trained as a religious scholar, and was later initiated into meditation and spirituality in the hands of his mother, who was a pious woman with strong determination. When their family faced hard times in Badaun, and after the early demise of his father, it was Nizam al-Din's mother who taught him the virtue of *tawakkul*—to endure suffering while remaining patient and steadfast in the way of God, the very first lesson of the Sufi path that Nizam al-Din carried with him for the rest of his life.

She also realized the importance of education, and never compromised on the quality of education her son received. Nizam al-Din started his education in Badaun, and later moved to Delhi to study under senior masters. His first instructor was Shadi Muqri, an expert in Quran recitation. Thereafter the shaykh trained with Maulana Ala al-Din Usuli for some years. It was during this training that he first heard about Baba Farid from Abu Bakr Kharrat, a *qawwal* who had come to Badaun after a visit to the *khanqah* of Baha al-Din Zakariyya in Multan and Baba Farid in Ajodhan. The description of Baba Farid's khanqah caught the imagination of Nizam al-Din. Thereafter he moved to Delhi for further studies and trained himself under Shamsul Malik who was a learned teacher of his time. In Delhi, Nizam al-Din stayed in the locality of Najib al-Din Mutawakkil, the youngest brother of Baba Farid.[33]

Najib al-Din Mutawakkil initially came to Delhi for education but decided to stay back for the rest of his life with no property or pension. He lived with his family, wife, and two sons, in a single room with a broken thatched roof.[34] Nizam al-Din had deep respect for Najib al-Din and visited him often for blessings. Nizam al-Din would often remark that

---

[33] Amir Hasan Sijzi, *Fawaid al Fuad,* 163–164, 169, in Rizvi, *A History of Sufism,* 154–155.
[34] Hamid Qalandar, *Khair al Majalis, Conversations of Shaikh Nasir al-Din Chiraghh-i-Dihlı,* 75, in Nizami, *Some Aspects of Religion,* 199. Henceforth *Khair al Majalis.*

he had not seen anyone like Najib al-Din, who would resign his life to God but remain happy with his family and companions.[35] On becoming qualified to be a *qazi*, Nizam al-Din requested Najib al-Din to pray for him, to which the latter advised him not to desire for a government position, but to seek another path. On his advice Nizam al-Din decided to give up trying for the position of a *qazi* and focused instead on spiritual training.[36]

In 1257–1258 he left for Ajodhan at the age of twenty. Nizam al-Din later recalled that when he arrived at the *khanqah* of Baba Farid, he was welcomed by the ageing saint with the following couplet:

Ah, the fire of separation from you has burnt many a heart
And the flood of yearning to meet you has ruined many a soul!

On hearing this, the young Nizam al-Din failed to give verbal expression to his feelings and could only manage to look overwhelmed, sharing his great desire to meet the Chishti master. To this Baba Farid replied that all newcomers to the *khanqah* are initially nervous. As a special treatment Nizam al-Din was not required to tonsure his head, and was allowed to keep his golden locks, and was also provided with a cot, a rare luxury in any Chishti *khanqah*. In the conversations that ensued, Nizam al-Din asked his master whether he should continue with his studies, to which Baba Farid replied that 'I do not restrain anyone from learning. Do both until one predominates. A dervish should have some measure of learning.'[37]

Nizam al-Din visited Ajodhan three times during the lifetime of Baba Farid. On the second occasion he read six chapters from the Quran, five chapters from the Sufi manual *Awarif al Maarif*, and other books. The last visit took place in 1265, when Nizam al-Din was conferred with the certificate of discipleship (*khilafatnama*) by Baba Farid with the following blessing, 'I have given you both the worlds. Go and take the kingdom of Hindustan ... you will be the tree under whose shadow people will find rest ... you should strengthen your spirits by devotion ... I have

---

[35] *Siyar al-awliya*, 167.
[36] *Fawaid al Fuad*, 32, in Rizvi, *A History of Sufism*, 156.
[37] *Siyar al-awliya*, 107; Nizami, *Some Aspects of Religion*, 195–196.

handed over all these things to you for at the time of my death you will not be present.[38] As foretold by his master, Nizam al-Din failed to remain present during the last hours of Baba Farid, the same way as the latter was away when his master Qutb al-Din Bakhtiyar Kaki breathed his last in Delhi.

In course of his training Nizam al-Din once heard from Baba Farid that fasting is only one half of the spiritual task, the other half consisting of prayer and pilgrimage. Following such instructions from his master, Nizam al-Din fully involved himself in ascetic exercises upon his return to Delhi. But at the same time he also continued with his studies in religious scriptures and works of theology.[39] The shaykh was a great believer in renunciation of worldly bonds and desires, not by just wearing a loincloth, but by being fully clothed and fed, yet distributing among the poor whatever came his way. For Nizam al-Din, it was only through proper worldly renunciation that regular prayers, fasting, and supererogatory prayers bore fruit.[40]

Initially the saint was undecided as to where he should settle in Delhi. After much deliberation and moving around, he decided to settle in Ghiyaspur, a small village near Kilokhri. It was a deserted place until Sultan Muiz al-Din Kaiqubad made Kilokhri his new capital. This shift of political centre made Ghiyaspur a bustling suburb of Delhi, where people thronged in large numbers to the hospice of Nizam al-Din. While the saint was contemplating a shift from that place, a strange incident happened which made him change his mind and stay back in Ghiyaspur.

Nizam al-Din would recall that on the very day he thought of moving out from Ghiyaspur, a handsome youth appeared before him after his noon prayers, and remarked,

That day that you became the moon, you did not know
That you would be the place to which the world looks

The Sufi master recalled later that the youth further added 'A person should not set out to become famous. If by chance one does become

---

[38] *Siyar al-awliya*, 116–117, 131–132.
[39] Ibid.
[40] *Fawaid al Fuad*, 10, in Rizvi, *History of Sufism*, 165.

Figure 1.3 Main Hall in the Khanqah of Nizam al-Din Awliya

Figure 1.4 Meditation Cell of Nizam al-Din Awliya

Figure 1.5 Qawwals performing at the khanqah of Nizam al-Din Awliya

famous, he should act in such a manner that on the Day of Resurrection he will not be embarrassed before the Prophet … what power is there in turning a deaf ear to people and busying oneself with God? True benefit comes from remaining in the midst of people while constantly remembering God'.[41] After this event Nizam al-Din decided to stay back in Ghiyaspur, where he found himself surrounded by people from all sections of society, from kings, scholars, and nobles to the poor and the destitute, who would throng to his *khanqah* to benefit from his spiritual wealth as a Sufi, together with his generosity and kind heartedness as a human being.

Chroniclers of the Delhi Sultanate like Zia al-Din Barani unhesitatingly exaggerate that people in Delhi turned towards piety and religion under the beneficial impact of Nizam al-Din's *khanqah* in Ghiyaspur. From the time Nizam al-Din opened the doors of his *khanqah* to all classes of people, irrespective of their social and economic position, the common masses of Delhi considered themselves to be disciples of the Sufi saint.

---

[41] Ernst and Lawrence, *Sufi Martyrs of Love*, 160.

Figure 1.6 Khanqah and Chilla of Nizam al-Din Awliya, Delhi

They refrained from sin and evil deeds and grew inclined towards prayer and religious practices. The general influence of Nizam al-Din's presence in the city of Delhi was visible at all levels of society, from the ordinary shopkeeper to the nobles.[42]

The spiritual domain of Nizam al-Din was secured and carried forward by a number of his disciples who spread out to different corners of the subcontinent, carrying with them the ideals of the Chishti order through the teachings of their renowned master. Nizam al-Din's lifetime saw the widest dissemination of Chishti principles through his disciples who incorporated within the spiritual map of Chishti Sufism places and individuals who had hitherto not come in direct contact with Sufi ideology. In a way, the words and practices of masters starting from Khwaja Muin al-Din Chishti onwards through Qutb al-Din and Baba Farid were transplanted from north India to regions in the east like Bengal, Deccan,

---

[42] K. A. Nizami, 'Attitude of Early Muslim Mystics towards Society and State during the Sultanate Period', in K. A. Nizami, ed., *State and Culture in Medieval India* (Delhi: Adam Publishers, 1985), 193–194.

Central India, and also western parts of the subcontinent. The network of Chishti spirituality initiated by Baba Farid and his disciples reached its culmination under the leadership of Nizam al-Din.

In Delhi, however, Nizam al-Din was succeeded by his most prominent disciple, Nasir al-Din Mahmud, also known as *Chiragh-i Dehli* (Lamp of Delhi). He was born in 1276/7 in Awadh to an affluent family. But ironically Nasir al-Din was drawn towards asceticism from early in his life, much in the way Baba Farid was. Though he was given a formal education by his family, he chose to spend his early days in the company of dervishes in Awadh, training himself in the art of contemplation and meditation in isolated places away from his home.

It was only after he had trained himself sufficiently in the practice of asceticism that he proceeded towards the hospice of Nizam al-Din in Ghiyaspur, desiring his tutelage. He was happily inducted into the ranks of Nizam al-Din's disciples, though Nasir al-Din Mahmud had problems making himself comfortable in the *khanqah* located in the middle of a bustling urban environment. His feeble request through senior members of the *khanqah* to retire to isolated places, like forests and mountains, was sternly turned down by Nizam al-Din, who in turn educated Nasir al-Din on one of the principle ideals of Chishti Sufism with the following lesson: 'Tell him that he should live in the city and bear patiently the tyranny and maltreatment meted out to him by the people and in return should undergo sacrifice for their sake and should be generous and kind to them'.[43]

Nasir al-Din could never ignore the instruction of his master and for the rest of his life had to yield to requests from the Sultan with much displeasure. He was asked to assist the royalty on various occasions, accompany the Sultan in his travels, as well as accept government positions. His *khanqah* faced severe poverty of resources, while the shaykh himself remained austere, immersed in prayer, meditation, and continuous fasting. He died in 1356 without appointing any successor to his spiritual domain. All his earthly remains—the robe (*khirqa*), his cap, the staff, his rosary, the wooden bowl, and the wooden sandals—were buried with him. For

---

[43] Sharib, *The Sufi Saints*, 74.

Figure 1.7 Hand-written genealogical tree (*shajara*)

those who looked forwards to a spiritual successor from Nasir al-Din, the Sufi master left the following message:

> *Tell them, they have to bear the burden of their own faith,*
> *There is no question of bearing the burden of others.*[44]

[44] Rizvi, *History of Sufism*, 187.

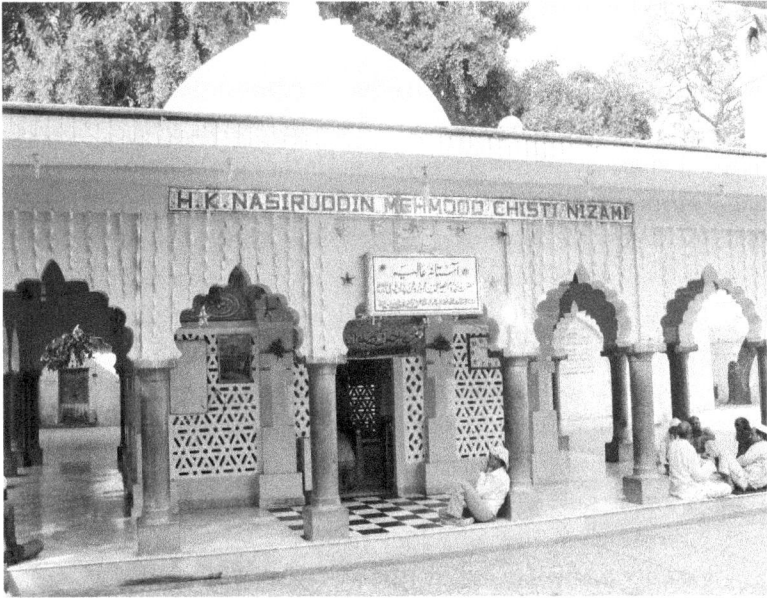

Figure 1.8 Dargah of Nasir al-Din Chiragh-i Dehli, Delhi

In the absence of a direct successor, the tomb of Nasir al-Din Mahmud became the last beacon of Chishti Sufism in Delhi, revered to such an extent that the locality came to be known as *Chiragh-i Dehli*. Though no contemporary source cites this epithet after his name, a number of reasons are cited as being behind the epithet, one of them being that after the transfer of the capital to Daulatabad by Muhammad bin Tughluq, Nasir al-Din was the only prominent Sufi master who sternly refused to migrate and leave behind the spiritual domain (*wilayat*) bequeathed on him by his master Nizam al-Din, and as a consequence was subjected to untold hardship, and his *khanqah* embodied the light (*chiragh*) of Sufi activities in a desolate Delhi.[45]

---

[45] K.A. Nizami, *The Life and Times of Shaikh Nasir al-Din Chiraghh-i-Dehli* (Delhi: Idarah-i-Adabyat-i-Delli, 1991), 148.

The Practice of *Sama*

With the rise of Sufism in South Asia, the Chishtis and Suhrawardis crystal-lized their position as foremost Sufi orders of this region, giving primacy to certain spiritual exercises over others. *Sama* in the form of listening to music and poetry came to be seen as the core spiritual practice among Chishti Sufis and their wide network of saints spread all over the subcontinent. Suhrawardis, with the exception of a few saints, remained largely indifferent to this ritual, prescribing instead more regularized and attentive recitation of the Holy Quran together with practicing *zikr*.[46] The Qadiri saints in general were opposed to the audition of music. They were particularly critical of instrumental music (*sama bi'l mazamir*), recommending silent contempla-tion (*zikr-i khafi*) as a more effective devotional exercise. The Naqshbandis, were even more rigid with regard to the inclusion of music and poetry in their spiritual regime. They too were in favour of *zikr* as a means of contem-plating and remembering God, thereby seeking spiritual union.[47]

In South Asia *sama* came to uphold the internal reality of union with God, through the efforts of the Sufi saint. Its permissibility and position in the hierarchy of rituals and practices—religious, as well as those meant for the pursuit of spiritual goals—has led to multiple debates. Whether Sufis of the subcontinent considered *sama* as superior to other religious practices, most importantly prayer (*salat*) and *zikr*, as a means of seeking nearness to God, is something that is open to debate.[48]

However, it remains undeniable that music came to constitute an in-separable part of spiritual contemplation, particularly for Chishti Sufis. As the order flourished across the subcontinent, Chishti saints and their disciples from time to time put forward a passionate defence for *sama* as an inseparable component of their spiritual training incumbent upon all Sufis of the order.[49] Legitimizing a ritual like *sama*—which has been

---

[46] Omar Khalidi, 'Qawwali and Mehfil i-Sama', in Christian Troll, ed., *Muslim Shrines in India: Their Character, History and Significance* (Delhi: Oxford University Press, 1989), 258.

[47] Ibid.

[48] While the Chishti Sufis considered *sama* to be a mystical exercise whose benefits sur-passed any known religious exercise of the Book, Suhrawardi masters like Shaykh Baha al-Din Zakariyya considered prayer to be the most important spiritual exercise, emanating from the folds of religious canons. See Qamar ul Huda, *Spiritual Exercises for Suhrawardi Sufis* (London: Routledge Curzon, 2003), 56–58.

[49] Lawrence, 'Early Chishti Approach', 73–74.

since early times a subject of intense debate among legists, scholars, and Sufis, in defence or in critique of the practice—required serious engagement with the exercise, at multiple levels of intellectual thought and practice. This is reflected through the teachings and experiences of individual Chishti Sufis in defence of *sama*. While there is a strong resistance towards any attempt to vulgarize the practice, at the same time it is upheld as a symbol of Chishti spirituality.

In the following discussion we turn towards examining how the early generation of Chishti saints engaged with the practice of *sama*, as a private spiritual exercise, a practice that attracted public scrutiny from the *ulama* and legists, questioning its legality in the eyes of *shariah*, together with its permissibility as a Sufi ritual.

In the absence of any reliable contemporary records, later sources claim that Muin al-Din Chishti, the founder of the Chishti *silsila* in India, had a great taste for *sama* which he inherited from his mentors. In an attempt to elevate his spiritual stature among peers, later sources like the *Siyar al aqtab*, compiled in the mid-seventeenth century, state—on the authority of Qutb al-Din Bakhtiyar Kaki—that the leading *ulama* and Sufis of the age, residing in and around Baghdad, like Shihab al-Din Suhrawardi, Muhammad Kirmani, Muhammad Isfahani, Burhan al-Din Chishti, Baha al-Din Bukhari, Muhammad Baghdadi, the great Khwaja of Sijs, Saif al-Din Majusi, Shaykh Jalal al-Din Tabrezi, Ahmed Wahid, Burhan al-Din Ghaznavi, Khwaja Sulaiman, and Abdur Rahman among others, often attended *sama* in the company of Muin al-Din. Many among them even sought his blessings. This tradition continued even after Muin al-Din's arrival in Ajmer, where he established the first Chishti hospice, though it is uncertain whether he allowed the use of musical instruments in the assembly.[50] Therefore, even when we sift through such apocryphal narratives, it is possible that the practice of *sama* constituted the primary Sufi ritual for Chishti saints, even before they arrived in the Indian subcontinent.

When Muin al-Din sowed the seeds of Chishti Sufism in north India during the thirteenth century, Ghurid military commanders and their deputies were out to secure their political and military position in the

---

[50] Currie, *Shrine and Cult*, 69; *Khair al Majalis*, 286.

Gangetic heartland. As it happens with new political centres, the tension between *mulki* (resident) and non-*mulki* (immigrant) status was yet to be dissipated. The Delhi Sultans from time to time became involved in severe faction fighting in order to secure their own authority. The onus towards socio-cultural assimilation was taken up by the Chishti Sufis, whose simple lifestyle and compassionate social attitude appealed to the diverse residents of the Indian subcontinent.[51]

In the course of interacting and cohabiting with the Indian masses, it is possible that Chishti Sufis adapted certain practices from within the immediate environment, the primary among which could have been the use of devotional music. Hindu practices of worship involve the use of vocal singing (*bhajan/kirtan*) as well as instrumental music in praise of their Lord. As Aziz Ahmad has thoughtfully observed, 'Music is perhaps the only art in which something like a synthesis between the Muslim and Hindu artistic traditions was achieved'.[52] I have argued above that music constituted a primary element in the spiritual practice of Chishti Sufis. Though conclusive evidence is yet to emerge regarding such early influence of Indian musical practices on Chishti saints, it can be assumed that the incorporation of Indian musical instruments in the exercise of *sama* might have occurred under the influence of Hindu devotional music, pointing towards a development which scholars have hinted at as a possible Indianization of *sama*. The ritual remained a hallmark of Chishti spirituality in medieval India, until the time it was theoretically challenged by the Naqshbandi-Mujaddidi order in the seventeenth century.[53] Comparing their position to salt in a dish of food, the sultans of Delhi encouraged attempts at bridging the cultural and civilizational differences between resident communities within these new socio-cultural and religious surroundings. At the same time they realized the crucial role towards this end played by Sufis in general and Chishtis in particular.

---

[51] K. A. Nizami, 'Impact of Sufi Saints on Indian Society and Culture', in S. S. Hameed, ed., *Contemporary Relevance of Sufism* (New Delhi: Indian Council for Cultural Relations, 1993), 139–168.

[52] Aziz Ahmad, *An Intellectual History of Islam in India* (Edinburgh: University Press, 1969), 143.

[53] Lawrence, 'Early Chishti Approach', 90.

Figure 1.9 Dargah of Qazi Hamid al-Din Nagauri, Delhi

A disciple of Khwaja Muin al-Din, Qutb al-Din Bakhtiyar Kaki, was a lover of *sama*. But surprisingly he found an unusual companion in the person of Muhammad Ata, popularly known as Qazi Hamid al-Din Nagauri. Hamid al-Din was originally from Nagaur, but settled in Delhi during the time of Qutb al-Din. Despite being a Suhrawardi saint, he shared a great taste for *sama*, as a result of which Hamid al-Din used to make regular visits to the *khanqah* of his fellow Chishti saint. Once when Qutb al-Din Bakhtiyar Kaki was engrossed in *mehfil i-sama*, Qazi Hamid al-Din Nagauri arrived at the *khanqah*. Seeing the mood of the assembly, and listening to the poetry from the *qawwal*, he was overcome with emotion and placed his head at the feet of Qutb al-Din Bakhtiyar Kaki. The latter was absorbed in the assembly and thus signalled to one of his attendants to gently lift Qazi Hamid al-Din's head.[54]

Years later, when someone referred to this event and enquired as to the reason behind this action, Nasir al-Din Chiragh-i Dehli remarked that, at that particular moment Khwaja Bakhtiyar Kaki had reached the station

---

[54] *Khatima*, 139.

of almightyness (*maqam-i kibriyai*). In such a state it was disgraceful for a Sufi to engage in any sort of physical action. Whenever a saint reaches such a spiritual station, it is advisable for him to hold on to that as long as he can, so that blessings of the Divine may descend upon him. At that moment he should only act under the will of God, rather than be distracted by any physical action. The latter could dilute the emotions experienced by the heart during those moments. The state in which a Sufi places himself should be seen as a Divine blessing, which falls only on the fortunate ones.

The above incident is significant as it brings forth fresh understanding with regard to Sufism in South Asia. One needs to look beyond Sufi orders as fixed impermeable entities engaged in rivalry and competition with each other. Rather a useful approach could be one where Sufi orders are seen as fellow wayfarers in the larger spiritual goal, within the geographical space of South Asia. In the above discussion a deep sense of cordiality among early Chishti and Suhrawardi saints is evident, beyond any narrow competitive spiritual hegemony.

Secondly, the ritual of *sama*, as a means for spiritual advancement, though avoided by Suhrawardi Sufis, cannot be taken as a normative position of the order. Qazi Hamid al-Din Nagauri, along with being a leading Sufi of the Suhrawardi order was, interestingly, also an emphatic supporter of *sama*. For those who confine a particular Sufi ritual to a particular order, Hamid al-Din Nagauri naturally stands out as an odd personality, and hence can be compared to an individual guilty of violating norms of behaviour laid down by the Suhrawardi order. A useful approach, elaborated in a later chapter, is to desist from identifying *sama* as a practice completely shunned by Suhrawardi Sufis and hence seen as a violation of spiritual conduct. Rather it is important to understand medieval Sufi orders as dynamic communities strengthened through the bond of the master-disciple relation, where cross-order interactions through training and spiritual practice were accepted, and exercises like *sama* and *zikr* were not strictly unacceptable across orders.

A famous incident validating the emotion of ecstasy in *sama* in the Chishti circle comes from the life of Bakhtiyar Kaki himself. The saint was once attending *sama* in the hospice of Ali Sanjari, where the *qawwal* recited the following couplet from a lesser-known Persian Sufi Ahmad-i Jam:

Koshtgan-i khanjar-i tasleem ra
Har zaman-az ghayb jan e deegar ast[55]

All those killed by the knife of submission;
Each are filled with new life from the Unseen

Qutb al-Din Bakhtiyar Kaki was overwhelmed by the intensity of the spiritual message the verse conveyed. Even after he returned to his *khanqah* he insisted that the verse be repeated to him. Every time on hearing the verse he would lapse into a semi-conscious state, only to revive momentarily during the five obligatory prayers. This state continued for four days, until on the fifth night he surrendered his soul to the Lord.

The verse brings out the spirit of Sufism in general and Chishti spirituality in particular by combining within itself different ideas and processes. It begins from the annihilation of the disciple in the master (*fana fil shaykh*) followed by annihilation in God (*fana fillah*). Those who achieve such stages journey towards God (*sayr ila Allah*) and then journey in God (*sayr fi Allah*). It is only with the completion of these processes that one can rest permanently in God (*baqa billah*). For Chishti Sufis the couplet was recited as part of a *sama* assembly, and appreciated by a senior Sufi master. As a result, the verse was recited continuously until the time it led to extreme spiritual nourishment, followed by union between the devotee and the Lord through the intervention of death.[56]

Among Chishti Sufis in South Asia the greatest patron of *sama* was none other than its most illustrious and influential saint from the fourteenth century—Nizam al-Din Awliya, fondly addressed as *Mahbub-i Ilahi* (Beloved of God). He remains the Chishti luminary not only for his ability to train and leave behind an entire generation of worthy successors spread across the Indian subcontinent, but also because his teachings and conversations have been recorded for posterity in the *Fawaid al Fuad*. This *malfuzat,* the first of its kind in South Asia, inaugurated a genre of mystical literature that eschewed miracles and hagiographical

---

[55] Amir Hasan Sijzi, *Fawaid al Fuad*, ed. Latif Malik (Lahore: Malik Siraj al-din and Sons Publishers, 1966), 140. Henceforth *Fawaid al Fuad*; Ernst and Lawrence, *Sufi Martyrs of Love,* 153–154.
[56] Ernst and Lawrence, *Sufi Martyrs of Love,* 15–16.

hyperbole for a more insightful and lively picture of medieval Indian society and culture, together with providing a mine of information on the legacy of Sufism.[57] Before we delve into the details of *sama* through the life and practices of Nizam al-Din, it is important to trace the lineage of this practice to his *pir*, Baba Farid al-Din, who was equally enthusiastic about *sama*.

Badr al-Din Ishaq recalled that once when Baba Farid was asked as to why individuals harbouring a taste for *sama* lose control over their senses, the shaykh replied that when such individuals hear the Divine covenant (*alastu bi rabbikum*) they lose control over their senses. Creation of humanity in the Sufi imaginary is located in the pre-temporal moment when *the Lord took from the Children of Adam from their loins their progeny and made them bear witness concerning themselves, 'Am I not your Lord?' they said 'Yes, we bear witness'—lest you should say on the Day of Resurrection 'Truly of this we were heedless'.*[58] The Day of Alastu is recollected by Sufis through the sealing of the primordial covenant (*mithaq*), signifying a moment before created time[59] when no veil existed between God and humanity. Since then, whenever Sufis are in *sama* listening to the *qawwal,* a feeling of senselessness comes forth from the depths of their hearts, and they cannot help but act otherwise. They are struck by the awe of the Divine so that they fail to control their senses, bringing their limbs into action.[60]

It is said that once Baba Farid wished to participate in *sama*, but unfortunately no *qawwal* could be found who could facilitate the spiritual exercise. Seeing no way out to fulfil his wish, Baba Farid asked Khwaja Badr al-Din Ishaq, the chief steward of his *khanqah*, to bring him the letter that Qazi Hamid al-Din Nagauri had written to him some days back. When the satchel containing the letters was brought to the shaykh he placed his hand inside and fortunately the first letter he took out was that of Qazi

---

[57] Bruce Lawrence (translated and annotated), *Nizam Ad-Din Awliya. Morals for the Heart, Conversations of Shaykh Nizam ad-din Awliya recorded by Amir Hasan Sijzi* (New York: Paulist Press, 1992), Introduction. Henceforth *Morals for the Heart.*

[58] Quran 7:172.

[59] For a discussion on the idea of time in Sufism, see Kashshaf Ghani, 'Time is in the Moment (*waqt*) and also in Eternity (*dahr*): Reflections from Sufi Islam', in Shonaleeka Kaul, ed., *Retelling Time: Alternative Temporalities from Premodern South Asia* (London: Routledge, 2022), 104–121.

[60] *Siyar al-awliya*, 540.

Hamid al-Din. Badr al-Din Ishaq was instructed to stand up and read out the letter to Baba Farid. The former stood up and started reading the letter, which opened with the following lines: 'This humble, weak and worthless beggar Muhammad Ata, who is the servant of the dervishes from head to toe is as lowly as dust under their feet'. Hearing this Baba Farid reached a spiritual state, where the love of God became manifest in him.[61] He was visibly moved by the deep humility expressed by Qazi Hamid al-Din in the letter, which upheld the obedience of a devotee towards a Sufi saint, and the community of dervishes. Overcome by a feeling of ecstasy, Baba Farid recited a verse from the letter:

> Where is the mind to grasp Your sovereignty?
> Where is the soul to mirror Your majesty?
> Beauty's face, I know, You could unveil
> But where are eyes to behold Your beauty?

This verse beautifully expresses Hamid al-Din's love for God through Divine attributes. But at the same time the verse is reflective of the limitations of the Sufi devotee to realize the Divine in His full glory. It is only by the mercy of the Lord that a Sufi can achieve the station where he is fully able to behold the beauty of the Creator.

In this context Nizam al-Din Awliya went on to remark that once Badr al-Din Ghaznawi too wrote a letter to Baba Farid, where he included a poem which he had composed for the shaykh. It read as follows:

> Farid has been, for the faith and the faithful, a mighty friend.
> That he spent his life bestowing wonders has been my prayer.
> But how I wish that my own heart could have been more composed,
> For I would have laid before him pearls of praise, layer upon layer.[62]

This verse extols the contribution of Baba Farid in the Sufi path. It describes him as a true friend of those faithful to God, and for those who have been courageous enough to tread the path towards knowledge and

---

[61] *Fawaid al Fuad*, 143; *Morals for the Heart*, 252–253.
[62] *Fawaid al Fuad*, 143; *Morals for the Heart*, 253.

truth. The entire life of Baba Farid was spent serving the needy and the common man, bestowing his blessings upon them.

The above incidents affirm with much exactness the reason why Nizam al-Din attached himself so deeply to the practice of *sama*, and once remarked that the ritual of *sama* was a touchstone of piety and a proving ground for men of spiritual prowess.[63] He considered *sama* to be permissible in itself, which cannot be termed as forbidden unless one finds anything in it that contradicts the *shariah*. If the content of *sama* goes against the spirit of the *shariah*, then it should be termed forbidden. Nizam al-Din, while upholding the conformity of *sama* with the *shariah*, elaborated on certain preconditions for organizing a successful assembly. First, the reciter must be a melodious singer. Second, the singer himself must have heard the poetry earlier, which he intends to recite in the assembly. Third, the listener must be a Sufi shaykh, and fourth, there needs to be a musical instrument which can be played as an accompaniment. Both the reciter and the listener should have sufficient understanding in spiritual matters so that disharmony is not created while listening. It is unsuitable to have young boys and beautiful women in *sama*, as they lead to sufficient distraction for those attending the assembly.

At times it may so happen that the reciter may be overcome with jealousy and greed while in *sama*. This can be taken as a trait of hypocrisy in his character under the influence of which, though he superficially conforms to the norms of the assembly, internally his heart is maligned with emotions harmful for the spirit of *sama*. The instruments that accompany *sama* are of various forms. Thus if the exercise of *sama* is pure on these grounds then it is permissible for all. It is suitable primarily for those who are trained in the spiritual path, so that poetry and verses hold little importance for them as elements of the assembly. For they are continuously in the presence of God, and do not need a medium to make them realize the majesty of the Creator.[64]

Depending on the degree of spiritual training, Nizam al-Din once categorized three kinds of listeners who participate in *sama*. First are those who are uninitiated (*mutasammi*). Second are those who are mature listeners (*mustami*), after which comes the third type, the perfected listener

---

[63] *Fawaid al Fuad*, 20; *Morals for the Heart*, 132.
[64] *Fawaid al Fuad*, 20; *Morals for the Heart*, 355–356.

(*sami*). The uninitiated listener participates in *sama* and listens to music through the moment (*waqt*) of his spiritual awareness, the mature listener hears music through the state (*hal*) of his spiritual progress, while the perfect listener listens to music in the assembly of *sama* from the direct agency of God (*al-Haqq*).[65]

Continuing on the subject, Nizam al-Din further categorized the nature of participants in *sama* into distinct groups, keeping in mind their intentions for participation. *Sama* is forbidden (*haram*) for those who listen with the aim of fulfilling their lust and worldly desires. Such a practice is compared to the pre-Islamic days of ignorance (*jahiliya*). For those who consider *sama* to be a permissible exercise, yet do not follow its etiquette (*adab*) by participating in it with the womenfolk of his family, they end up in playful and worldly activity. Though *sama* in itself is permissible, it can easily degenerate into a sensuous exercise if not carefully conducted. However, if someone listens to *sama* with a pure heart which reflects his spiritual state, and under an urge for proximity with God he is emotionally overcome through weeping, then his participation is permissible (*halal*). The above categorization concerning participants in *sama* came to be borrowed by many later Sufi shaykhs.

Nizam al-Din categorized *sama* into two types: invasive (*hajim*) and non-invasive (*ghair hajim*). Invasive *sama* is that which invades the human body quite easily, stirring it towards agitation. This is likened to the reaction a heart may have on accidentally hearing a verse or poetry. Non-invasive *sama* is that in which the intellect of the listener comes into play. In such an audition, whenever one hears something that agitates him, he is drawn into a particular fold of contemplation where he equates verses of poetry to a different non-material realm.[66] These can be the attributes of God, or that of his spiritual master. It is this feeling which rules his heart. But the shaykh also made it clear that the first form of *sama* is more impulsive and hence cannot be explained by logical faculties.

Gisu Daraz once narrated that during *sama* Nizam al-Din listened to a variety of verses in Arabic, Persian, and Hindavi, which filled his heart with feelings of deep love for the Divine beloved (*mashuq*). Nizam al-Din

[65] Ernst and Lawrence, *Sufi Martyrs of Love*, 37.
[66] *Fawaid al Fuad*, 121–122; *Morals for the Heart*, 212.

was bestowed with the ability to enjoy the flavour (*zauq*) of *sama*, which became a rare quality after his time.[67]

Depending on the varying emotions of the heart, Nizam al-Din categorized *sama* as *halal* (lawful), *haram* (forbidden), *makruh* (abominable), and *mubah* (permissible). Elaborating on these categories, the shaykh remarked that in the assembly of *sama*, if the heart of the listener (*sahib-i wajd wa hal*) is orientated more towards the truth of God, then his practice of *sama* is *mubah*. If greater attention is devoted to the worldly concerns (*majaz*) of the individual, that *sama* is then termed *makruh*. If the heart is consumed by affairs of the material world, then that practice of *sama* is *haram*. If the heart of the mystic is focused entirely towards the proceedings of the assembly, together with contemplating God, then *sama* is *halal*.[68]

In the above description, while enumerating the finer qualities of the ritual, Nizam al-Din clearly emphasized that participants in *sama* need to be clear on the difference between *halal*, *haram*, *makruh*, and *mubah*, so that the participant does not indulge in actions that do not conform to the ethics of the ritual.[69] The shaykh further stated that for an assembly of *sama* to be *mubah*, certain conditions need be adhered to—primarily the *qawwal* should be a mature individual, and should never be a young boy or a woman.[70] It is incumbent on the audience (*mustame*) to immerse their hearts in the thought of God, and to keep away from any form of distraction. The content (*masmu*) of the ritual, precisely the verses recited, should not be of frivolous or puerile character (*fahash, hazal*), nor incur banter and lightheartedness in the mind of the listener. The ambience of *sama* should be strictly maintained as in the case of any other spiritual exercise. Hence musical instruments (*ala-i sama*) should be kept away from such an assembly.[71] Nizam al-Din Awliya censured the use of musical instruments, particularly *chang* and *rabab*. Such were the parameters laid down by the shaykh within which the exercise was to be performed for it to be recognized as *halal*. Else it should be termed questionable. After such elaborate regulations Nizam al-Din questioned

[67] *Khatima*, 130.
[68] *Siyar al-awliya*, 511.
[69] Ibid.
[70] Ibid.
[71] Ibid.

the non-permissibility of *sama*, stating that when *sama* is a sacred rendition of the voice, then why should it be termed as unlawful in the eyes of religion.[72]

However, despite adhering to all the norms in an assembly of *sama*, the state of ecstasy may elude participants. Such was an occasion once when Qazi Hamid al-Din Nagauri engaged himself in an audition assembly (*mehfil-i sama*) and a renowned *qawwal* was conducting the affairs of the gathering. Unfortunately none of the participants felt the desired effect, and feelings of spiritual arousal were missing. The head of the assembly, while taking a serious note of this, enquired whether any individual harboured feelings of animosity for his fellow participant. If so, then he should sort things out immediately through the medium of dialogue. When none of the participants responded, the shaykh further enquired whether any vagabond or people with worldly preoccupations had entered the assembly. That could have been the cause behind the ineffectiveness of the exercise. But after a thorough search none of that sort was found. Hence the assembly was dissolved.[73]

The above instance is reflective of some intrinsic truths regarding the practice of *sama*. First, as emphasized by Nizam al-Din, *sama* is essentially an engagement with the feeling of compassion, which comes into play only when there is a bestowal of Divine mercy. No amount of poetry, verse, and musical instruments can make the 'heart stir in the love for God'. Only when it is divinely ordained does an assembly of *sama* reach the heights of success. The arousal of the heart therefore depends on the will of the Lord. Secondly, *sama* should be carried out with noble intentions. Any individual participating in this ritual should cleanse his heart of all worldly thoughts, feelings of hatred, and desires of the flesh. It is only under such circumstances that *sama* carries beneficial effects on the heart of the listener, stirring it towards spiritual realization. Else, not only does he involve himself in an unworthy act, but he disturbs the spirit of the entire assembly by polluting the sacred ambience and depriving fellow mystics of the benefits of such a deeply spiritual exercise. Third, the most important lesson to be adhered to is the eligibility for participation. *Sama*, being a highly structured ritual intended

---

[72] Ibid.
[73] Ibid., 520–521.

for experiencing the Divine, cannot be allowed for all and sundry. Only individuals who are trained in the spiritual path are allowed to participate in it, thereby enhancing its effect both on the individual and the gathering at large. But if a lay individual or a novice chances to attend such an assembly he places not only himself at risk, but also the spiritual gains of the entire gathering. Since the individual has little training in the art of interpreting verses of poetry, he might attribute them to worldly matters. At the same time he remains unaware of the methods to control his emotions, should they arise in him after listening to such verses. On occasions of intense spiritual turmoil he may lose control over his self, and thereby risk his own life. Lastly, one should never strive for forced emotions from such an assembly. *Sama* is meant to be a natural way of deriving spiritual benefices by listening to poetry and verses. Therefore, if feelings of ecstasy do not come naturally to the participant, the guardian of the assembly should not continue with it, hoping for its arrival. Rather the assembly should be dissolved with the belief that such is the will from the Unseen.

Sufi saints attest that assemblies of *sama* are blessed from the Unseen. Once Nizam al-Din was sitting in the courtyard of his *khanqah* listening to the *qawwal* recite verses for the shaykh. Hearing the words of the *qawwal*, the shaykh was gripped by a sense of ecstasy, while his heart moved towards a remembrance of the Divine. But none among those present were ready to do dance (*raqs*). The shaykh was greatly saddened by the passiveness of the assembly, as he felt the urge to engage in *raqs*. In such a moment a man entered the assembly and after prostrating to the shaykh, started doing *raqs*. The shaykh immediately rose up and joined him in the exercise. For some time both continued with the exercise of *raqs*, until they were completely lost in the mood. When the assembly ended the person left immediately. Nizam al-Din asked his disciples to bring him back. People went out searching for the person, but he could be found nowhere. Those present in the assembly remarked that the individual must have been from the Unseen.[74] Nizam al-Din once remarked that when a person while listening to the verses of the *qawwal* gets overwhelmed in his heart with the feeling of love for the Divine Beloved,

[74] Ibid., 532.

and is agitated by the remembrance of God, then Divine enlightenment (*anwar*) descends upon him. In such a situation it is obligatory that some-body from the Unseen is sent to participate in such an assembly of *sama* to heighten its spiritual flavour, thereby transforming a passive gathering into a spiritually stimulating one.

It is accepted that *sama* does not have a uniform effect on all listeners. The spiritual maturity of a Sufi is a precondition for the benefits he seeks from such an exercise of audition. When asked about the reason for his success in *sama*, Nizam al-Din replied that each time he participated in *sama* he attributed whatever he heard from the *qawwal* to the virtues and dispositions of his shaykh, Farid al-Din. So that once when he was at-tending *sama*, he heard the following verse from the *qawwal*:

> Do not walk like this
> Lest you be hurt
> By an evil eye

Nizam al-Din said that when he heard these lines he was at once re-minded of the virtues of his shaykh, which constituted piety and right-eousness, excellence in learning, and his captivating grace. Whenever he recalled these attributes of his master, Nizam al-Din was moved to tears with such emotional intensity that it remained beyond expression. He requested the reciter to repeat those two lines again and again, until he became completely exhausted under continuous emotional upsurge.[75] Thereafter Nizam al-Din emphasized that whenever one hears something in *sama*, he must attribute it to his *pir*, or to God. For it is only through the blessings of the *pir* and the Lord that an individual benefits in *sama*. The love for one's *pir* and the Lord helps the listener fix his heart on the spir-itual content of *sama*. On the Day of Judgement, when the listener will be questioned whether or not he listened to *sama*, he will say 'yes'. And when asked as to how he could attribute the transient qualities he heard in *sama* to the permanence (*qadim*) of Divine essence, he will answer that he did it out of nothing but the extremity of his love for the Creator. On this the Divine command would proclaim 'As you did that out of sheer love for

[75] Ibid., 515.

Me, I shower My mercy upon you'.[76] While recalling this, Nizam al-Din, with moistened eyes, once remarked that if such was the chastisement with one immersed in the love of God, then it was quite understandable as to the fate of others.[77]

Nizam al-Din possessed a strong taste for *sama*. He once remarked that in *sama* when he was drawn into folds of ecstasy, he felt like he was being transported into a state of bewilderment. He completely lost himself in the emotions that arose from within the depths of his heart. In such circumstances he surrendered himself at the feet of his mentor, Baba Farid al-Din. Once, the shaykh, on hearing a Hindawi verse from the *qawwal*, became so engrossed that he went into a state of ecstasy. He started doing *raqs*, all the while listening to the verse. After few hours, when *sama* ended, Nizam al-Din still could not overcome his ecstatic state. Seeing this, the *qawwal* decided to start the assembly afresh.[78] In this context, Nizam al-Din later remarked that if the effect of *sama* does not get dissipated from the heart of an individual after the assembly ends, then it is incumbent for the *qawwal* to continue.[79] Given his deep love for *sama*, many around him suggested that Nizam al-Din should not aspire for the position of a *qazi*, and that he was more suited for the spiritual path, and deserved to be the *Shaykh-ul Islam*.[80]

Chishti Sufis argued that even if *sama* were to be unambiguously permitted in the eyes of law and religion, sceptics who kept themselves aloof from such an exercise on the pretext that it was forbidden would never have engaged in it, for participation in *sama* required a certain conditioning of the heart, which only the mystics attained through prolonged rigour in the path of God.[81] Those of the material world find little flavour and hence success in it, and thus remain deprived from the taste of *sama*.

Nizam al-Din, while enumerating the effects of *sama* on the listener, remarked that for those who maintain a taste (*zawq*) for *sama* the effect from the Unseen was such that they often lost control over their senses.

---

[76] Ibid.
[77] Ibid.
[78] Ibid., 532.
[79] Ibid., 533.
[80] *Fawaid al Fuad*, 205; *Morals for the Heart*, 111.
[81] *Fawaid al Fuad*, 190; *Morals for the Heart*, 336.

At the same time there are others in the Sufi path who experience similar ecstasy but never lose control over their senses. In the opinion of Nizam al-Din, true spiritual seekers are those who, in spite of a severe surge of emotions, never lose control over their actions in *sama*.[82] Some individuals experience such intense ecstasy that they forget the world around them, while engaging in *raqs*. During this time, even if they are stung by a thorn they do not feel the pain. Some Sufis, on the other hand, while remaining deeply engrossed in the contemplation of their Lord, never lose their senses even for a moment. So that even if a rose petal comes under their feet, they are fully aware of its presence. In the words of Nizam al-Din, this should be the identity of a true Sufi shaykh.[83] Even when he is lost in the contemplation of God, he remains in complete control of his senses and faculties.

Nizam al-Din passed away in 1325 during the reign of Muhammad bin Tughluq. His spiritual mantle in Delhi was handed over to Nasir al-Din Mahmud, who later came to be popularly known as *Chiragh-i Dehli*. He combined in himself the rare qualities of being an erudite religious scholar, a deep believer in Chishti spirituality, an ascetic, and a teacher who strongly believed in the spiritual principles. Nasir al-Din was well aware of the growing impact of Ibn Taimiyya's ideology in South Asia. However, the saint was a great believer in *sama*, much like his master. Thus his own position on *sama* ran counter to that of Ibn Taimiyya.

Nasir al-Din Mahmud believed in the 'spiritual efficacy' brought upon participants in *sama*, and hence organized such gatherings in his *jamaat-khana*. However, in his *malfuzat*, the *Khair al Majalis*, Nasir al-Din Mahmud strictly condemned the use of any form of musical instruments in *sama* assemblies. When asked about the use of musical instruments like a single drum (*duf*), reed pipes (*nai*), and rebec (*rubab*), Nasir al-Din Mahmud remarked that there remains a consensus (*ijma*) according to the Sufi path (*tariqa*), and religious law (*shariah*)[84] that musical instruments and *qawwals* in the form of young boys and women are not permissible in *sama*. Though *sama* together with dance was

[82] *Siyar al-awliya*, 535.
[83] Ibid.
[84] Nizami, *Some Aspects*, 113; *Khair al Majalis*, 42–45.

permissible under certain conditions, it should only be for those who are trained to participate in it, whose hearts are immersed in the remembrance of God, and when the content does not violate the norms of the *shariah*.

The shaykh considered *sama* as a practice that carried an individual, trained in the spiritual path, to higher realms. Such was his own experience when he participated in *sama* at his *khanqah* that on multiple occasions ecstasy overpowered him and he began to do *raqs*. The energy with which the shaykh participated in *sama* and performed *raqs* amazed his contemporaries. However, he attributed his ecstatic behaviour to the verses he heard from the *qawwal*, like the one below:

> You promised not to subject your lovers to torture, but did it;
> You promised not to erase the name of those who have lost their
> hearts, nevertheless you did it.[85]

Confrontation with the *Ulama*

Sama is a spiritual practice undertaken primarily by those who cherish a taste for it. Chishti records capture from time to time the sceptical attitude of the *ulama* towards the practice of *sama*. For Chishti saints, an exercise like *sama* held at the Sufi *khanqah* does not cross the limits of religious and ethical sanctity. Even if the *ulama* condemned such a practice, they could not impose a ban on it, nor could they stop Sufis from participating in *sama*. Nizam al-Din once remarked that the *ulama* are not always opposed to the practice of audition. While some are accommodating towards such an exercise, many tend to act brashly without taking into consideration the standards which regulate such a ritual. He further continued that Sufis and dervishes are blessed from the Unseen. Hence it is not judicious to get into a forced confrontation with them.[86]

Even in the early days of the Delhi Sultanate, the *ulama* took offence at the practice of *sama* by the early Chishti saints, particularly Qutb al-Din

---

[85] K. A. Nizami, *The Life and Times of Shaikh Nasir-ud-din Chiraghh-i-Dehli* (Delhi: Idarah-i Adabiyat-i Delli, 1991), 60–61, 107–108.
[86] *Fawaid al Fuad*, 190.

Bakhtiyar Kaki and his fellow-saint from the Suhrawardi order, Qazi Hamid al-Din. They complained on the matter to Sultan Iltutmish. The accusation was led by two muftis, Qazi Sa'ad and Qazi Imad, who implored the Sultan as a zealous supporter and protector of the faith, appealing that Qutb al-Din Bakhtiyar Kaki be summoned to the court and condemned for practicing *sama*. Sultan Iltutmish agreed to call an arbitration council (*mahzar*) to deliberate on the issue. Qutb al-Din decided to visit the royal court accompanied by Qazi Hamid al-Din, who argued in favour of the permissibility of *sama*, meant only for those who are trained in the spiritual path, but not for untrained individuals. In the discussion that followed, Sultan Iltutmish was convinced about the spiritual pedigree of Qutb al-Din and that his practice of *sama* was not in contradiction to the *shariah*. His display of deep respect towards Qutb al-Din dampened the spirits of the *ulama*, who had hoped for a ruling against the ritual of *sama*.

However, it would be simplistic to justify the decree from the Sultan only on the verbal defence of the Suhrawardi saint, Qazi Hamid al-Din. Sultan Iltutmish was well aware of the spiritual stature of Qutb al-Din, the principal *khalifa* of the Chishti saint Khwaja Muin al-Din. When the former arrived in Delhi the Sultan extended him a hearty welcome, offered him the post of *Shaykh-ul-Islam*, and requested him to stay near his palace. The shaykh declined both requests, and being trained in the Chishti tradition distanced himself from the bureaucracy, but not from the people at large. The physical presence of Qutb al-Din, together with his popularity among the masses in Delhi, were significant factors which Iltutmish could not afford to ignore. The presence of important Sufi saints in the capital city strengthened the legitimacy of the ruling house by securing the support and participation of the common masses. It was perhaps all of this combined that led Iltutmish to override the allegations of *Shaykh-ul-Islam* Najm al-Din Sughra against Qutb al-Din Bakhtiyar Kaki. Instead Iltutmish submitted himself at the feet of the Chishti master, begging him to stay back in Delhi.[87] Being a pragmatic ruler, Iltutmish realized the efforts of the Chishti Sufis to create an environment of social harmony among the large population residing in and around Delhi, through an attitude of compassion.

---

[87] *Siyar al-awliya*, 54–55; Nizami, *Some Aspects,* 189.

Baba Farid al-Din too was not immune to the hostility from the *qazi* of Ajodhan, who disapproved of Farid's practice of *sama* in his *khanqah*, as well as his attending *sama* assemblies in other hospices. However, the *qazi* was unsuccessful in manipulating the *ulama* to issue a decree prohibiting the practice of *sama* by Baba Farid al-Din.

Nizam al-Din considered it an irony that while the *ulama* wore attires emulating fakirs, they considered spiritual practices of fakirs, like *sama*, to be unlawful in the eyes of law. The shaykh further remarked that should *sama* seem to be an unlawful exercise for the *ulama*, they should practice self-restraint and not participate in the ritual, rather than stop others from participating in it. It is not in the character of dervishes to create enmity with others. He further added that it is possible that everyone may not carry a taste (*zawq*) for *sama*. Hence such people label *sama* as forbidden for all. Nizam al-Din remarked that even if *sama* were permissible in their eyes, they would not have participated in it.

It was during the high-noon of Nizam al-Din's career in Delhi that the most controversial confrontation on the issue of *sama* occurred between the saint and the *ulama*, during the rule of Sultan Ghiyas al-Din Tughluq.[88] The latter already had some differences with the saint, the root of which lay in the distribution of large grants by Khusrau Khan when he usurped the throne after the murder of Sultan Qutb al-Din Mubarak. While some Sufi saints refused to accept the grant, Nizam al-Din accepted it and distributed the amount among the *faqirs* and poor ones of the city. When Ghiyas al-Din Tughluq ascended the throne after defeating Khusrau Khan, he sought to revive the state treasury by recovering the grants given by his predecessor. While some Sufi saints who kept the amount unspent readily returned the same, Nizam al-Din replied that he had distributed the sum among the poor and the needy as the money belonged to the public treasury (*bayt al mal*). There was nothing left for him to return to the Sultan. Ghiyas al-Din could not take any measures against the saint, but he became antagonized against him.

It was this animosity which the *ulama* wished to utilize. Led by an immigrant, Shaikhzada Husam al-Din Farjam, who had once been a disciple

---

[88] Raziuddin Aquil, 'Music and Related Practices in Chishti Sufism: Celebrations and Contestations', *Social Scientist*, 40/3–4 (Mar.–Apr. 2012), 26–31.

of the saint, and Qazi Jalal al-Din Saqanji, the Deputy Governor (*Naib Hakim*), some of them turned hostile towards Nizam al-Din and spoke ill about him to the Sultan. Out of disregard towards Nizam al-Din, they disrespected his *khanqah* life. Matters came to a head when the *ulama* started to criticize the practice of *sama*. They repeatedly tried to convince Sultan Ghiyas al-Din Tughluq to call an arbitration council (*mahzar*) to debate on the legality of *sama* practiced by the shaykh, with the intention of a possible ban on the practice. Nizam al-Din was asked to be physically present in the council to defend the practice.

It is interesting to note that earlier Shaykhzada Farjam was not opposed to Nizam al-Din. Rather he was attached to the Sufi saint through a bond of deep love and respect. But strange are the lurings of power and fame. In a gradual shift of circumstances, Shaykhzada Farjam was invited by Sultan Qutb al-Din Mubarak Khilji to take residence in Delhi under the patronage of the Sultanate. The Sultan planned to check the popularity of Nizam al-Din through this ploy, and as a mark of state support a *khanqah* was built for Farjam to act as the second spiritual centre in Delhi. However, the plan failed to achieve fruition, and Farjam was gradually drawn under the influence of the *ulama* who held Nizam al-Din responsible for the Shaykhzada's failure. Thereafter the latter began to show disrespect towards the Sufi master. He neither had any knowledge about *sama*, nor was he interested in the practice. All he wanted was to bolster his position in the court by organizing an arbitration council to deliberate against *sama*, and humiliate Nizam al-Din.

In this exercise he was supported by Qazi Jalal al-Din Saqanji, Qazi Kamal al-Din, the *Sadr-i Jahan*, and Abul Hai. The latter was equally well known for his animosity towards the shaykh. They were joined by other scholars of the time, many of whom had great disrespect for Nizam al-Din that arose from their jealousy of his popularity. At a suitable time, and under the leadership of Shaykhzada Farjam, this group met the Sultan and presented their case. They argued that *sama* was forbidden according to *Shaykh-ul Azam* Abu Hanifa. Yet Nizam al-Din, who is supposed to be the leader of *mashaikhs*, and a highly respected Sufi master, indulged in this forbidden exercise together with his disciples.

In spite of the strong accusation levelled by the *ulama*, Sultan Ghiyas al-Din Tughluq was ill-equipped to decide on the issue of whether the practice of *sama* was acceptable (*halal*) or forbidden (*haram*). However, he was surprised as to why a revered Sufi master of the stature of Nizam al-Din indulged in unlawful (*be-shariah*) practices. On the other hand, the Sultan was constantly pushed by the faction led by Shaykhzada Farjam to call an assembly of all the leading *ulama* of the city, community elders, along with senior scholars, and present before them the issue of the legality of *sama*, as practiced by Nizam al-Din. Ghiyas al-Din Tughluq had to concede.

When the followers and disciples of Nizam al-Din, attached to the royal court, received the news, they shared it with their master. Nizam al-Din, however, did not react strongly upon hearing this. On the other hand, the section of the *ulama* closely attached to Nizam al-Din decided to collect all legal and religious evidence in support of *sama* as an acceptable exercise. Even then the shaykh did not show much concern. The companions of the shaykh were assured of his success in defending the practice.

Eventually Nizam al-Din was called to the court. He decided to visit alone, without taking along any of this disciples or companions. However, Maulana Muhi al-Din Kashani and Maulana Fakhr al-Din Zarradi accompanied him to the court voluntarily. On arriving there, Qazi Jalal al-Din, instead of receiving the shaykh with respect and warmth, started addressing him in harsh language. Nizam al-Din and his companions chose to ignore this, while behaving with etiquette and restraint.

Matters reached a point where Qazi Jalal al-Din warned Nizam al-Din of strong punishment if any complaint concerning *sama* reached his ear. At this point the shaykh rebuked him, warning him not to become intoxicated under the influence of power and authority. Incidentally, after a period of twelve days from the day of the arbitration, the warning of Nizam al-Din turned out to be true. The qazi was dismissed from his position and died soon thereafter. Realizing the inability of his companions to corner the shaykh on the issue of *sama*, Shaykhzada himself decided to face Nizam al-Din. The Sufi master was accused of organizing *sama* in his *khanqah*, where participants and disciples of the shaykh indulged in some form of dancing and shouting out loud under the influence of ecstasy.

Nizam al-Din warned Farjam not to indulge in false reports and hearsay. When the shaykh asked him to explain the meaning and significance of *sama*, the Shaykhzada expressed his ignorance on the subject. On this the shaykh refused to speak to him as he did not know anything about *sama*. Neither was he familiar with the inner truth of the exercise. Farjam went silent on hearing this retort from the Sufi shaykh. The Sultan, too, listened with singular attention to what Nizam al-Din had to say on *sama*. He even sternly warned Shaykhzada Farjam that instead of exaggerating facts and narration he should listen attentively to whatever Nizam al-Din had to say. The assembly felt silent and listened with attention what the shaykh had to say on *sama*.

Once the Shaykh finished his defence, Qazi Kamal al-Din referred to the canons of Abu Hanifa while emphasizing that the jurist decreed *sama* to be forbidden. Similar was his opinion with regard to dance (*raqs*). At this time Maulana Fakhr al-Din Zarradi came to the defence of the shaykh. Just as he was presenting his opinions, Maulana Alim al-Din Banassi and Shaykh Ilm al-Din, the grandsons of the Suhrawardi Sufi Baha al-Din Zakariyya of Multan, arrived at the court. Sultan Ghiyas al-Din Tughluq turned towards them and asked their opinion on the ongoing debate—whether *sama* was sanctioned or forbidden. The Sultan stressed that since they were men of deep spiritual scholarship and experience, and had been to places like Baghdad, Rum, and Damascus, they may throw some light on how such an issue on legality of *sama* is addressed in those places by learned *mashaikhs*.

At this Maulana Alim al-Din said that he had written a book on the issue titled *Maqsad*, in which he debated whether *sama* can be labelled as *halal* or *haram*. He began by stating that in an assembly of *sama* of those who listen by the heart, the exercise is permissible for them. It is forbidden for those who participate in the assembly for worldly pleasure. The latter gives rise to desires of the flesh within the individual. Shaykh Ilm al-Din went on to add that in all the places he visited in course of his travels, Mecca, Medina, Egypt, and Syria, he saw the learned and the Sufis enjoying *sama*. On many instances such assemblies were accompanied by musical instruments like tambourines (*duff*) and flutes (*shehnai*). *Sama* in these places upheld the lineage of Shaykh Junaid and Shaykh Shibli from Baghdad, who were great patrons of the exercise.

On hearing this, Ghiyas al-Din Tughluq fell silent. On seeing the Sultan vacillate, Maulana Jalal al-Din stressed that the Sultan should take into consideration the legal canons of Imam Abu Hanifa and proclaim *sama* as forbidden (*haram*). However, Nizam al-Din, who was seated close to the Sultan, advised him to refrain from passing any final decision on the legality of the issue. Sultan Ghiyas al-Din took this advice to heart and chose not to pass any final judgement on the issue of *sama*. The assembly continued until the time of lunch when it was dismissed without any final decision.[89] Ghiyas al-Din Tughluq, with great humility and respect, bade farewell to Nizam al-Din as he left the court for his *khanqah*.

A second version of the event, albeit a later and weak construction, stresses that Ghiyas al-Din Tughluq did pass a judgement on the debate and permitted Nizam al-Din to convene an assembly of *sama* whenever the shaykh felt an urge. However, for those who listened to *sama* for worldly desires, like Qalandars and Haydaris, their participation was forbidden. It was adjudged as *halal* for the shaykh. At this Nizam al-Din replied that if *sama* is forbidden (*haram*), then it should be forbidden for all, and if it is allowed (*halal*) then it should be allowed for all. On the use of instruments it was said that Imam Shafi considered the use of musical instruments like *duff* and *shehnai* as permissible (*mubah*) while participating in *sama*.

On his return to the *khanqah*, Nizam al-Din met Amir Khusrau and Maulana Muhi al-Din Kashani before afternoon (*asr*) prayers, and shared with them his experiences at the royal court earlier in the day. He felt that the learned elite of Delhi were filled with animosity and jealousy towards the shaykh and hence tried to humiliate him at the court. However, what pained Nizam al-Din most was the fact that no scholar and *ulama* at the assembly were ready to listen to his arguments based on the traditions (*hadith*) of Prophet Muhammad. They refused to attach any importance to references from the *Hadith*. Rather they placed more importance on traditions of *fiqh* or Islamic law. When traditions from the Hadith were cited in support of the legality of *sama*, the *ulama* and scholars present in the assembly refused to acknowledge the importance of it. They stood up in protest and prepared to leave the assembly on the premise that this tradition of *Hadith* originated from the school of Imam Shafi, who was unacceptable to the *ulama* and scholars present in the assembly inclined towards the Hanafi law.

This amazed Nizam al-Din greatly, and he remarked that only those people will have the proclivity to organize such arbitration councils

---

[89] K. A. Nizami, *The Life and Times of Shaikh Nizam ud din Auliya* (New Delhi: Oxford University Press, 2007), 80, 82, 129.

who are completely disrespectful towards the traditions of *Hadith*. The shaykh went on to remark that people like these are only interested in arm-twisting others into following what they think is right, without any consideration for established religious traditions. He considered it unfortunate that during the assembly he had to face these *ulama*, devoid of any sense of etiquette. He feared the city of Delhi may face Divine wrath due to the presence of such individuals, who refused to accept the traditions of the Prophet.

It so happened that in course of time when Muhammad bin Tughluq became the Sultan, this entire group of scholars and *ulama* were transferred to the new capital in Devagiri, renamed Daulatabad, as an attempt on the part of the Sultan to populate the new city as the second imperial capital after Delhi. The new city was struck by drought and epidemic. Disciples and followers of Nizam al-Din attributed this calamity to a curse from the Unseen for subjecting their master to great humiliation and refusing to give due importance to the traditions of Prophet Muhammad.

Such an overtly legalistic attitude of the *ulama* through an increasing reliance on the schools of Islamic jurisprudence (*majhdhab*), particularly the Hanafi School, was symptomatic of the contemporary religious mentality in the Sultanate of Delhi. Until the late thirteenth and early fourteenth century, the works and teachings of the Islamic scholar-philosopher Ibn al-Arabi (1165–1240) held sway over large parts of the Islamic world, not to mention the Indian subcontinent.[90] The Chishti saints of South Asia too were trained in Arabi's school of thought. But sometime from the fourteenth century onwards the concept of *Wahadat ul-Wujud* (Unity of all Beings) was being debated at various levels, accentuated by the intense polemic of Imam Ibn Taimiyya (1263–1328) whose bitter criticism was levelled against pantheism and shrine practices, like music, *sama*, prostration before the shaykh, praying during tomb visits, pilgrimage to shrines etc.[91] Quite naturally it began to have a significant effect across the Islamic world, not to mention South Asia. With this, the religious atmosphere of the subcontinent was shifting more and more towards a conservative interpretation of the *shariah*, reflected in the juristic

---

[90] Muhammad Suleman Siddiqi, *The Bahmani Sufis* (Delhi: Idarah-i Adabiyat-i Delli, 1989), 33.
[91] Ibid.

works of the period. As a result, the *ulama* armed themselves with the doctrines of Islamic jurisprudence, refusing even to recognize the words of the Prophet (*Hadith*), as seen above.

Chishti mystics too began to feel the change in the religious climate. The numerous injunctions and regulations of Nizam al-Din with regard to the proper observance of and participation in the exercise of *sama,* as elaborated above, need to be located in the context of such a changing ambience concerning religious legal discourses in north India. Being the head of the Chishti order in the subcontinent, Nizam al-Din realized the necessity of engaging with this trend from within the spiritual order itself and took various steps towards the same. First, he laid down detailed regulations and instructions concerning the practice of *sama,* so that his successors did not face further trouble in practicing and defending the same. Second, he diligently trained his disciples like Nasir al-Din Mahmud in the ways of *shariah, fiqh* (Islamic jurisprudence), and the leading schools of religious and philosophical thought. This was done with the possible intention to equip later Sufis of the Chishti order to fight back against any conservative attack, the prominent example being Muhammad Husayni Gisu Daraz—ably trained in the scholarly and spiritual tradition by Nasir al-Din Mahmud. Third, by decentralizing the Chishti order Nizam al-Din ensured that his successors and their progeny reached the farthest corners of the subcontinent and carried with them the principles of Chishti mysticism.

With the death of Nasir al-Din Mahmud, the first cycle of Chishti Sufism in north India came to an end. The legacy of Nizam al-Din continued through the regional centres established by his disciples across the Indian subcontinent. It is through one such disciple, Burhan al-Din Gharib, that Chishti Sufism flourished from Khuldabad in the Deccan. In a remarkably similar manner, it was one of Nasir al-Din Mahmud's foremost disciples, Gisu Daraz, who later established the second major Chishti centre in the Deccan at Gulbarga. In our study of *sama* as the core Chishti practice, we turn towards its career in the Deccan through the life and teachings of these masters.

2

Defending the Practice of Audition

Maulana Fakhr al-Din Zarradi's *Usul al Sama*

Under continuous insistence from a section of his courtiers, Sultan Ghiyas al-Din Tughluq ordered an arbitration council (*mahzar*) to deliberate on the issue of legality concerning the practice of *sama*. Not only were fingers raised at Nizam al-Din's practice of *sama* at his *khanqah*; the seriousness of the matter required the most reputed Chishti master in Delhi to accede to a rare summon from the court, and be physically present in front of the sultan to defend *sama*—the core practice in the Chishti spiritual tradition. The saint was accompanied by one of his most erudite disciples, Maulana Fakhr al-Din Zarradi, who penned the treatise *Usul al Sama* for the occasion, with the aim of enunciating in detail a defence of the mystical practice, starting from its historical antecedents.

Trained in the intellectual environment of Delhi under the tutelage of Maulana Fakhr al-Din Hanswi, Fakhr al-Din Zarradi, much like his spiritual mentor Nizam al-Din, was a brilliant scholar of Islamic law (particularly the *Hidayah*) and Islamic jurisprudence (*fiqh*). As a scholar of the Islamic sciences, Fakhr al-Din was initially dismissive of the Sufi tradition and spiritual knowledge. This was until one day, when Nasir al-Din Mahmud, the spiritual successor of Nizam al-Din, who frequently visited the seminary of Fakhr al-Din Hanswi, convinced Fakhr al-Din Zarradi to visit Nizam al-Din at his *khanqah*. Rather than spiritual matters, Zarradi was more interested in discussing with the saint the problems he was having in understanding some parts of the *Hidayah*. On hearing Zarradi's issues, Nizam al-Din comprehensively explained the points raised by Zarradi regarding the *Hidayah*. This discussion brought about a radical change in the attitude of Fakhr al-Din Zarradi, and he decided to explore the spiritual path under Nizam al-Din's guidance, without leaving his

Sufi Rituals and Practices. Kashshaf Ghani, Oxford University Press. © Kashshaf Ghani 2024.
DOI: 10.1093/oso/9780192889225.003.0003

intellectual pursuits. Such was the impact of the Chishti master on Fakhr al-Din Zarradi that the latter too decided to remain celibate.

Spiritual training did not overshadow Fakhr al-Din Zarradi's scholarship in branches of Islamic knowledge, which subsequently came to include the Hadith tradition, along with grammar. He continued to teach in the madrasa run by Mir Khwurd's father in Delhi, along with expanding his breath of learning on various subjects like medicine. Such was his repute as a teacher that, on the occasion when Siraj al-Din Usman was denied spiritual succession by Nizam al-Din on grounds of insufficient education, it was Fakhr al-Din Zarradi who took up the responsibility of training Siraj al-Din. Helped by his disciple Rukn al-Din Indpati, Fakhr al-Din Zarradi trained Siraj al-Din, over six months, in major branches of Islamic sciences, including Arabic grammar, by compiling the text *Sarf-i Usmani* in order to facilitate Siraj al-Din learning.

Fakhr al-Din Zarradi did not share a particularly cordial relationship with Sultan Muhammad bin Tughluq. Once when the sultan was planning the transfer of the capital to Devagiri in the Deccan, and a military expedition against the descendants of the Mongols in Central Asia, he summoned some of the leading scholars and Sufis in Delhi to seek their advice. Fakhr al-Din Zarradi visited the court in spite of great hesitation, fearing harm on his life if he behaved tersely with the sultan. Though the meeting did not turn out to be a pleasant one, Zarradi was spared from the sword of the sultan through the appropriate intervention of Qutb al-Din Dabir, the disciple of Nizam al-Din, and a student of Zarradi. After the death of his master, Zarradi travelled towards Daulatabad and thereafter proceeded to Hajj. After completing the pilgrimage, he died in a shipwreck as he was on his way back through Baghdad.

Written in Arabic, *Usul al Sama* is divided into ten sections elaborating on specific aspects of *sama*, accompanied by an introduction and conclusion. Zarradi introduces *sama* as an exercise of listening, for the masses, that which is meant to be listened to, while the spiritual elite listen to whatever originates from the truth and focus on the hidden meanings. Sufis, for Zarradi, are the best among those who follow the sunnah of the Prophet, the other two sects being the legists and scholars of Hadith. The superiority of the Sufis lies in their complete dependence on God for guidance and sustenance, which thus allows them to rise above the limitation of individual sects. Zarradi argues for seeking knowledge through argument and analysis rather than through predetermined opinions of individuals and sects—an approach he undertakes in the *Usul*. He claims to have verified the information and traditions on which the arguments of the text have been built, thus leaving aside the non-verifiable ones.

Each of the ten sections elaborates one principle concerning the permissibility of audition. The author begins by discussing what he terms 'the truth behind *sama*'—which analyses the etymological root of the word, the literal meaning of the term, and the actions attached to it. The core action constitutes the combination of well-measured rhythmical verses with a melodious voice which is listened to carefully by Sufis so that the proper meaning is unveiled. Zarradi identifies this practice as radically different from popular singing, which may contain frivolous content. The author supports his position with Abu Talib al Makki's *Qut ul Qulub* when arguing that spiritual training and proper conduct determine the focus of Sufis in an assembly of *sama*, which then becomes very different from a popular gathering of music and singing.

A beautiful voice is considered important in an assembly of *sama*, since the quality of a melodious voice is a blessing from God. Therefore listening to such a voice involves recognizing the beneficence of the Lord towards human beings. Audition through such a voice, then, is considered a pious act and attracts the mercy of God upon listeners. This is supported through a Hadith where Prophet Muhammad confirmed good voice as an attribute of all prophets. This is further supported by the Quran, where Allah reminds human beings to be grateful for the sweet voice, and pray to him while reading the Quran in such melodious voices. Zarradi thereafter cites popular traditions of Prophet Daud that extol the miraculous beauty of his voice. Based on the above, the author then argues for the importance of a good voice in the exercise of *sama*. In *sama*, a beautiful voice is often accompanied by musical instruments, which is permitted depending on the occasion. For non-spiritual assemblies, Zarradi argues, musical instruments should not be combined with a melodious voice since it influences listeners towards non-permissible actions. Only when the lower self of the listener is pure does singing combined with musical instruments have a beneficial effect, acting as nourishment for the soul. The author goes on to discuss the qualities of musical instruments.

The content of *sama* is poetry and verse, whose quality for the occasion is ascertained through whether they are composed in a well-measured and rhythmical way and thus bring out the inner meaning with clarity. For recognizing such qualities in a verse, the reciter needs to have 'pure nature and good qualities'. Zarradi attributes the element of ingenuity in a verse to the blessing of God, which inclines the heart of the listener towards what is listened to. Such an inclination of the heart is useful for creating harmony between the mind and the body, stirring them in remembrance of God. The impact that verse and poetry create on the listener is recognized as a blessing of God which descends on a particular occasion. The author cites Hadith traditions in support of the above position, and also argues that poetry in itself is not a bad exercise unless in situations where it conveys obscenity.

Since listening to a melodious voice when it recites poetry and verses is permissible for an individual who is in control of his senses, the author argues that by such logic *sama* is a permissible exercise for Sufis and mystics. This is supported through Hadith traditions mentioned above, as when the Prophet encouraged recitation and audition of the Quran in a melodious voice, as well as listening to poetry in a good voice which gives rise to deep emotions in the heart of the listener. It is thus clear from the foregoing discussion that Zarradi argues in defence of *sama*, and the ritual needs to adhere to certain conditions in order to be permissible among Sufis. Most importantly, *sama* needs to adhere to its character and not turn into something frivolous. Zarradi, on the authority of Sufi saints like Nizam al-Din, enumerates the conditions that allow *sama* to be performed as a regulated exercise through a harmonious existence amongst the *qawwal*, the poetry recited, and the audience of Sufi saints. In situations where such conditions are not met, *sama* is against the spirit of the *shariah*, and is a non-permissible exercise.

Zarradi collates proof from the Quran, through verses where God extols His servants to listen to things that glorify the Creator and His words, which establish the permissibility of listening to good things which celebrate the glory of God and are thus considered pure for all beings. Evidence is also cited from the Quran where God warns his subjects against indulging in wrongful things, like *sama* which is performed in a bad voice and thus brings immoral thoughts to the mind of the listener. The author considers such acts as similar to the practice of singing (*ghina*), which is different from the practice of *sama*. The latter, according to Zarradi, also involves poetry, verse, and singing, but it is performed in the spirit of the *shariah* conforming to spiritual standards of the assembly. Hence the message which is presented in a beautiful voice does not bring frivolity in the mind of the listener. The acceptability of *sama* is also attested through important Hadith traditions from multiple dependable authorities, which narrate that the Prophet allowed singing and music with instruments to celebrate special occasions. The Prophet himself appreciated the recitation of poetry and verses by his companions, who were reputed poets and recited in beautiful voices. This is followed by arguments put forward by important Sufi saints in favour of *sama*, from the very earliest ones to Nizam al-Din. The latter distinguishes three forms of listeners of *sama* with three different attributes: those who make others listen carry the attribute of empathetic ecstasy (*tawajud*); those who say something in *sama* have the attribute of momentary ecstasy (*wajd*); while those who are listeners in *sama* benefit from durative ecstasy (*wujud*). Zarradi's last principle constitutes the longest section, which elaborates on the experience of empathetic ecstasy that falls on the listener, beyond his control, leading to agitation within the body.

The following translation of Zarradi's treatise into English aims to introduce this important work on the subject of *sama* that survives, among a few others, to a wider readership on this much contentious subject.

Usul al Sama—Principles of Listening to Music[1]
of Maulana Fakhr al-Din Zarradi

Introduction

In the name of Allah, the most Merciful and the most Compassionate

All praise to God who has counted the eminent saints (*awliya*) among His chosen subjects and commanded upon them acts of devotion and piety.

---

[1] Maulana Fakhr al-Din Zarradi, *Risala-i Usul al Sama* (Delhi: Matba-i Muhibb-i Hind, 1889).

There are two commands with regard to *sama*: the first is 'sama' which means 'to listen to that which is meant to be listened to', and the second is 'husn e sama', which means listening to that which originates from God and truth, that is 'the old and truthful kalam'. The latter is preserved especially for saints, since they listen to nothing but the word of truth. If they listen to anything that is against this, then they commit a sin.

> *In an intense yearning (for you), the walls (of my heart) have*
> *become a mirror,*
> *In every direction that I turn to, your splendor is on display.*

Keeping in mind the taste and interest of the reciter in sama, hidden meanings should be emphasized upon, and while listening the audience should be provided with delight through such verses so that they listen with attention. The hearts of the listeners should be addressed through traditional verses so that the veils of secrecy are unveiled upon them. Blessings and prayers are for Hazrat Muhammad (SAW), the leader of the prophets, as well as for his family and followers.

According to the dictionary, 'muqaddimah' is one who is the leader of the army, and in scholarly usage it is whatever that is mentioned in the beginning of a text or treatise, as an introduction.

It is important to know that the *ahl i sunnah* has three groups: the legists, the traditional scholars of Hadith, and the Sufis. Legists have labeled the scholars of Hadith as externalists (*sahiban i zahir*), since these scholars of Hadith engage with those Hadith traditions that originated in and have been received from the era of Prophet Muhammad (SAW). They refer to these Hadith records on the ground that their transmitters are reliable individuals. The latter have been called *faqihan i sahiban*, since they depend on their intellect, and work through it, while rejecting those Hadith records even when they have been transmitted through a single chain. Thus it is known that, on the contrary, they adhere more to reasoning and intellect. Only when a Hadith tradition is confirmed by multiple transmitters it is considered permissible for reference. But it is not permissible for the scholars of Hadith.

Compared to these two sects Sufis are better and more capable, since they depend only on God for all things, and they look to none else other than God. Thus Sufis trust in the protection from God and do not subscribe to a fixed *madhhab*. It is said that such individuals do not become Sufis unless they go against the idea of a fixed *madhhab*. They also follow the saying of Prophet Muhammad (SAW), *there is a room for discord within my community*. When this situation of discord arises, then the authority of the *madhhabs* will diminish. For that *madhhab* which is allowed in the faith, constricting it is synonymous to ignoring it. And for anyone this is similar to refusing to follow the faith. Prophet Muhammad (SAW) has forbidden this—*do not associate anyone with God*. And peace and blessings of God be on Prophet Muhammad (SAW). Prophet Muhammad (SAW) further remarks that *your inquiry has constricted the openness of the heart*.

Thus it is proven that adhering to *madhhab* is not a good thing, and that it is the path of the masses, as is confirmed by the Quran and Hadith. And this is the truth of the *muhaqqin*. And God says in the Quran that *if you are unaware about any issue then ask about it from ahl i zikr*. Thus it is a command from God that without verification from an *ahl i zikr*, questions on *madhhab* should not be raised. It is mentioned by the Prophet Muhammad (SAW) himself that *my companions are like the stars. Among them whomsoever you choose to follow will show you the correct path*. Thus drawing lessons from the Hadith is as much recommended as from the Quran. On any issue or question there has to be consensus (*ijma*), rather than the opinion of any individual belonging to a sect. It is important to pay attention to the sayings of a *mujtahid*, since he can differentiate between various opinions.

The principles of sama have abundance of piety and intense passion since it is the path for seeking knowledge, and acquiring knowledge by rightful means is mandatory for all, as emphasized in the introduction of this text through Hadith citation. It is mandatory on every Muslim male and female to acquire knowledge. So, following *taqlid*, or the opinion of any particular sect or a predefined path, is discouraged. And following *qiyas*, or using one's intellect to argue on an issue, is also similar to following a particular *madhhab*, because all *madhhabs* in reality make claims without any strong argumentative basis. This author has elaborated all the arguments and positions of legists on this issue.

The *madhhab* of the Sufis is such that they do not follow the individual positions of the different sects, since not only do Sufis and saints pay attention to legists and scholars of Hadith, but on every aspect of each issue they take a careful approach. Thus the norms of *fiqh* are not binding on them, as they follow a deeper sense of understanding. Thus, note very carefully that I have elaborated in great detail the issues of sama that make it permissible (*mubah*)—meaning that following which you do not receive virtue, neither are you at sin if you are not following it. And I am leaving behind this book, *Usul al Sama*, written on this issue. And I have written this work on the foundations of original traditions (*asl riwayat*). I have also taken precaution not to include in this work useless information which lacks strong foundation.

First Principle

The first principle narrates the **truth behind sama**—which part of it is from literal or conventional meaning. Sama is a homonym (*mushtarik*) with interpretations (*mani*). To some it is a primitive or concrete noun (*ism-e jamid*). According to some vocabulary, like the Taj al Sami, sama can be applied to happiness. Ism-e Jamid is meant for those words from which no other words are formed, nor is it derived from any other word. For most, its origin is from the action of hearing or listening (*shanidan*). And it is used as a passive participle of the word 'masmu', meaning that which is 'heard, or listened to'. For example, it is said that 'this book is sama', meaning it has been listened to. This is the reality of its derivation (*siga*) and literal meaning. However, according to conventional meaning sama is a phrase that is listened to. Sweet and rhythmical verses (*mauzun kalam*) are combined with melodious voice so that hearing (*sama'at*) can take place properly. And the essence of sama lies in understanding what is being said by the reciter. And as per the conventional practice of Sufis, careful observance (*ri'ayat*) of literal meaning has to be done, and this constitutes the fundamental principle. And this is in contradiction to singing, since playing music while listening to verses and phrases (*kalam*) can be interpreted as being expressive of (*ibarat*) that which is sung in a good voice while referring to young and beautiful women. Those women are called *gawani* who are fearless and indifferent (*be parwah*) due to the grace of their beauty.

Abu Talib al- Makki, in his treatise *Qut ul Qulub*, has indicated towards this. The truth is, these musical instruments are played by women with the beating of their hand. Women also elaborate on the merit of these musical instruments and are often seen with them. These instruments, when played, ignite sensuality and desire, and the heart is led towards bad thoughts and unsuitable jest. The words spoken by the shaykh are proof of his adab. The wealth and abundance of his knowledge are the foundation of his abstinence. That is why sama is not forbidden (*haram*), while ghina, which is playing of music and instruments, is forbidden. Since all the wrong and indecent things that are present in ghina do not apply to the meaning of sama.

Are we not aware of the truth that if someone vows not to consume meat and thereafter consumes the meat of fish, then according to Imam Abu Hanifa (RA) he will not be considered a liar. Since the word 'lahm' is derived from the word 'ilteham', whose quality is toughness and perpetuity (*hameshagi*), that is not associated with the meat of fish. Therefore the meat of fish is not included in the usual category of meat. In the same way sama is excluded from the category of ghina, since phrases of ghina comprise of the beauty and grace of women, which does not fall in the category of sama. So, words of sama are unrestricted (*mutlaq*) while ghina is restricted (*muqaiyad*), and what is unrestricted is dissociated from what is restricted.

For example, the use of red colour is prohibited in the shariah while other colours are allowed. That is because being restricted it is forbidden, for it is not in accordance with being unrestricted. So when sama is freed from the description (*wasf*) of ghina, that is from those words and phrases used in ghina, in such a condition sama is concurred (*ittifaq*) to be permissible (*mubah*). Since all genuine arguments concerning (*mut'alliq*) sama being permissible (*jayez*) have been collected, that is sama is borne through a good voice and well-measured verse (*kalam mauzun*), the hearing of the above is permissible in the eyes of the shariah. That is because there is goodness in such actions whose meaning is the essence of the practice.

Second Principle

The second principle is regarding the **audition of a beautiful voice**. A beautiful voice is a gift from an individual who has been created by

Allah with a human nature. So its observance is better. And a beautiful voice is a gift that is bestowed from the Divine on an individual. So a beautiful voice is in itself good in nature, and listening to it is equal to a pious act since the mercy of the Lord on his humble creation is great, like it is mentioned in the Quran that among his creations Allah bestows upon those he likes. Some would interpret the bestowed thing as good voice. Some readers have read *fi al khaliq* with a 'pesh' with 'kh', which is considered one of the uncommon styles of recitation (*qir'at*).

Of all the Prophets, the most chosen one (*bar guzida*), Hazrat Muhammad Mustafa (SAW), has stated that *no prophet has been sent by Allah but with a good voice*. That is, in the voices of prophets a charm is to be found. So, words said in a good voice are a gift to be thanked for, and such words spoken are binding (*wajib*), conforming to the Lord. That is, God has said in the Quran to *converse with the Lord through the gift of the sweet voice he has bestowed upon you and express your gratitude to the Provider for this gift*. So the decree according to the Hadith tradition is that acquiring tasteful delight (*lazzat*) is obligatory. Bad and distasteful voice has been rejected.

If the Lord has mentioned that the worst of all voices is that of the donkey, it is proven that compared to bad voices beautiful voices are preferred. This is evident and cannot be erased. And also because good voice is a miracle that was bestowed on Prophet Daud (SAW). Of all the signs of God, a good voice is one of His signs, and it has a very beneficial effect on the heart. And this is the reason why in all funerals there are arrangements to read the Quran in a beautiful voice.

And from among the dependable authorities it is stated that when Prophet Daud (SAW) read the Zabur in a beautiful voice, humans, animals, four-legged creatures, grazing animals, and birds—all would listen spellbound. Such would be the condition in Prophet Daud's (SAW) assemblies that listeners, under the effect of his beautiful voice, lost control over their lives. It is said in traditions that in one of Prophet Daud's (SAW) assemblies his beautiful voice had such a spellbinding impact on listeners that 400 individuals lost their lives.

Hafiz al Tirmidhi, in his book *Nawadir al Usul*, has narrated a tradition on the authority of Ibn Abbas that Prophet Muhammad (SAW) once said that Prophet Daud (SAW) recited the Zabur in seventy different intonations with such beautiful voice that even insects would listen to him spellbound. And at times when he wept, animals from both land and sea congregated to hear him weep. Since good voice is a miracle of prophets and it is incumbent to listen to it.

Interpreters of traditions have said, based on reports from earlier generations, that a good voice is liked even by God. For example, it is found in the Hadith that a person was once praying to God with weeping and crying. Then angel Gabriel pleaded with God *oh Lord, this servant of yours is praying to you. Please accept it.* The Lord replied *I know it. You need not mention. But the delay in accepting his prayers is due to the fact that I like his voice very much.* So it became evident that one should not hurry in prayers.

The same also applies for sama. That is, its listening is obligatory at that moment when there is a beautiful voice. Since the work of truth is to reveal miracles, to show them, and to believe in them. Prophets have said that two types of voices are cursed (*la'nat*). The first is the voice of crying, wailing, and lamenting; and the other is the sound of musical instruments (*mizmar*) that are played on occasions of happiness. The proof that is presented for the above saying is allowable. The sound of musical instruments is meant for people only when it is allowable. The argument for distinguishing (*makhsus*) good voice from musical instruments is that musical instruments without voice are allowable, otherwise its reality is to be rejected. So understand it this way.

Third Principle

The third principle is on the issue of **musical instruments (*mazamir*)**. Musical instruments are a means for weighing voices, and it is allowable in its nature. This is because it has already been said that a good voice is a miracle of prophets, and its audition is binding. However, it is forbidden for a different reason when it is listened to at the time of consuming alcohol. Trustworthy (*mo'tabar*) transmitters of tradition from the time of Prophet Muhammad (SAW) have said that at the time when alcohol became forbidden, musical instruments were forbidden as well. The reason for this being that people used to play musical instruments under the intoxicating influence of alcohol. So the playing was made forbidden, since at the time of the playing it would remind people of wine-drinking (*sharab noshi*). Due to this, musical instruments came to be termed as bad. There are no reasons apart from this. It came to be forbidden due to wine. So, if this reason is not there, then it is not to be forbidden. That is, if the cause of forbidden-ness is not found, then that exercise will not be forbidden. In this way, the playing of the kettledrum (*naqqara*) during war and the playing of music to announce the five times of prayer is also allowable. Therefore, it becomes proven that when the defect or malady (*illat*) of a thing is changed, due to this reason its nature also changes. In this way, for those who aspire to witness the countenance of the Lord, the purity of their lower self is important and they should keep their hearts pure and clean from all forms of amusement (*lahw-o-la'b*), greed, and avarice. So the sound of musical instruments is an invitation from foulness (*kudurat*) to cleanliness, and its sound takes one from lowness towards highness.

Melodious sound is nourishment for the soul. In the realm of angels this nourishment does not equal forgetfulness and frivolity (*ba sar o tafri*). And this is confirmed by the words of Dhun Nun Misri (RA). When he was questioned on the issue of good voice he replied that these are such signs which God has bestowed on every pious man and woman. So, listening to it is allowable for both men and women. And bringing forward the reason for this sanctity, an analogy needs to be drawn with the playing of kettledrums during battles. Are we not aware that the Prophet of God allowed the playing of duff to announce marriage? It is mentioned in the Hadith that one can *announce marriage through the playing of duff*. Likewise, in similar Hadith records the playing of duff is permitted on joyful occasions as a means of expressing happiness (*izhar masarrat*).

It be known that duff has two kinds of qualities. One is the quality of creating happiness, and the other is the quality of manifestation. So happiness comes from its quality of being well-measured and rhythmical, and its quality of manifestation comes from the sound being high-pitched. So the duff is allowable on these two qualities. And playing of the duff is allowable for congregating people who would listen to the message of Prophet Muhammad. For other issues, analogy can be drawn from musical instruments, since the malady of wine-drinking is the reason for which musical instruments are forbidden. If wine-drinking lessens, so will its malady, and if there is no malady due to wine-drinking then the act will also not be forbidden. Through such reasoning Imam Ghazzali has drawn an analogy between sound from musical instruments and that of animals. For instance, listening to animals like birds who have a sweet sound is allowable.

So in this way there are people who are completely intoxicated in the passion for sama, when the sound of musical instruments reaches their ears in such an assembly. But the shaykhs keep themselves pure from such frivolity. The passion which overcomes them is without musical instruments; it is merely from the voice of the singer who recites poetry and verses in such a manner that it showcases an example of the wondrous workmanship (*karigari*) of God. And our mashaikhs are enraptured by such sound.

Fourth Principle

This is on **poetry and verse**. *Sher kalami* is that kind of poetry whose verses are well-measured and rhythmical, and which brings out with clarity (*wazahat*) the fine and difficult meanings. One who brings out the clarity in the verses, that is, the reciter, has to be a person in whom pure nature and good qualities are found. What comprises the ingenuity and message of the verse is an example of the handiwork of God, and the heart is inclined (*ma'il*) towards listening to it. And the increasing passion of the individual gets agitated for the real creator of the verse that is God and His mystical knowledge (*ma'rifat*). It is stated in the Hadith that some verses have their foundation in ingenuity. That is, things that are beneficial have an effect on the heart, and this is due to their quality of being well-measured. And the hidden ingenuity in this is that it leaves an impression on the heart. And the harmonious condition of the mind and body is the grace (*inayat*) from the Lord that is bestowed on whomsoever He wishes. If someone wishes that the abundance be bestowed upon him at all times, that does not happen. Good voice is the workmanship and the result of the abundance of God that is bestowed upon His servants. And verses in which the harmony of the mind and the body is to be found is better than a good voice, because the harmony of the mind and the body is a special attribute for humans. Here the good voice of animals is also included as an attribute.

Apart from this the other issue is on the various kinds of musical instruments. That is also a special favour from God for His servants. There is no bad element in poetry, since poetry in itself is a better thing. Are you not aware that the Prophet (SAW) of God himself had ordered his companion Hasan bin Thabit to recite poetry for him? Hasan abided and recited poetry in the assembly of the Prophet. As a result of being present in front of the Prophet (SAW) when Hasan began reciting poetry, the Prophet (SAW) said to Hasan, *Oh Hasan the sanctified soul angel Gabriel is with you in your defense and assistance.* So Qasim Qasiri has used this Hadith in his book with all the available authorities (*isnad*). Thus whenever there will be an angelic impact on the recitation of poetry, it will be recognized as the assistance of angel Gabriel. And this cannot be refuted. The words of the Prophet (SAW) also support the saying that below the throne of God the treasure lies with humans and its keys are in the shape of the reciters of poetry. For this reason, the Prophet (SAW) called it *she'r*, since like the shariah it is ingenious. The reason being that it descends from the station of the exalted that is the throne (*arsh*).

Thus it has been proven that poetry is a good thing because its nature relates to the intellect. In the same way as good voice, the nature of poetry has no badness in it. Except due to certain reasons; like obscene and indecent talk is not allowable, neither are describing and praising things that are forbidden as per the shariah, saying bad things about the Prophet to reprove a favour, or making fun of the faith of Islam.

On one occasion a reciter said bad things about the Prophet (SAW) from a particular treatise full of infidelity, obscenity, and immorality. And by defending wrongful and misled individuals the reciter placed himself under the burden of sin. On such false reciters there is the curse of God. And their poetry cannot be in agreement with the signs and indications of faith. And poetry that is mixed with good advice is recorded mostly on the unanimous authority of the companions of the Prophet (SAW). And the manifestation of the heart is in that where poetry is read from both layers—that is, from the Prophet (SAW) and his companions. It is said that the Prophet (SAW) himself recited poetry. And this argument manifests itself on the issue of poetry being allowable.

Fifth Principle

The fifth principle is concerned with **good voice and well-measured verses**, and the means by which both these things are allowable. So, it has been proven that good voice and audition of verses through one's senses, that is, a clear indication of the workmanship of the pious being, is permissible. So, from this it is also proven that sama which contains good messages in a good voice, and for that reason leads to the increase in virtue, is allowable. For this reason, both sama and its audition are good activities. And this also indicates the saying of Prophet Muhammad (SAW), *read the Quran with a good voice*, since due to the good voice there is an increase in virtue which is gained from the reading of the Quran. The Quran itself is good by nature, and its cantillation in a good voice is the reason for increase in virtue. And this is the reason that there is a deep impact on the mind of those who listen to the recitation of the Quran in a good voice.

Thus, whenever verses are in conformity to the meaning of the Quran it will be included in the order of the Quran. Such recitation of poetry is in accordance with the Quran, and if this is done in a good voice then it will be said that this is in accordance with the order of the Quran. So, poetry is not bereft of two meanings: first, it is mixed with advice, and second, it is melodious to listen to.

If verses that are recited contain descriptions of beautiful women and minor girls then it is a sin. And if verses contain descriptions of angels and virgins of paradise then their audition is good. As a result, it gives rise to passion and lamentation in the heart of a believer, refreshing his thoughts for the Day of Judgement. For reciting poetry, a good voice is strictly enjoined (*takid*), so that it becomes the foundation for audition, and reminds one strongly of the Day of Judgement. And this is a good thing that such audition becomes the reason for augmenting taste and passion. And it is truthfully proven that Prophet Muhammad (SAW) listened to the odes (*qasida*) of Qa'ab bin Zahir. Originally though, such odes used to have references to beautiful women.

It is mentioned in the shariah that reciting poetry in a good voice is a good thing, since its audition and acceptance is approved by the traditions of Prophet Muhammad (SAW). He has stated that whoever memorizes this ode will be blessed with heaven. There is also a tradition that

Prophet Muhammad (SAW) listened to this ode in a good voice inside a mosque.

And Sufis (*mashaikh*), based on the tradition of these arguments, have presented their case in favour of sama being allowable. And to some Sufis hand-clapping is also a good act, since it brings happiness to the hearts of the listeners. But playing the duff with the hand in such a manner that it leads to a state of ecstasy (*wajd*) in the listener is a sin. And it is narrated in traditions that an Arab villager, while reciting poetry in front of the Prophet (SAW) with a good voice, used to play the drum with both hands in such manner. And the Prophet (SAW) would be moved into a state of ecstasy in the company of his companions from such a good voice.

Sixth Principle

This principle is on the **conditions (*shurut*)** that testify sama to be allowable. Both Sufis and scholars of Hadith concur on this principle that if sama is according to its character, then it is allowable. Otherwise, if it is related to frivolity and cheap play, it will be forbidden. And those legists (*fiqaiyah*) who have declared sama as forbidden based on Hadith traditions have related it to sins like frivolity and cheap play. If its malady is decreased, then its dignity also will surely be increased.

So, it is remarked by Shaykh Nizam al-Din Awliya that sama is allowable in its character itself, and there is never a disagreement in this position, unless something is found in it that is against the shariah. And it is important for sama that there is someone to recite, that is, the singer, and secondly that the singer should have himself heard the verses that he wishes to recite for the assembly. Thirdly, the listener has to be a Sufi, and fourthly, any instrument related to sama should be kept there. And the qualities that are present in a listener must also be present in the reciter, so that there is no possibility of mischief being created. Minor boys and girls must not be present, for both of these are causes of mischief. During the assembly of sama no such thing must be said that is against the word and spirit of the shariah. At times it so happens that feelings of greed, lust, and avarice may arise within the reciter, and this action by him shall be explained as hypocrisy. And the instrument that is used in sama is also a kind of musical instrument. Thus, if sama is pure from such a position, then it is agreed by all as allowable. And the argument for this is given from knowledge of the intellect (*ma'qul*), and transcribed knowledge (*manqul*). Details of the knowledge of intellect have already been mentioned before, and detail on transcribed knowledge is forthcoming.

Seventh Principle

This principle is on the **proofs on sama**. The verse of the Quran related to this issue states that, in the first verse, God commands *give good tidings to my servants that they should hear such things that are best in obedience to me*. Its related argument is that God Himself has praised those of his servants who out of submission to Him listen to good things that are in accordance with the principles of the Creator. Of all the good things, the best of the sayings are of God. And it is proven that whatever comes out from the mouth of the servant in accordance with the principles of the Lord is not the word of the servant, but actually that of the Lord.

If *alif* and *lam* are joined and used in place of *aliah*, as indicated in the tafsir of Zahiri, it will mean the wish that *my servant should himself give me glad tidings by listening to my words*. So, words that are in accordance with God will also be included in that order of things.

The second verse is *all the pure things on earth have been made legal and lawful for you so that your senses derive happiness. And unlawful things have also been manifested for you.* And all things that are apart from these are pure. And among all these things sama is the purest and best of them, since the heart and the soul receives happiness from it. And as per proofs, this is legal and lawful.

In the third verse the command of God is *following my orders you offer your gratitude to me with your ears, eyes, and heart.* And it is the beneficence of God that He has bestowed the quality of good audition to His servants, so that through it all things can be heard. But regarding things whose audition leads one towards immoral conduct (*fisq*), adulterous behaviour (*fajur*), and bad things, such an audition is forbidden. All these things are forbidden by the shariah (*mamnu'at e shariah*) and under the command of the Lord. By prohibiting His servants from such harmful things, He has done a favour for them. It is also the command of God that some of His servants become interested in harmful deeds and words that create a strong desire and passion within them for playfulness and frivolity.

And in the last verse it is the command of God that *for such servants is the punishment and torment from God that is despicable and ruinous*. And the command from God is also for those kafir servants who will be punished, because all these playful, frivolous, and sinful acts are the invention of kafirs, and by following these actions one faces punishment. But for the believers who stay away from such immodest and obscene activities, God has even commanded Satan that using whatever power you have mislead my servants with your bad voice. Due to this reason, legists have labelled such sama that focuses on immodest and obscene thoughts as forbidden. In this regard interpreters have also said the same. Many among them are of the opinion that playfulness and frivolity lead to desires. And it is mentioned in a treatise entitled Samud that playfulness and frivolity result in laughter and jest. Of this all is related to playfulness and frivolity that gives birth to unrest and harmful things.

And many commentators have said that it leads to desires of singing (*ghina*). Thus all of these opinions mean that not one thing can be fixed to the issue of playfulness and frivolity. Also related to this issue, it has been noted in the past about Sufi saints that they are not followers of a single legal school (*madhhab*). And if their sayings are understood, then in the context of all the above discussions an agreement in their sayings can be found. This is because singing (*ghina*) can lead to desires of *kufr*. Listening to singing in the pre-Islamic (*jahiliya*) period that narrated the bravery of the *kafirs* during war, stories of their glory and grandeur, of their love and passion, and their praise, is similar to listening to poetry.

The reality of singing is that it is related to playfulness and frivolity, as well as unrest during the age of ignorance (*jahiliya*). And its legality can be seen from the verses of the Quran. *Ghina* deviates people from the path of God and misleads them. And it is evident that in the age of ignorance, *ghina* was the necessary cause for people being misled.

So, sama opens the ear of the listener so that his eyes and ears open up for the benefit of weeping and invites them in the way of the pure and sacred. Such attention and courtesy that is available from the above is not part of the order of *ghina*, which is misleading. Similar interpretation is given on the issue of poetry by Ibn Masud. The audition of poetry is not forbidden by its own nature, since Prophet Muhammad (SAW) too listened to poetry, and even recited it. And similar actions can be seen from the companions of the Prophet in his presence. Whatever is forbidden in poetry is against the spirit of the shariah. In issues of playfulness and frivolity, these can be misleading. These are presented in a beautiful manner so that thoughts of kufr and sin place themselves in the heart of Muslims. Thus we have elaborated many things on poets who are misled.

However, even during singing the audition of poetry is allowed as a command, that is, *ghina* is not forbidden in its own nature. Rather its ingenuity is due to the reason of unrest it creates, through the playing of song and music with musical instruments by minor girls or women. So, if *ghina* is kept away from unrest and playfulness and frivolity, then all will concur to render it as allowable.

Eighth Principle

This principle is on the **proofs of sama according to famous Hadith traditions**. Among these there are some accounts that have been narrated on the correct authority of Hazrat Ayesha (RA). Once when Abu Bakr (RA) entered the house of Ayesha (RA), he saw two young women singing and playing duff. The Prophet (SAW) was lying down with the bed sheet covering his face. When Abu Bakr (RA) reprimanded them and asked them to stop doing such things, the Prophet (SAW) uncovered his face and told Abu Bakr (RA), *O Abu Bakr let them go, today is their Eid.*

The other tradition says that Abu Bakr (RA) told them again that singing and playing instruments is the work of Satan, then Prophet Muhammad (SAW) told him, *O Abu Bakr let them go, since every community has their Eid, and today is their Eid.* Abu Bakr's (RA) instruction to stop such acts is because of the direction of *ghina* and its ingenuity, which is the reason for unrest and playfulness and frivolity. This kind of chaos and unrest used to be found in *ghina* during the age of *jahiliyah*. There are directions from Prophet Muhammad (SAW) towards this being allowable, when the voice is good and the verses well measured, bestowed with wisdom, advice, and grace; and which is the reason for love towards God and His Prophet. So in the age of *jahiliyah*, the reason for *ghina* to be forbidden was that it distracted the heart towards intoxication.

Therefore we can compare such *ghina* with verses that contain the mention of God Almighty, and His unending beneficence (*niamat*). It contains the message of salvation for those people who by their actions become the cause of gracing Islam. And in whose hearts there is a longing (*talab*) for God, the knower of the Unseen, so that the seeker finds a place in paradise. And in this regard, Sufis also say that sama is such a practice that agitates the heart towards God. If someone says that sama is allowable only on days of Eid, then how can we reject the argument for its audition on other days. We can say that Eid is the day of desiring happiness, and its proof is based on the mention of such days as when the Prophet (SAW) said that the day is of Eid, that is, happiness, rather than saying it is the day of Eid ul Fitr, when the event took place. And this can be related to the word of God in the verse of the Quran which means that *O Provider bestow upon us with a tray of food from the heaven so that it becomes a day of Eid and happiness.* Thus the meaning of Eid is meant to return again and again. This is proven that every day of happiness is the day of Eid.

And many renowned Hadith scholars agree that there is a tradition of Hazrat Ayesha (RA) where she says *I had an Ansari girl whom I married to an Ansari boy.* On this occasion the Prophet (SAW) asked Ayesha (RA), *O Ayesha why didn't you not do singing and instrument playing, since people of the Ansar tribe like this practice.* Thus this Hadith relates to the proof of *ghina* being allowable, since the Prophet (SAW) appreciated the *ghina* of the Ansar tribe and praised it. And for the companions of the Prophet such is the command from God that *you are greatly loved by Allah because He has bestowed the grace of faith within your hearts as a result of which you dislike kufr, sin and immoral activities.* So if *ghina* would have been a truly sinful action, then it would have been disliked by the companions as well.

Thus it has been proven that in all times and days the audition of *ghina* is desirable (*mustahabb*). And it is not special only during weddings, as no special moment is fixed (*ta'id*) for this. Thus it is legal and beneficial at all times, whether it is the moment of a wedding, day or night time, or any other occasion for happiness. And its permissibility is supported by a number of Hadith traditions that act as proof. The exact number of these Hadith traditions cannot be ascertained. We have based our proofs on the above two Hadith traditions, which is sufficient.

And those traditions that legists have narrated on the Hadith records of Abu Amamah and Jabr Razi on sama as a forbidden practice do not match with the Hadith records received from proven (*sahih*) authority. And scholars of Hadith traditions (*muhaddis*) do not have any faith in these kinds of Hadith narrations. Like Shaykh Majid al Din has mentioned it in his book *Sirat al Mustaqim*, even if we believe in such Hadith records, then it also does not relate to the traditions narrated by Hazrat Ayesha (RA) because the tradition of Hazrat Ayesha (RA) is more famous and valuable than the Hadith records of Abu Amamah and Jabir. And if these two individuals carefully analyse the Hadith record that has originated from the Prophet, then they too would be seen arguing for *ghina* as allowable.

So the first issue is, in the Hadith tradition that has been mentioned on the authority of Abu Amamah, he says that, according to the command of Prophet Muhammad (SAW), there is none who during sama raises his voice and God does not send for him two satans who sit on his left and right shoulders. So the meaning of Eid is to increase the pitch of the voice in *ghina*, and not just its audition. And there is no denying and arguing against its ingenuity because increasing the pitch of voice creates hindrance for *ghina*. Since by listening to this there is a desire for intimacy, and it is prohibited to raise the voice for those individuals who raise their voices during *ghina*. And this is the proof of its legality.

Are you not aware that at the time of reciting the Quran it has been commanded to listen to it quietly? Since talking at the time of eloquent recitation of the Quran hinders the exercise of its audition. The second Hadith is from the authority of Jabr Razi, where the Prophet remarked that any individual who cries, sings, and laments is a primary form of Satan. This Hadith has been interpreted in the sense that crying and lamenting is similar to showing off (*numayish*), and singing and playing music is similar to frivolity and playfulness. The reason being, Satan cries and laments and focuses on singing and playing music. And this is the tradition of frivolity and playfulness that is meant here. But shedding tears when someone passes away is similar to worship, and singing on such an occasion is meant to bring happiness to the heart.

So this cannot be resemblant of *nauha*. Since *nauha* is jest, frivolity, and playfulness, and *ghina* that invites one to unrest and chaos is allowable as proven earlier. So through these words and proofs, the Hadith traditions are conformed to, in principle.

But the arguments of legists (*faqiha*)—that singing and playing music is forbidden, and sitting in such assemblies is immoral and taking pleasure from these assemblies is *kufr*—prove the words and statements of the Prophet (SAW) as false. Compared to the words of the Prophet (SAW), there is no worth and desire in their words. Since acquiring taste from anything is unlawful, even if it is by feigning. But in the eyes of the *ahl sunnat wa jamaat*, that is not kufr. So this saying is for those who take pleasure from the desires of the lower self that is according to the belief of the heretics and dissenters. One guilty of greater sin is a *kafir* in their eyes. So their faith is not worthy of being trusted.

Ninth Principle

The ninth principle is on the famous **Hadith traditions whose authorities/narrators are competent and dependable.** The master gnostic Abu Talib Makki (RA) has narrated that numerous virtuous men of the past, the noble companions, the *tabi'in*, and many other noble individuals besides have stated that sama is allowable (*mubah*), and its audition has been done by many who are companions of the Prophet and the *tabi'in*. This statement of Abu Talib Makki (RA) is thus held in high regard (*mo'tabar*), since he had reached the great station of (spiritual) knowledge, and he was aware of the position of the virtuous men of the past.

Related to sama, traditions has it that if any individual refuses sama on abstract and relative grounds, fixes it on any particular day, or has narrated its characteristics and benefits, one could say that the person has ignored eighty such noble individuals mentioned above who are pious and have placed the seal of authenticity on sama. And although we know the kind of refusal, it is closer to the nature and hypocrisy of the reader.

And the truth is we never reject it since we know the things that those individuals do not know. And we have heard these things from virtuous men of the past (*salaf al saleh*), who have not been heard by these people. And he also says that those who are in denial of sama are not free from three types of calamities and problems. First is that they are not aware of the traditions and narrations of the Prophet, that is he is illiterate. Second is that he is short-sighted and self-centred regarding all those good deeds that have been permitted for him, and adhering to which great virtue can be obtained. And thirdly, he is either dull or has no taste and passion and interest in these commands, more like a donkey on which books are piled up. And it has been mentioned in the *Kitab al Bayan* on the science of jurisprudence (*fiqh*), and narrated on the authority of Hazrat Usman Ghani (RA), that the truth is two handmaids used to sing to him every morning. He would say 'khamush', meaning 'be silent', since this is morning time. And Shaykh Abd-al-Rahman al Sulami (RA) has narrated and documented from Ibn Umar (RA) that his research about singing was questioned. Then he said that it is not scary when he does not have wine with him. Also it is mentioned in the *Tehzeeb ul Akhlaq* of Imam Shafi on the authority of Hazrat Umar (RA) that when he was unoccupied in his own home, that is, when he was alone, he would sing with one or two verses. He then requested permission from Abd-al-Rahman bin Auf, that is, he expressed his will to come closer to him. And while he was singing he said, 'Did you listen O Abd-al-Rahman?'. He said 'Yes, when I become unoccupied I will myself do in the same way as you do'. Thus it is proved that singing (*ghina*) to make oneself happy is permitted and this is well known among them. And Imam Ghazali has mentioned from Yunus bin Abul Ala that it is said his research was questioned. Imam Shafi said about the people of Medina making sama permissible, 'I do not know anyone from the scholars of Hejaz who considers sama objectionable unless there is someone who has denied something'. But the saying of Ibn Masud (may God be pleased with him) that singing (*ghina*) produces hypocrisy in the heart just as water produces greenery, is therefore the reason why it is permitted. Since hypocrisy does not have the ability unless in a virtuous matter. In a way that the doer has a corrupt intention, then it corrupts the act as well.

Thus from this evidence it can be proven that by nature *ghina* is a pious activity. But the saying of Usman that *neither did I sing nor did I desire for it nor did I touch my private part with the right hand while taking oath from the Prophet*, has been compared/reasoned with *ghina* in the age of jahiliya, and all things similar to this have been compared/reasoned in the same way. So in the age of jahiliya the fulfilment of adhering to *ghina* has been conformed according to these Hadith traditions, that is somewhere in between the two above sayings. And this is in principle.

Of the two sayings, the first one that emerges from Usman, that his daughter used to sing and play instruments in front of him, is allowable. The second saying is non-allowable. Thus it is the saying of Sultan al Mashaikh[2] that in sama there are things which are permitted, forbidden, and ambiguous. So for individuals who listen to sama just for the desire of their lower self, fame, and worldly senses, this is a forbidden exercise, since by means of this it can be compared to *ghina* that was prevalent in the age of jahiliyah.

And for that individual who, knowing that sama is allowable, listens to it from his daughter or wife out of desire, then this form of sama will be considered similar to frivolity and playfulness. Since by nature sama is allowable but resembles playfulness. If someone listens to sama that is founded on playfulness, with the purity of his heart as a result of which his being acquires a taste of passion and through which he becomes aware of sayings that bring tears and grief to him and increases the desire to meet God, then this sama is allowable (*halal*). Sayings of Sufis too point towards this direction.

Dhun Nun Misri said that sama is a revelation from God that increases within one's heart the love for God. The individual who orientates himself towards that direction, that is, towards sama, in reality orientates himself towards truth. And those who out of sheer desire of their carnal selves orientate themselves towards sama, they are *kafirs* and *zindiqs*. Similar is the saying of Shaykh Shibli when he was asked about sama. He replied that in the exterior sama is chaos (*fitna*), but in the interior sama is good counsel. For the individual who understands this by its signs, it is permissible. For those to whom these signs make no sense, sama is chaos, trouble, and torment.

Thus it is proven that for people of the mystical path sama is the most delicious nourishment of the soul, and is good in its own nature. It is not bad, since through it the soul receives pleasure, and its emotions are stirred. As it has been said by Abu Ali Daqqaq, sama is the most delicious nourishment for the soul for people on the spiritual path, but its command for approach is through the exercise of audition. That is, the intention with which individuals participate in sama for deriving benefits will decide whether the exercise be termed as halal or haram.

---

[2] Shaykh Nizam al-Din Awliya (d. 1325).

Whoever verifies sama through truth, for him it is truth. Those who think it otherwise, for them sama is against the spirit of truth. So sama is like those trees which sway from the blowing wind, and by passing through them the cool breeze brings relief to the gardens and also perfumes (*mu'attar*) the mind with its sweet fragrance. That same breeze when it passes over filth and impurity by its nature acquires a bad odour. So while listening to sama, such a degree of caution is mandatory so that whatever benefits the listener draws from the audition are according to his mental aptitude (*iste'dad*) and destiny. And in this regard Sultan al Mashaikh has said that there are three types of listeners in sama: first is the *mutasammi*, or those who make others listen, second is *mustami*, or those who say something to be heard, and the third is the *sami*, who are the listeners. The attribute of the *mutasammi* is empathetic ecstasy (*tawajud*), that of *mustami* is momentary ecstasy (*wajd*) and that of *sami* is durative ecstasy (*wujud*). And all of these are forthcoming in the following discussion.

Tenth Principle

This principle narrates the **reality of tawajud**. Empathetic ecstasy (*tawajud*) is a form of agitation that befalls an assembly as a result of its well-measuredness from the *mustami* without his choice/control. And it almost overpowers the assembly of sama. So it is proper because it appeals to the condition of ecstasy that arrives on the heart unexpectedly, and seeks the condition of an increased ecstasy. So that he can feel ecstasy on the existence of his Beloved.

And this is also confirmed by the saying of the Prophet (SAW) that when Muawiya related frivolity and playfulness to empathetic ecstasy, the Prophet (SAW) remarked *O Muawiya there is no elder who does not come under ecstasy while listening to the zikr of the names of the Friend*. When Junaid Baghdadi was questioned on the issue of empathetic ecstasy, he said that surely Allah on the day of mithaq, that is on the day of oath, while addressing the souls remarked *Am I not your Lord*? Then due to the reason of being able to converse with their Lord all souls danced in joy, and came under ecstasy. Because in the words of the Lord there was much sweetness and grace (*latafat*). Thereafter, whenever they listened to sama their bodies were agitated while listening to the voice.

Thus during sama the agitation of the body is not ignored because the Prophet himself did this, and all his companions have followed this accordingly. It is mentioned in the traditions that Prophet Muhammad (SAW) once told Hazrat Ali *you are from me and I am from you.* On hearing this Ali got physically agitated out of pleasure that he encountered ecstasy. And it is also mentioned in the traditions that the Prophet once told Zafar *in creation you are like me. That is your limbs and organs are similar to what I have and your habits and morality and personality is also similar to mine.* Thus, on hearing this from the blessed tongue, Zafar went into ecstasy. The tradition on Hazrat Zayed is the same. Once, the Prophet on meeting him told him that *you are my brother and very dear to me.* He too went into ecstasy on hearing this. On occasions of happiness it agitates the body, and it is the quality of the soul. Shaykh Junaid has indicated towards this direction that together with the heart the soul too remains agitated. So the soul becomes agitated and brings agitation to the heart.

Whenever the soul becomes agitated because of songs and melodies, the heart remains captured in this feeling, and while trusting this comes into agitation. But those who are in ecstasy cannot express this except through relevant agitation. Because songs and melodies have well-measuredness and rhythm, and there is no possibility to ignore it, because it is to be found in those who are in ecstasy without any choice or control.

Thus empathetic ecstasy is different from *raqs*, since *raqs* is a form of agitation that manifests itself in a controlled, thus preferred, manner, and this is the style of fools and show-offs. They are overcome by the desires of their lower selves, and this is absolutely forbidden. But those who feel empathetic ecstasy have various forms of ecstasy that are related to their specific conditions. That is, their agitation can take many forms. One form of agitation is manifested from those who do sama during moments of proximity and restlessness from discomfort. This is an agitation that is found in animals at the time of their slaughter. The second type of agitation is the tremble that appears in the body of an individual while presenting himself in front of the ruler of the age when summoned by the ruler. This agitation resembles that of a fish when it sees the seashore. Another agitation is that which arrives unexpectedly on someone on the occasion of happiness, and this agitation is like the moth when it sees a glimmer of light.

So, for the desires of the lower self it is like digging, and for the heart it is a search for the heart, and happiness for the soul. So, the desires of the lower self (*nafs*) are destroyed, the heart finds the path, and the soul reigns supreme. For men of wonders this is a special agitation and gesture. Thus, the Prophet too participated in agitation with his companions while listening to poetry full of love:

> *The serpent of love has bitten my liver,*
> *Now neither is there a doctor nor medication.*
> *Due to this reason I have sacrificed myself to this friendship.*
> *And this is both the medicine and the poison for me.*

Listening to this verse the Prophet (SAW) went into ecstasy so that the sheet of cloth slipped from his shoulders. Since empathetic ecstasy was practiced by the Prophet (SAW) and his companions, it is therefore a good practice. And if we try to point out the negative elements that manifest in it, then it would relate to the practice of Amir Muawiya, since it was he who considered it to be frivolity and playfulness, for which the Prophet (SAW) stopped him and asked him to refrain from saying such things. This has been mentioned above.

The manifestation of ecstasy happens both in the outer (*zahir*) and in the inner (*batin*). Its outer form is those actions which can be publicly seen, and its inner form is overpowering. That is, within the inner such actions take place which cannot be seen. So for the outsider it is frivolity and playfulness for the lower self, unaware of the significance and state of the inner. They have no feeling and sense of what passes over the state of the heart. They only see the face of external agitation.

And it is the effort of the *ahl e batin* that whatever overpowering spiritual treasure lies within them they witness it internally, so that none of its external manifestation is visible. Conditions of outer and inner have been narrated from Hadith traditions with proof, and without any doubt this is correct. But on the authority of Muawiya the relation of empathetic ecstasy to frivolity and playfulness has raised such doubts that men of the spiritual path have been in a dilemma. These shaykhs are grateful for the beneficence and gifts of God, paying no attention to such issues.

Like the angels they are engaged day and night in the remembrance of God, silently or loudly. But they are beyond any longing for the condition of love and beyond any realization of the verses read out in sama. Since for them it is not important to have equality between the two things. It is not so that without one the other cannot function.

It has been mentioned by Nizam al-Din Awliya in the *Fawaid al Fuad* on the basis of a conversation with Shaykh Najib al Din that the gift that is possible for men is present in his existence. The gift of love and sama is only for those on whom these things have an effect, and he gets lost in them. He should lose himself in worshipping and contemplating God to such an extent that he annihilates himself in the exercise and thus loses himself. So, his (Amir Muawiya) problem offers proof in the direction that the Hadith tradition he presented in support of his position is weak (*za'if*) and this is well indicated. Since the author of *Qut ul Qulub* has included that Hadith tradition in his book, and his period was closer to that of the Prophet and he was a learned and erudite individual, hence he was mindful of the genealogy and trail of the Hadith.

Conclusion

Know that sama is a matter of difference of opinion (*ikhtilafi masla*) among those groups and sects whom I have mentioned. So its allowability is not fixed (*muta'aiyin*) from one generation to another. In this way its allowability and forbidden-ness is not proved through revelation. And after the period of Prophet Muhammad (SAW), the age of revelation has ended. For those individuals who disapprove of sama, their sayings can be correct since their sayings are from those traditions that claim to be based on truth. They say that though sama was allowable in earlier generations, it is forbidden now, and provide proof that such pious souls of God are no longer to be found in our times. And making such claims is transgressing the realm of revelation and the Unseen. Since nowadays the fact that there are no pious souls of God cannot be confirmed for certain except on the basis of those two claims. And this is unanimously *kufr*, since revelation has ceased, and knowledge of the Unseen is only known to God.

Thus in accordance with the saying of those who reject sama it has been proven that they hold the grandeur of sama to be misleading (*gumrahi*). But except for those misled and heretic sects, none say these things. So, *oh my dear brothers understand these things and pay attention to them. And browse through this treatise on sama with fairness, so that you may dissociate from discord, and the real message be manifest (wazeh) on you. And may God grant you divine guidance, and may also favour us with the same so that we may follow our forefathers and those pious beings who are the pious and virtuous sons of Prophet Muhammad (SAW). The End.*

3

Far from Delhi

Sama in the Deccan

Nizam al-Din Awliya passed away in 1325, marking the beginning of the end of an era of the five great Chishti masters who contributed towards strengthening Chishti Sufism in north India. Nizam al-Din's career in Delhi also marked the culmination of the steady process of decentralization of the Chishti order that had begun during the lifetime of Baba Farid al-Din. Aimed towards a greater dissemination of Chishti teachings, Farid al-Din allowed his disciples to position themselves in the Gangetic heartland of north India. Nizam al-Din extended his hand of mentorship to a large number of disciples, and hence could command a spiritual network spread over a wide geographical area—across north, east, west, and the Deccan region. Over the fourteenth century, Chishti centres in South Asia overlapped with administrative centres of the Delhi Sultanate, whereby important capital cities and administrative towns also became the seat of an important Sufi saint teaching and preaching to the common masses. A majority of these Sufi centres were headed by disciples of Nizam al-Din, thereby strengthening an ever-expanding network of Chishti Sufism. Nasir al-Din Mahmud stayed back in Delhi, Akhi Siraj al-Din Usman was sent to Bengal, Muntajib al-Din was sent to Khuldabad in the Deccan, followed later by his brother Burhan al-Din. Others were sent to various regions across west and central India.

After the demise of Muntajib al-Din, Burhan al-Din Gharib was instrumental in establishing the Chishti order in the Deccan, operating from the small town of Khuldabad adjacent to Daulatabad, the second capital of the Delhi Sultans in the Deccan. Later, with the arrival of Muhammad Gisu Daraz, the influence of the Chishti order penetrated deeper into the Deccan, with the Bahmani capital of Gulbarga emerging as the major centre of Chishti activity. Before we turn our attention to Chishti spiritual

Sufi Rituals and Practices. Kashshaf Ghani, Oxford University Press. © Kashshaf Ghani 2024.
DOI: 10.1093/oso/9780192889225.003.0004

practices in the Deccan, it is necessary to explore the historical context which led to the rise of the Chishtis in the Deccan, the roots of which can be traced to the imperial policies of one of the most powerful rulers of Delhi, Muhammad bin Tughluq.

After Ghiyas al-Din Tughluq died in an accident in 1325 when his pavilion collapsed, prince Ulugh Khan ascended the throne of the Delhi Sultanate. Taking the title of Muhammad bin Tughluq, he became the ruler of a domain that was geographically larger than what the Mughals controlled in their heyday. Even before his accession Ulugh Khan was constantly engaged in the Deccan, subduing the kingdoms of the Yadavas (Devagiri), Kakatiyas (Warangal), and Hoysalas (Dwarasamudra). After ascending the throne, one of his major policies involved the setting up of an administrative centre of the north-Indian Sultanate in the Deccan in 1327 that would, in all means, operate as the second capital. The city of Deogir, or Devagiri, in the heartland of Yadava territory in western Deccan was chosen as the site and renamed Daulatabad in 1328. The successful completion of this project was ensured through the physical transfer of the Muslim elite from Delhi to the new capital city. This involved the transfer of intellectuals, scholars, nobility, clergy, administrators, warriors, revenue officers, poets, and artisans to the Deccan capital, who, it was expected, would inaugurate a new era in the socio-cultural and political life of the region.

With the rise of Muslim power in the Deccan, centred around its second capital at Daulatabad, Sufi activities too started drifting from the north to the south. Sufis formed a considerable section of this migrant population, who were expected to spread the worldview of Islam in Daulatabad, and subsequently the larger Deccan region, thereby advancing the agenda of the Sultan to fuse Islamic religious symbolism with the rhetoric of empire. This, Muhammad bin Tughluq hoped, would reaffirm his authority within the realm, and, as a result, he paid little heed to the strong resentment from the Sufis at Delhi towards this imperial transfer.[1]

One of the noted Sufi saints who dared to resist his transfer from Delhi to Daulatabad was the spiritual successor of Nizam al-Din in

---

[1] Mahdi Husain, *Tughluq Dynasty* (Calcutta: Thacker Spink & Co., 1933), 144, 173; H. K. Sherwani, *The Bahmanis of the Deccan* (New Delhi: Munshiram Manoharlal Publishers Pvt. Ltd., 1953), 19–22.

Figure 3.1 Dargah of Muntajib al-Din Zar Zari Zar Baksh, Khuldabad

Delhi, Nasir al-Din Mahmud, who refused to leave the spiritual territory (*wilayat*) bequeathed upon him by his master. Nizam al-Din had passed away in 1325, a couple of years before the transfer took place. Being the most illustrious Chishti Sufi in Delhi, the hospice (*khanqah*) of Nizam al-Din attracted a large number of visitors—disciples, as well as lay devotees who sought guidance from him. Such individuals also included notable names from the royal court, like the poet and scholar Amir Khusrau, the royal chronicler and historian Zia al-Din Barani, and the poet Amir Hasan Sijzi, among others. In the course of time the spiritual successors of Nizam al-Din spread far and wide, carrying the legacy of the Chishti order to various corners of the subcontinent. One such disciple was Muntajib al-Din, who went to the Deccan and settled there much before the new capital was established. It was his death in 1309 that created a vacuum in the leadership of the Chishti order in Deccan.[2]

Perhaps the experienced eyes of Nizam al-Din could foresee the inevitable. Having survived seven consecutive sultans of Delhi with an attitude of non-reciprocation towards the royal court, the Sufi master

---

[2] Ghulam Ali Azad Bilgrami, *Rawzat ul Awliya* (Hyderabad: Matba i Karimi, 1926–27), 14, in Muhammad Suleman Siddiqi, *The Bahmani Sufis* (Delhi: Idarah-i Adabiyat-i Delli, 1989), 41.

could sense the shift in the political climate of Tughluq north India. So that before his death in 1325, he summoned one of his eldest disciples, Burhan al-Din Gharib, the younger brother of Muntajib al-Din, and said 'I have appointed you in place of your brother, and it is binding upon you to leave for Khuldabad.'[3] Burhan al-Din was shaken by this instruction and pleaded with the master to allow him to stay back in Delhi. He further added that he would miss the master and the company of his august assembly. Nizam al-Din comforted an unwilling Burhan al-Din by saying that he could take all those sitting in the assembly along with him. Trained in the Chishti ethics of master-discipleship, Burhan al-Din chose not to invoke the displeasure of Nizam al-Din through further reluctance.

On an earlier occasion, Burhan al-Din had already survived the ire of Nizam al-Din when a rumour spread that the former was styling himself as a shaykh in the lifetime of the latter. Burhan al-Din, due to his extreme old age and failing health, had difficulty sitting on the ground. As a result, he four-folded his blanket and leaned against it while sitting. When this reached the ears of Nizam al-Din, he instructed his steward Khwaja Iqbal that Burhan al-Din should leave the hospice immediately. Burhan al-Din was left completely distraught, and it was only after the personal intercession of Amir Khusrau, who appealed to Nizam al-Din in a posture of seeking forgiveness for Burhan al-Din, that the latter was pardoned and allowed to return to the hospice.[4]

Nizam al-Din left his earthly abode in 1325, and in 1327 Burhan al-Din finally set off on his long journey towards Khuldabad, a few miles from the imperial capital of Daulatabad, accompanied by a large congregation of Sufis and scholars, popularly believed to be 1,400. In the group were Amir Hasan Sijzi (d. 1337), the author of *Fawaid al Fuad*, Pir Mubarak Karwan (d. 1333), Khwaja Hasan, Khwaja Umar (d. 1349), Kamal al-Din Samana, Kaka Sa'd Baksh, Rukn al-Din Kashani, Imad al-Din Kashani, Khwaja Majid al-Din, Khwaja Burhan al-Din Kashani, Khwaja Jamal al-Din Kashani, Farid al-Din Adib (d. 1337) and Maulana Rukn al-Din.[5] Over the next century, Sufi masters in the Deccan carved out their

[3] Ibid.
[4] *Siyar al-awliya*, 289–291.
[5] Bilgrami, *Rawzat ul Awliya*, in Siddiqi, *Bahmani Sufis*, 41.

Figure 3.2 Khuldabad Valley showing the mosque of 1,400 saints

domains of activity—spiritual and material—through various equations with powerful Deccani ruling houses, as well as by training disciples, pursuing their spiritual goals, and literary production.[6]

Burhan al-Din's establishment in Khuldabad kept alive the Chishti spiritual line in the Deccan, sanctified by the handing over of the sacred insignias (*tabarrukat*) of Nizam al-Din, which included a staff and a rosary that was carried to Khuldabad. This transfer of spiritual authority through training in the ethics of spirituality, moral conduct, and ritual practice, together with the possession of the sacred regalia used by the Sufi master, confirmed the authority of the succeeding saint. All of this was central to the master-disciple (*pir-murid*) relation that bound a disciple to his master right from the days of initiation. The scope of this relation was believed to be limitless, as a master was able to guide and protect his successor even after leaving the material world. The bond between the

---

[6] Kashshaf Ghani, 'Succeeding the Master: Locating Chishti Sufis in the Political and Social Environs of Peninsular India', in N. Chandramouli, ed., *Religion and Society in Peninsular India (6th–16th Centuries CE)* (New Delhi: Aryan Books International, 2015), 216–230.

master and the disciple is strengthened through sincere devotion, dutiful obedience, and utmost respect from the disciple towards the Sufi master. One can get a sense of this attachment even between Burhan al-Din and his chief disciple and successor Zain al-Din Shirazi (d. 1369). The bond between the two was close, resting on a sense of deep respect which Zain al-Din had for his master, to the extent of portraying him as a representative of the Prophet, and hence the supreme spiritual figure of his time (*qutb-ul alam*):

> Prophet Muhammad at this time is in the veil. His representatives such as Imam Jafar Sadiq, Hasan Basri, Uways Qarani, Bayazid, Junayd, Shibli, Shaykh ul Islam Nizam al-Din and Shaykh ul Islam Burhan al-Din have taken care of his position after him. Each of them was in his time the representative of the Prophet. With their protection they bring people to fulfill their religious and worldly goals, so one should entrust oneself to their protection so that following them all one's affairs should be in order.[7]

It was perhaps keeping in mind the high standards of succession set forth by Nizam al-Din and Burhan al-Din, resting on strict adherence to codes of spiritual training, moral conduct, and ethical norms, that Zain al-Din refrained from appointing a successor (*khalifa*). Scholars in the circle of Burhan al-Din, and even later, would recognize the end of one major branch in the Chishti spiritual genealogy with Zain al-Din. Hence going by his position in the genealogical table he is recognized as the twenty-second master (*bais khwaja*), starting from the founder of the Chishti order. All the spiritual regalia that were handed down to him from his ancestors were laid to rest with him, along with the robe of the Prophet that passed through all the Chishti masters. Only after the arrival of Khwaja Muhammad Gisu Daraz in the Deccan was a parallel line of Chishti Sufism activated.

The strong foundation of the Chishti order in the Deccan can be traced to the task begun by Muntajib al-Din. However, it was Burhan al-Din

---

[7] Mir Hasan, *Hidayat ul Qulub* (Khuldabad: Farid al-Din Saleem, Compiled 1344–67), 52–53, in Carl Ernst, *Eternal Garden: Mysticism, History, and Politics at a South Asian Sufi Center* (New Delhi: Oxford University Press, 1992), 134–135.

who was primarily responsible for completing this task already begun through all the struggle and hard work, setting standards of spiritual practice and discipline he inherited from his master in Delhi. Similar to his master, Burhan al-Din too was a great believer in the qualities of love and compassion that his predecessors practised. He is said to have once remarked, 'Our order is known for two things: love and compassion.'[8] For Burhan al-Din, love for only God flowed in the heart of an individual who successfully controlled his worldly desires, turning his face away from distractions and attachments. Burhan al-Din can be seen as a Sufi saint who with all humility immersed himself in passionate love for God, rather than a scholar on the spiritual path occupied with sterile debates on canons and traditions.

Following the Chishti practice of dissociation from the royal court, neither Burhan al-Din nor Zain al-Din sought any support from the Bahmani sultans. While entrusting the responsibility of the Deccan to Burhan al-Din, one of the principles to which Nizam al-Din asked him to adhere strictly was 'No refusing, no asking, no saving'. While Nizam al-Din could never dissociate himself fully from the shadows of the royal court in Delhi, he did his best to uphold the practice of royal dissociation laid down by his master Farid al-Din: 'If you aim to achieve the spiritual position achieved by our elders, keep away from the princes of the blood'.[9] Trained in this ideology, Zain al-Din Shirazi was careful to respect the guidelines laid by his spiritual elders, dutifully avoiding royal company as well as soliciting any state support. Throughout their lifetimes both Sufi saints steered clear from any form of association with Bahmani rulers, to the extent of openly defying them on many political matters.

Sama in the Circle of Burhan al-Din Gharib

Burhan al-Din made two major contributions as the master of the Chishti order in the Deccan. First, the rise of Chishti Sufism in the Deccan began from the period of Burhan al-Din, around his *khanqah* in Khuldabad.

---

[8] Ernst, *Eternal Garden*, 126.
[9] *Siyar al-awliya*, 75.

Second, the practice of *sama* as the defining spiritual exercise of Chishti Sufis was firmly established in the Deccan.

Among all the disciples of Nizam al-Din, Burhan al-Din Gharib was an ecstatic enthusiast of *sama*, among other spiritual practices. Sources attest that he followed 'a distinctive style' of dancing (*raqs*) at moments of ecstasy, which came to be known as 'Burhani', after the shaykh.[10] Opinions differ as to what was precisely meant by the term 'Burhani'—whether it signified the style of dance or the epithet given to the disciples of Burhan al-Din who participated in such a style of dance. Such was the intensity of Burhan al-Din's participation in *sama,* accompanied by passionate limb movement (*raqs*), that he often used to lose control over his conscious self. Some participants in *sama*, who were probably not direct disciples of Nizam al-Din, passed terse remarks on Burhan al-Din's demeanour after his participation in *sama* and *raqs*. It is possible that some in the circle of Nizam al-Din may have also expressed reservation along similar lines. To this Burhan al-Din retorted that such was the practice of the great masters of the Chishti lineage and that it was incumbent upon him to adhere to that hallowed tradition, even if it did not conform to the highly respected Sufi manual from the Suhrawardi order, the *Awarif al- Maarif.*[11]

Burhan al-Din's attitude illustrates the Chishti attachment to *sama* as an intrinsic spiritual exercise that conditioned the state of the heart, allowing the Sufi saint to seek proximity with the Divine. Chishti Sufis repeatedly emphasized the essentiality of *sama* as the ecstatic core of their spiritual order, regarding it as an indispensable exercise towards the goal of spiritual union. Burhan al-Din, being one of the senior disciples of Nizam al-Din, was trained in the spiritual tradition of the Chishti order; it is improbable therefore that he would be deterred from participating in *sama*, the *sine qua non* of the Chishti spiritual path, due to reservations from some fellow Sufis.

The popularity of *sama* in the spiritual circle of Burhan al-Din in Khuldabad, together with voices of reservation against this practice, meant that a framework of strict guidelines had to be laid down within which the ritual needed to be practiced, quelling any doubts regarding its permissibility.[12] The careers of Burhan al-Din and his disciple Zayn

---

[10] Ibid., 289.
[11] Ruknuddin Kashani, *Nafais al-Anfas,* 49, in Ernst, *Eternal Garden,* 149.
[12] Ernst, *Eternal Garden,* 153.

al-din Shirazi contributed greatly towards upholding the sanctity of *sama* in the eyes of fellow mystics, both within and beyond the order, and most importantly to keeping at bay any form of legal objection from the ruling authorities and the clergy.

Depending on the psychological and spiritual frame of mind of the seekers of God in *sama*, Burhan al-Din, quite like his master Nizam al-Din, categorized *sama* into four types. First, lawful (*jaiz*) *sama* is that in which the mystic directs his heart completely towards God, longing only for Him, without leaving any room for distraction in his devotion towards the Beloved. Secondly, *sama* is permitted (*halal*) under conditions in which the listener, whether a Sufi adept or novice, orientates himself towards God, longing mostly for Him and little for His creation. Third, such an exercise of *sama* is disapproved (*makruh*) where the listener feels attracted mostly towards the creations of the Almighty, rather than longing for the Creator Himself. But lastly, the most heinous and forbidden (*haram*) is that type of *sama* where the listener does not care to pay any heed to the Beloved Lord, but focuses all their attention on matters of the material world, engrossed in thoughts of flesh and blood.[13] Such actions add little worth to his spiritual pursuit, instead pushing him towards heresy.

Following the tradition of his spiritual mentor, Burhan al-Din was in favour of elaborate norms and regulations for the exercise of *sama*. The rules for practicing *sama* in Khuldabad incorporated guidelines from Islamic law and theology, in an attempt to regulate the attitude, motivation, and psychology of the listener.[14] It needs to be remembered, however, that rather than being a religious scholar, Burhan al-Din Gharib was a lover-mystic at heart. Once in the *khanqah* of his mentor Nizam al-Din, Burhan al-Din expressed his inner desire to live his life more like a *dervish* than a preacher (*khatib*). The saint expressed little interest in the tiring debates of scholars on mundane issues like the correct way of ablution and washing hands during ablutions, or the proper way of reading *suras* (chapters) from the Quran, among other things. All Burhan al-Din desired was to sacrifice oneself through love and compassion for the benefit of others, in continuing to follow the path towards God.[15]

---

[13] Ruknuddin Kashani, *Shamail al-Atiqiya*, 347–148, in Ernst, *Eternal Garden*, 149.
[14] Ibid.
[15] Kashani, *Nafais-ul-Anfas*, 116.

Such an attitude of Burhan al-Din was also reflected in his approach to *sama* as an exercise of love and compassion. Once, he is said to have remarked that *sama* constitutes two things—contemplation, or reflection (*fikr*), and weeping (*girya*). Anything else that surfaces in the practice is nothing but chaos (*fitna*). Verses read in *sama* give rise to compassion that stirs the heart of the listener. If the listener is one among those trained in the spiritual path, he will relate whatever he listens to the Divine truth. It is important for the listener to clearly know with whom he is going to relate whatever he hears in *sama*.

It was the genius of Nizam al-Din that he saw the imminent, in spite of foretelling that Burhan al-Din will remain a dervish. The rising fervour of orthodoxy pervading the religious ambience of the Delhi Sultanate under the Tughluqs did not escape the seasoned eyes of the Chishti master, who spent many springs under consecutive sultans of Delhi. He taught Burhan al-Din the value of accommodating Islamic legal and theological doctrines into his spiritual training, so that Chishti Sufism in the Deccan did not face an uncertain future in the face of religious conservatism. Thus, despite encouraging ecstatic states in *sama*, Burhan al-Din took great care to incorporate Hadith, law, and theological learning in his circle of training. Works produced from his *khanqah* in Khuldabad include extensive references from the Quran, its classical commentaries, Hadith, law, treatises on Sufism etc. Burhan al-Din, while training his disciples like Zayn al-din Shirazi on the essentials of Chishti mysticism like *sama*, took care to train them in the religious sciences, Hadith, and legal subjects as well. Before moving into the circle of Burhan al-Din, Zain al-Din Shirazi had received training as a scholar and was strongly critical of *sama*. Burhan al-Din undertook great efforts to ensure that the Chishti order sunk deep roots in the little-known environment of the Deccan. His organizational abilities did not to allow sultans and the clergy any opportunity to criticize the spiritual practices of the order in the name of *shariah* and religious doctrines.

As a Sufi order, Chishtis allowed novices to take part in *sama* gatherings meant for the spiritually mature, with the intention of familiarizing them with the core ritual of the order.[16] For novices training in the path, such participation allowed them to observe and therefore learn

---

[16] Ernst, *Eternal Garden*, 149.

from their spiritually adept peers. This training took many forms, such as observing correct behaviour or *adab* from senior masters, as well as observing various expressions of ecstasy among participants. At a certain point of maturity in their training and participation, novices were allowed to exhibit ecstasy even if they had not achieved that state (*hal*). They could show such feelings by imitating the physical actions of a senior participant who had already achieved that state. This was termed *tawajud*, or empathetic ecstasy, in Chishti circles, and was made permissible for novices. From the days of Nizam al-Din the necessity of grading ecstasy commensurate to the maturity of listeners in *sama* was realized by Chishti Sufis. Hence, *tawajud*, rather than being a deterrent to the pure and undiluted feeling of ecstasy (*wajd*), came to be acknowledged as a permissible method for inducing ecstasy.[17]

Burhan al-Din initially thought differently. Being a strict adherent to *sama*, he regarded it as a ritual only for those with a pure heart, so that the resultant effects it ensued was also pure in origin.[18] Thus for Burhan al-Din empathetic ecstasy was a defect in *sama* that should never be indulged in, as it diluted the spiritual ambience of the assembly. Nizam al-Din, however, held little disagreement with some of his senior disciples, like Maulana Fakhr al-Din Zarradi, when they voiced their support for empathetic ecstasy (*tawajud*) as a permissible response to *sama*.[19] Thereafter it came to be recognized in Chishti circles as a legitimate form of emotional expression, alongside the exhibition of ecstasy (*wajd*) during *sama*.

Thus, in spite of strong reservations against allowing such superficial emotions in *sama*, Burhan al-Din had to follow the precedent set by his master Nizam al-Din—if a participant in *sama* does not experience ecstasy, he should practice *tawajud*, that is empathetic ecstasy, whereby the participant forces himself into ecstasy. In addition he should continuously remember God as *al-wajid*, the giver of ecstasy.[20] Sufis believe that true ecstasy emanates only from the beneficence of God, and individuals cannot force it within their hearts. If a listener in *sama* is blessed with a few moments of rapture and compassion, he can spend the entire day

---

[17] Ibid., 150.
[18] Ibid., 149.
[19] Ibid.
[20] Hammaduddin Kashani, *Ahsan ul-Aqwal*, 132, in Ernst, *Eternal Garden*, 150.

under its influence. However, the fervour and passion which result from *sama* can be diluted only under two circumstances—physical movement and weeping.[21]

Though Burhan al-Din eventually accepted the practice of *tawajud*, he stressed that it should be a permissible form of behaviour only during *sama*. Under such circumstances the novice who is yet to experience the state of ecstasy should recognize and conform to the same feelings when it is aroused within a spiritually mature companion. When the latter is moved by feelings of ecstasy, it is incumbent on the part of the novice to imitate and provide companionship by standing 'with the people of ecstasy and conform with them'.[22] Chishti Sufis assert that in an assembly of *sama*, whenever a Sufi rises up under the influence of his spiritual state and demonstrates ecstasy, all his companions should rise up in similar manner in conformity to his feelings.

Even if the novice does not successfully attain spiritual ecstasy but remains confined to the intermediate experiences of 'rapture' (*jazb*) and 'taste' (*zawq*), he should nonetheless stand up conforming to others in the assembly, or remain seated if the rest of the assembly does so. This in turn helps in enhancing the spirit of companionship in *sama*.[23] If one is overcome by the feelings of ecstasy on experiencing the Divine, then the blessing thus derived benefits all participants in the assembly. Empathetic ecstasy therefore becomes a means for capturing Divine benefaction during the practice of *sama*.

Attempting to downplay any controversy around the inclusion of musical instruments in assemblies of audition (*sama*), early Sufis repeatedly spoke on the importance of poetry and verse as the central foci of *sama*. While poetry created an opportunity to contemplate on the Divine beloved, the exercise of interpretation became crucial for a novice participating in *sama*. Chishti Sufis repeatedly emphasized the need to interpret poetry and verses recited by the *qawwal* during *sama* in the true spirit of the path, concentrating on the praises and attributes of God. Words and phrases became the important medium that steered the thoughts of the Sufi listener towards contemplating the Lord. It became

---

[21] Kashani, *Ahsan al-Aqwal*, 102.
[22] Ernst, *Eternal Garden*, 150.
[23] Kashani, *Shamail al-atiqiya*, 360.

crucial that the allegorical interpretation (*tahmil*) of the verses needed
to be done with respect to the Divine, and also the spiritual master
(*murshid*). It was emphasized on many occasions that while listening
to the verses the listener should focus his thoughts on the qualities of
his master, so that his mind is focused on the virtues of his *pir*. The Sufi
mystic benefits from such an assembly of audition as long as he continues
interpreting the verses of poetry through such a method that helps in
understanding its inner meaning (*batin*), thereby aiding his spiritual efforts. But most importantly this interpretation has to be done in a correct
manner. For it is important to be able to equate the negative and positive
aspects of the verse with similar attributes of the Lord or the master of
the assembly. So that description of beauty should be attributed to Divine
beauty and glory. Likewise, the darkness of the curls could indicate qualities of Divine wrath.[24] This is a process intended to train the novice to
become receptive to ecstasy, naturally or through imitation of that which
becomes visible in the physical behaviour of the adept.

In *sama*, when the listener interprets the verses of the *qawwal,* he is
overcome with emotions of 'rapture' (*jazb*). Burhan al-Din once remarked that the nature of such experience becomes evident in the colour
of the listener's face.[25] *Sama*, when leading to a countenance of the
Divine, leads to two kinds of manifestations in the face of the listener.
First, when misfortune descends on the listener in the form of wrath and
separation, the face turns pale. The turmoil which the heart experiences
due to separation from the Beloved is evident through this pallid face.
Thus the first colour of *sama* is yellow. Second, when the listener gains
Divine mercy his face blushes with happiness, revealing his nearness to
the Lord Beloved. Hence the colour is red. Emotions within the heart of
the Sufi saint find expression in the hue of his face.

Sama is a facilitator in the spiritual path towards seeking the Divine.
However, there arrives a stage when the Sufi has matured enough and
hence is no longer dependent on poetry and music as a spiritual aid.[26]
He is able to perceive Divine attributes in everything that he sees around
him. Witnessing the creation makes him remember the Creator. In such

[24] Ernst, *Eternal Garden*, 151.
[25] Ibid., 358.
[26] Ibid.

a spiritual station poetry and music are of little help.[27] What Sufis hear on reaching such adeptness is not from the mouth of the *qawwal*, but directly from the Unseen, a process which Sufis recognize as internal listening through the ear of the heart.

Burhan al-Din ensured that strict discipline and ethical standards were maintained by participants seeking spiritual benefits from *sama*. That insistence was placed on proper interpretation of verses as well as practice of *adab* in *sama* assemblies. While regulating participation in *sama*, Burhan al-Din emphasized on the elimination of ego from the heart of the participant. While upholding standards of discipline laid down by early Chishti masters, Burhan al-Din Gharib and Zain al-Din Shirazi were instrumental in giving a new lease of life to the Chishti order in the Deccan, which continued to inspire young Sufis in the way towards higher spiritual experiences.

Deccan after Burhan al-Din Gharib

Burhan al-Din passed away in 1337. The situation in Deccan was heading towards a point where the Tughluq experiment with the second capital at Daulatabad had begun to crumble. The situation was accentuated due to the attitude of high-handedness the Tughluqs showed towards the residents of Daulatabad, who had left their home and hearth in Delhi to populate the new capital. Slowly but steadily, resentment began to crystallize among local Hindus as well as immigrant Muslims who rose in recurrent revolts in areas of Mabar, Warangal, Bidar, and Bharpur. Notable leaders of these revolts were Harihara and Bukka to the south of the river Krishna, and Zafar Khan to the north, in Daulatabad. Within a decade of Burhan al-Din's demise, the political landscape of the Deccan had changed dramatically. By 1347–1348, one can witness the rise of the two powerful kingdoms of Vijayanagara, established by Bukka, and the Bahmani, founded by Zafar Khan, who ascended the throne as Sultan Ala al-Din Hasan Bahman Shah.[28]

---

[27] Kashani, *Shamail al-atiqiya*, 357.

[28] Richard M. Eaton, *A Social History of the Deccan, 1300–1761: Eight Indian Lives* (New York: Cambridge University Press, 2005), 33–58.

Figure 3.3 Dargah of Burhan al-Din Gharib, Khuldabad

Shortly after his ascension, Ala al-Din shifted his capital from the erst-while Tughluq capital of Daulatabad to the centrally situated ancient town of Gulbarga. The foundation of the new Sultanate through rebellion against the parent Tughluq Empire is recorded in later Sufi chronicles as a direct outcome of the physical presence and blessing of Zain al-Din. An anecdote, inserted in later Chishti hagiographies, traces the succession of Zafar Khan to the throne of the Bahmani kingdom to the direct blessing of Nizam al-Din. It describes how one day, as he was seeing off Muhammad bin Tughluq, who had come to visit the shaykh at his *khanqah*, Nizam al-Din noticed the young Zafar standing on the doorway of the hospice. The shaykh is said to have remarked, 'One sultan has left my door, another is waiting there.'[29]

Sultan Ala al-Din's patronage of Chishti shrines, particularly those of Burhan al-Din Gharib and Zain al-Din Shirazi, the former being the direct spiritual successor of Nizam al-Din, is understandable. The Sultan ordered a donation of 200 pounds of gold and 400 pounds of silver to the shrine of Burhan al-Din, thereby deeply entangling important Chishti

---

[29] Muhammad Qasim Ferishta, *Tarikh i Ferishta*, vol. 1, trans. J. Briggs, *History of the Rise of the Mahomedan Power in India* (Calcutta: Editions Indian, 1966), 274.

shrines of the Deccan, connected to the spiritual legacy of the great Nizam al-Din Awliya, with the rising political fortunes of the Bahmani Sultanate.[30]

Such acts need to be analysed at multiple levels, in quite the same way as the remark of Nizam al-Din foretelling Zafar Khan's rising political fortunes. First, they need to be read in tandem. These donations seem justified as acts of reverence towards premier Chishti shrines of the Deccan whose lineage can be traced to the revered Nizam al-Din Awliya in Delhi. Secondly, Nizam al-Din's remark seems to reinforce a common theme in the tradition of medieval Persianate kingship where Sufis, as real sovereigns of both the worlds, were believed to possess the power to make and unmake political fortunes through an act of leasing out worldly authority to the one deserving it.[31] Burhan al-Din's and Zain al-Din's blessings for the new Sultanate thus continued the sanction bestowed upon the Bahmani Sultanate by the Sufi master in Delhi. Seen in this context then, neither Nizam al-Din's remark nor the lavish donations made by the new Bahmani Sultan to the Chishti shrines in Khuldabad seem out of place.

However, none of these Chishti masters sought any support from the royal court. Throughout their lifetime, not only did Sufi saints of Khuldabad avoid any form of association with the Bahmani court, but they were also accused at times of openly defying the court on many political matters. On one occasion, Sultan Muhammad Shah I (1358–1375), after succeeding Ala al-Din Hasan Shah to the Bahmani throne, rode out against Bahram Khan, the governor of Daulatabad, who rose in revolt. The governor sought refuge with Zain al-Din, who advised him to flee to Gujarat to escape the Sultan. Muhammad Shah was extremely disappointed with the shaykh, and later, together with other Sufi saints, asked him to pay homage at the royal court. Zain al-Din refused, and the Sultan sent a royal messenger to bring the Sufi saint to the court, to which Zain al-Din replied 'I am resigned to the king's resentment, but will neither come to his presence nor acknowledge allegiance to him'.[32] Angered by

---

[30] Ibid., 277.

[31] Eaton, *A Social History*, 45; Simon Digby, 'The Sufi Shaykh as a Source of Authority in Medieval India', in Richard Eaton, ed., *India's Islamic Traditions 7111750* (New Delhi: Oxford University Press, 2003), 234–262.

[32] Ferishta, *Tarikh i Ferishta*, vol. 2, 200–202.

Figure 3.4 Dargah of Zain al-Din Shirazi, Khuldabad

this defiance, the Sultan ordered Zain al-Din to leave the city, at which the saint moved across the street to the shrine of his master, Burhan al-Din Gharib. The Sultan chose not to escalate matters.

However, this was not to remain the model of Sufi conduct in the Deccan vis-à-vis the royal court. While Chishtis from Khuldabad refused to pay homage to the Bahmanis, Sufis of the Junaydi order were more than obliging in this regard. Siraj al-Din Junaydi (d. 1380) coroneted the first Bahmani Sultan Ala al-Din Hasan at the grand mosque in Daulatabad. The shaykh occupied a position of great reverence at the royal court. All sultans, three to be precise, were coroneted by the Sufi saint, who presented each Sultan with a coarse shirt, a belt, and a turban made out of his headgear, as symbols of spiritual blessing and recognition of authority through the handing over of royal regalia. Similarly, before marching to war all Bahmani sultans took the blessings of Siraj al-Din Junaydi. On many occasions, after returning victorious from the battlefield, Sultan Muhammad Shah I would visit the hospice of the Sufi master, donating large portions of the war booty to be distributed among the syed and holy men. With the shift of the capital, Siraj al-Din too shifted from Kodchi to Gulbarga during the reign of Sultan Muhammad Shah I to spare the Sultan the trouble of travelling every time to meet the saint. In return the shrine of Siraj al-Din received handsome donations in the form of land grants (*jagirs*), which continued under the descendants of the saint.[33]

In the period that followed Siraj al-Din Junaydi's demise in 1380, none of his successors could rise to his spiritual standard, and the Bahmani Sultanate was once again left without a patron Sufi saint. Once more we see history repeating itself, almost in the manner it had done during the early days of this Sultanate, when spiritual patronage arrived from north India. This brings us to the last phase of our discussion, where, once again, it would be the spiritual successors of Nizam al-Din who extended their blessings and support to a flourishing Indo-Persian political authority in the Deccan.

While Burhan al-Din represented Nizam al-Din in the Deccan, the latter's spiritual domain in Delhi was under the care of his successor Nasir al-Din Mahmud. After the death of Nasir al-Din in 1356, his mantle passed on to his successor, Sayyid Muhammad Husayni, more popularly known as Gisu Daraz (one with the 'long locks'). As a child Gisu Daraz had visited Daulatabad when his family moved with the caravan of Tughluq migrants from Delhi. He returned a few years later, began training under Nasir al-Din, and finally succeeded him to the position of the primary Chishti Sufi master of Delhi. For forty years Gisu Daraz stayed in Delhi, until the time when Timur's approaching army signalled an imminent disruption in north India. Once again, the elderly Shaykh left Delhi with his family and followers in December 1398.

In the meantime, Firoz Shah Bahmani, the eighth ruler of the Bahmani dynasty, had succeeded to the throne in 1397. When the news of the arrival of Gisu Daraz in Daulatabad reached the Bahmani capital in Gulbarga, Firoz Shah lost no time in sending his governor to convey his deepest regards to the Sufi shaykh. Not content with this, the Sultan himself rode at the head of a contingent to Daulatabad, where Gisu Daraz had taken shelter at the shrine of his father, Sayyid Yusuf al Husayni, also known as Shah Raja 'Qattal', the epithet probably indicating the severe

[33] Ibid., 202–204; Suleman Siddiqi, *The Junaydi Sufis of the Deccan: Discovery of a Seventeenth Century Scroll* (New Delhi: Primus Books, 2014), 201–205.

Figure 3.5 Khanqah of Gisu Daraz, Gulbarga

austerities he undertook to slay (*qatl*) his material desires. Acceding to Sultan Firuz Shah's invitation, Gisu Daraz decided to move ahead to the imperial capital at Gulbarga in early 1400, where the Sultan out of gratitude built a hospice (*khanqah*) for the Sufi saint near the western gate of the fort.

Gisu Daraz and the Practice of *Sama*

Gisu Daraz—Deccan's most charismatic Chishti Sufi—had already established his reputation in Delhi when he completed his training under Nasir al-Din Mahmud, Burhan al-Din Gharib's spiritual mate, and began to accept his own disciples. However, very little is known to us regarding the career of Gisu Daraz in Delhi. After arriving in the Deccan as the fountainhead of the Chishti order, he continued to build on the foundation laid down by Burhan al-Din Gharib and Zain al-Din Shirazi, following a two-fold method: guiding newcomers in the spiritual path, and leaving behind a large corpus of work on various aspects of Sufism and Islamic philosophy, which came to constitute the most significant body of scholarly contribution by any Chishti Sufi up to his time.[34] Much like his predecessors, Gisu Daraz too was attached to the practice of *sama*, and contributed to the institutionalization of this core Chishti practice through articulation of rules and regulations.[35]

As an ardent lover of *sama*, Gisu Daraz considered it to be no ordinary musical gathering. Rather, for him, *sama* signified an assembly where Sufis seek spiritual progress and proximity to God. Going beyond ordinary forms of worship, *sama* represents a 'specific path' leading to God, and therefore a primary means of seeking the Divine Beloved.[36] Gisu Daraz conformed to views expressed by Sufis of earlier generations that, together with the regular religious practices of prayer (*salaat*), fasting (*sawm*), and reciting of the Quran (*tilawat*), *sama* too leads an individual closer to God.

In the above context, Gisu Daraz once remarked that unfortunate are those Sufis on whom *sama* has no effect. Of all the rituals prescribed for a Sufi, *sama* is the best way of turning one's heart towards God. Any other assembly organized in the manner of *sama* but focusing only on music and seeking pleasure cannot be equated with the *sama* that Sufis practiced.

Spiritual intoxication and happiness of the heart that Sufis experience in *sama* does not depend only on the performance of the *qawwal* or the element of music. Sufi shaykhs of higher spiritual stature who participate in *sama* focus fully on the contemplation of God and have little to do with the music being played. They seek pleasure and intoxication from a mere word or verse that touches the inner chords of their heart, resulting in weeping and wailing and exclaiming loudly words like *hu ... haqq*. At times when greatly overwhelmed, Sufis rend their clothes and enter into a happy and joyful state, sometimes losing consciousness, though this is not considered a preferable behaviour. Such is the impact derived from *sama* that even a single word when uttered in a particular manner can agitate a Sufi to heights of ecstasy. It is said that once Nizam al-Din was walking by the fields when he saw a herdsman trying to stop his cattle from roaming away far. He gave a cry, 'go back ... do not go ahead'. These

---

[34] *Khatima*, 20–21.
[35] *Khatima*, 19.
[36] *Siyar al-awliya*, 492.

words threw the shaykh into a state of ecstasy. His disciples Khwaja Iqbal and Khwaja Mubasshir, who were accompanying him, continued to repeat this line, which kept Nizam al-Din in that state for the rest of the journey. Even in a *sama* assembly it may so happen that Sufi listeners become attached to a particular verse, as in the case mentioned earlier with Qutb al-Din Bakhtiyar Kaki becoming ecstatic. Sufis then request the *qawwal* to repeat the specific verses so that they can hold on to their spiritual state.

According to Gisu Daraz, the preferred state for any Sufi shaykh in *sama* is when he is with his *self*, yet at the same time without his *self*. One who experiences this duality is placed in such a state that he no longer has control over his bodily movements. Whatever he does is not in his control, nor can he restrain himself. However adept and perfect a Sufi shaykh might be, it is difficult to control oneself during that state. While the heart of the Sufi derives pleasure and happiness from that state of ecstasy, his body is powerless to restrain its movements. The aim of *sama* is to bring the thoughts of the Sufi together, and turn his heart towards God. The greatest benefit to be derived from *sama* is emptying the heart of all worldly desires, and focusing on God.

In the light of the importance attached to *sama*, the question which arises concerns the reason for such importance. What sort of advantage, spiritual and otherwise, does *sama* have over mandatory religious practices? Why is it considered more effective in realizing spiritual goals? And, lastly, why do Sufis prefer it over other spiritual practices? The answer provided by Gisu Daraz in his writings is based on the premise that the primary requirement for a Sufi travelling on the spiritual path is to interiorize qualities of contemplation and thought—by focusing on the attributes and essence of the Lord. As an assembly of audition, *sama*, for Gisu Daraz, was the best way to achieve unity of thought and contemplation (*tawajuh*), which in turn leads to the best of all fortunes (*jami i- sa'adatha*) a mystic can hope to achieve in the way to God. Gisu Daraz further asserted that 'triumph in my affair' (*fath-i kar-i man*) was achieved through extensive recitation of the Quran and participation in *sama*.[37]

---

[37] Muhammad Ali Samani, *Siyar-i Muhammadi*, ed. S. N. Ahmad Qadri (Hyderabad: Matbuah Ijaz Printing Press, 1969), 90.

Gisu Daraz borrowed the views of Nizam al-Din, and earlier Sufis, who argued that multiple benefits descend on the Sufi when he participates in *sama* where recitation of the Quran (*tilawat*) is combined with *sama*. Such an exercise carries more benefit than simple observance of daily prayers and recitation of the Quran. Routine religious exercises are meant only for those who spend their thoughts between opposing emotions of 'fear' (*khawf*) and 'hope' (*raji*).[38] Mystics, who engage themselves in nothing but love of God, prefer the earlier exercise. Gisu Daraz always began and concluded the assembly of audition with a recitation of the Quran.

While differentiating between regular religious practices and *sama*, Gisu Daraz referred to Maudud Chishti, who, when asked about the efficacy of *sama* over prayers, replied that when a person observes prayers following all the prescribed rules he swings between extreme emotions of fear and hope. He remains unsure whether his prayers will be accepted or not. *Sama*, on the other hand, reflects a passion (*jadhbah*) in the form of a ritual emanating from the all-Merciful (*al-rahman*).[39] While prayers are doubtful of being heard and accepted (*qabul*), proper participation in *sama* is an acceptance within itself (*ayn- i qabul*).

It is probable that Gisu Daraz was deeply influenced by his master, Nasir al-Din Mahmud, who argued that 'passion' (*jadhbah*) was actually 'Divine love' (*muhabbat- i khwass*) bestowed exclusively on those who are brought closer to the Almighty through deep meditation (*muraqaba*).[40] Thus, according to Gisu Daraz, 'remembrance' (*zikr*), 'meditation' (*muraqaba*), and 'prayer' (*salat*), being essential religious practices, cannot supersede *sama*, which is an exercise in the presence of the Divine.[41]

Such a strong position in favour of *sama* was bound to invite criticism from those who considered it nothing more than a means to indulge in pleasure and frivolity.[42] Gisu Daraz was quite severe regarding such critics, arguing that such individuals were men of the world, and their opinions were based on worldly parameters, incapable of looking beyond

---

[38] *Khatima*, 70.
[39] Muhammad Husayni Gisu Daraz, *Asmar al-Asrar* (Hyderabad, 1931), 103–04.
[40] *Khair al-Majalis*, 28.
[41] Gisu Daraz, *Asmar al-Asrar*, 103.
[42] *Khatima*, 34–35.

into the sphere of the Unseen. As they were alien to the path of spiritual enlightenment, they were oblivious to emotions like pain (*dard*), seeking (*talab*), and burning (*suzi*), as understood by the Sufis. Since they were unaware of the means and aims that *sama* catered to, they had little right to declare it unlawful. It is prudent for them to observe silence on such matters. The position of Gisu Daraz is evident in his remark where he retorts, 'What a strange (*ajab*) he is! He refers to agitation (*idtirab*), crying (*giryah*), grief (*andih*) and sorrow (*huzn*) as a sport'.[43]

Intolerance of the *ulama* regarding *sama* rested on the pretext that *sama* was an innovation by Sufis within the prescribed religious practices of Islam, and their indulgence in such a practice with the accompaniment of music was completely illegal in the eyes of *shariah* and hence should be forbidden for any Muslim. Time and again the *ulama* approached the sultans of Delhi to issue verdicts condemning the practice of *sama* by the Sufis. One of the grounds, though historically untenable, for criticizing *sama* was that it was influenced by the devotional music practiced by the resident Hindu population, and thus polluted the faith of Islam by attempting 'a synthesis between the Muslim and Hindu artistic traditions'.[44]

While in Delhi, Gisu Daraz too had to face the ire from the *ulama* whose intolerance for *sama* was stoked up during the reign of Sultan Firoz Shah Tughlaq (r. 1351–1388). The *ulama* complained on the issue of prostration by disciples and devotees, which they performed by placing their heads on the ground before Gisu Daraz during the assembly of *sama*. Although they tried their best to impose a ban on the *sama* assemblies of the Chishti master, the Sultan refrained from taking such an extreme step, and requested the saint to participate in *sama* in seclusion, so that the ambience of the assembly did not become polluted through such practices. Gisu Daraz acceded to the request and henceforth enjoyed *sama* from within a cell, with a curtain separating him from the rest of the participants.[45] It is to be noted that Nasir al-Din Mahmud, the spiritual guide of Gisu Daraz, strictly disallowed any prostration before him by devotees and disciples.

[43] Ibid.
[44] S. S. K. Hussaini, *Sayyid Muhammad al-Husayni i-Gisudiraz (721/1321-825/14222): On Sufism* (Delhi: Idarah-i-Adabiyat-i-Delli, 1983), 124.
[45] Samani, *Siyar-i-Muhammadi*, 87–88.

Gisu Daraz was quick to learn from the changing religious environment of the Delhi Sultanate. After moving to the Deccan, he worked earnestly to bridge the gap between *ahl-i zahir* and the *ahl-i batin,* which had broadened as a result of *wujudi* doctrines.[46] While carrying the mantle of Chishti Sufism in Gulbarga, Gisu Daraz combined it with erudite scholarship reflected in commentaries on the Quran, Hadith, *fiqh*, and Sufi treatises, together with original works on Sufi practice.[47] His spiritual and intellectual efforts turned Gulbarga into the most important centre of Chishti Sufism in the Deccan, where core Chishti practices were retained even after Gisu Daraz incorporated certain new elements into his teaching.

Two important achievements resulted from the charisma and influence of Gisu Daraz in the Deccan. First, he succeeded in silencing critics, primarily the *ulama*, who were ever-inclined to raise a finger at the Chishti practice of *sama* on grounds of legal permissibility and religious sanctity. Second, by enlisting the support of the Bahmani Sultan Firuz Shah, and his brother, Ahmad Shah, Gisu Daraz secured a strong patronage for the Chishti order. The Bahmani sultans in turn drew legitimacy from the spiritual charisma of the premier Chishti saint. The patronage extended to Gisu Daraz was intended to serve the purpose of legitimizing the Bahmani Sultanate vis-à-vis the powerful north Indian empires, as well as in the eyes of the local population, who thronged at the door of Gisu Daraz for spiritual guidance and blessings. Gisu Daraz was also unique in his patronage of local language and culture, so that during his lifetime we see the use of Dakhni (or Deccani) Urdu both as a language for communication and for writing verses which were read out in *sama*.

The legality of *sama* being a recurrent issue of contention, Gisu Daraz categorized *sama* into four strict types, depending on the intent and spiritual maturity of the listener.[48] *Sama* became permissible (*halal*) when the thoughts of the listener focus exclusively on the remembrance of the Divine. It is completely forbidden (*haram*) when the listener allows his mind to stray towards worldly thoughts. When the listener vacillates between the Divine and the material world, and is not able to fix

---

[46] Siddiqi, *Bahmani Sufis*, 49.
[47] Ibid., 58.
[48] Hussaini, *Sayyid Muhammad*, 127.

his thoughts on either, then *sama* is desirable (*makruh*). However, *sama* is permissible (*mubah*) when the listener focuses his thoughts more towards the Divine than on affairs of the material world.[49] It is thus evident that Gisu Daraz, being a strong defender of the practice, did not consider *sama* to be suitable for all. Rather, for him, participants in *sama* need to be chosen keeping in mind their spiritual orientation, emotions of the heart, and degree of devotion towards the Divine.

As far as participation in *sama* is concerned, the firm intervention of Gisu Daraz brings forth two issues. First, there is the problem of the common masses participating in *sama*. Following his illustrious predecessors in north India, Gisu Daraz too did not impose a complete sanction on the participation of the lay individual in *sama*. However, while elucidating on the qualities of listeners in *sama*, the shaykh insisted that the listener (*mustami*) should be an individual of high intellect (*sahib-i firasat*). Importantly, to be worthy of participation in such a spiritually charged exercise the listener should have an experience of suffering in love (*ba-dard*), which in the mystical connotation is very different from worldly love and attraction.[50] Thus the above preconditions make a clear distinction between lay individuals and those on the spiritual path who possess an understanding of the assembly together with a receptive heart. Gisu Daraz is unambiguous that *sama* is not for everybody, and a Sufi who holds a taste (*zawq*) for participation in *sama* should stay away from any such assembly where all sorts of people (*har jins*) gather to listen to verses of poetry.

The reservations of Gisu Daraz on the issue of common masses participating in such a spiritual assembly are made amply clear when he states that *sama* is 'desirable' to the proficient (*muntahiyan*), 'allowable' to the beginners (*mubtadiyan*) and intermediate (*mutawassitan*), but completely 'undesirable' for the common masses. This categorization leads us to the second point in discussion—that of the participation of novices in the assembly of *sama*. From the above it is evident that Gisu Daraz advocated *sama* for 'beginners'. But at the same time he created some ambiguity by referring to Junaid, the famous Sufi saint from the Baghdad school of Sufism, who was a sceptic regarding the practice and argued

---

[49] This categorization basically follows the pattern of Nizam al-Din Awliya elaborated earlier.
[50] *Khatima*, 34.

that if a novice showed fondness for *sama* it signified that there was an element of idleness left in him.[51] Thus if Gisu Daraz followed the principles of Junaid in this respect, and at the same time advocated participation of newcomers in the ritual of *sama*, the two positions seem opposed to each other.

Yet at the same time Gisu Daraz also emphasized that participation in an assembly of audition had the power to purify the soul of the novice from impurities of the material world. Thus *sama* acted as a cleanser for the heart of a young listener in the spiritual path. While Suhrawardi mystics voiced their resentment regarding the audition of *ghazals* and descriptive poetry (*al- awsaf*) in *sama*, Chishti Sufis like Gisu Daraz himself defended the practice of listening to poetry and verse as a means of stirring up emotions within the heart.[52] But as a mode of precaution against distractions, and misinterpretation of the same, he stated that the young disciple (*murid*) should focus all his attention on the personality of his master (*pir*).[53] Therefore for the novice *sama* remained an essential spiritual practice for guiding him towards the realm of the Divine.

Sama for Gisu Daraz was no ordinary musical assembly for the pleasure of the heart. It was a powerful ritual which elevated the hearts of men seeking spiritual nourishment through poetry and music. Those who favoured *sama* knew it was no commonplace gathering of men, but a highly structured ritual capable of taking a person away from his lower self. Following the renowned Egyptian Sufi Dhun Nun, Gisu Daraz qualified *sama* as an exercise towards the Divine, and stated that those who participated in it with a pure heart would receive 'visitations' (*warid*) from the Unseen (*ghayb*), which would draw their hearts towards a realization of the Divine Truth (*haqq*).[54] Hence any individual who listened to *sama* through Truth (*ba haqq*) reached God (*tahaqqaqa*), while those who listened through their carnal self fell into heresy (*tazandaqa*).[55]

Although Gisu Daraz conformed to the ideology of Dhun Nun in interpreting the essence of *sama,* his important contribution lay in the realm of elaborating the concept of Truth (*haqq*). Gisu Daraz states that

[51] Hussaini, *Sayyid Muhammad*, 129.
[52] *Khatima*, 158.
[53] Ibid., 68.
[54] Hussaini, *Sayyid Muhammad*, 135.
[55] Ibid., 136.

there are multiple implications attached to the idea of Truth. In an assembly of audition (*mehfil-i sama*), when a listener finds himself attached to the quality of Truth he naturally becomes an adept (*muhaqqiq* and *mutahaqqiq*) in the path of Truth. Under such circumstances, whatever he listens to in the assembly, it is essentially this quality of attaching himself to Truth that places him closer to God.

The next level concerns the implied meaning of Truth, which is often mistaken by the listener. A participant in the assembly of audition thinks that by virtue of his presence in the physical space, where others have congregated to realize the Divine Truth, he is closer to the realm of Truth.[56] But a mere attachment to the attribute (*sifat*) of Truth is not enough, for the listener must realise the essence of Truth in order to benefit from its attributes. Thus although the listener thinks he is listening to the Truth, in actuality he remains engrossed with his own self (*khudi*) and the carnal self (*nafs i nafsaniyat*), rather than getting rid of his lower self (*be khudi*).[57]

When a listener becomes genuinely involved in the assembly of audition, he is likely to receive 'visitations' (*warid*), as mentioned above, from the Unseen (*ghayb*). This experience equips the listener with a sense of power (*quwwat*) which can be achieved only in the exercise of *sama*. He no longer remains in possession of his worldly senses (*sahih quwa*), and in the process he is taken away from his conscious self. It is only when he is away from his *self* that he feels the emotional upsurge brought about by Divine beneficence that stirs latent feelings within his heart, and on many occasions agitates his calm demeanour (*dar tasarruf i- khud awurdah*).[58]

Gisu Daraz considered the experience of Divine visitation as crucial for a complete realization of the beneficence of *sama*. Based on this approach, he categorized reactions arising from the assembly of *sama* into three kinds. First, aggressive *sama* is a reaction where the listener is affected by the proceedings of the assembly from the very beginning.[59] Such is the power of recitation and emotional outburst of the *qawwal* that the listener is overcome instantly through severe agitation within his heart, which immediately takes control of his senses, and spreads rapidly to his limbs. Under such an influence individuals become uncontrollable,

---

[56] Ibid., 135.
[57] Ibid.
[58] Ibid.
[59] *Khatima*, 37.

which is evident through brisk movement of their limbs and shaking of the head. In the second category, *sama* takes control of an individual and does not leave him until he has achieved perfection through a continuous process of contemplation and *tahmil*. It is only when the individual is blessed from the Unseen that the effect of *sama* completely dissipates.[60] The listener too considers such *sama* as a Divine blessing and accepts it willingly as a spiritual gain (*ghanimat i tasawwuf*). The third type of *sama* is that where the listener achieves his spiritual destination through the process of confrontation and conformation with other companions in the assembly of *sama*.[61] Though Khwaja Gisu Daraz did not pronounce this explicitly, it is probable that he refers to the idea of 'empathetic ecstasy' (*tawajud*), discussed above. The latter elaborated on the practice of *tawajud* while stating that the conformity of the individual was necessary for an inducement of ecstasy (*wajd*) through *tawajud*, and at the same time for achieving actual conformity (*wifaq*) through imitation (*tawafuq*).[62]

Thus Gisu Daraz does not completely undermine the possibility of *tawajud* in an assembly of audition. Rather he is open to such conditions, and acknowledges it by incorporating the same in the practice of *sama*. In a way it is seen to be in accordance with the Prophetic tradition that people in proximity to blessed individuals should try and imitate their actions so that Divine grace will indirectly affect them when they are unable to attract blessings from the Unseen. But, more importantly, it upholds one of the ritualistic positions of the Chishti order that recognized the worth of empathetic ecstasy as a means of seeking Divine beneficence during *sama*.[63] It is due to the uniqueness of the Chishti order that their practice of *sama* recognized variations in the spiritual maturity of the participant, being empathetic towards those who strived to reach heights of spiritual experience. Being a reputed Chishti Sufi, Gisu Daraz could not have overlooked this crucial ideological disposition of his masters.

Being a mystic at heart and a scholar in practice, Gisu Daraz nonetheless had much to say about the rules and regulations meant for an

---

[60] Ibid.
[61] Ibid.
[62] Ibid., 38.
[63] Hussaini, *Sayyid Muhammad*, 135.

assembly of *sama*. A proper compliance with these tenets was strongly advised if the gathering was to be transformed into a unique exercise for spiritual pursuit, rather than being just a congregation for seeking pleasure. The details of rules and moral conduct will be discussed later. We now turn towards exploring the legacy of Gisu Daraz on performing *sama* that has been preserved across generations through the practice of his modern-day successors.

Sama in a Private Assembly

Honouring the memory of Khwaja Gisu Daraz and his deep attachment to the ritual of *sama*, even to this day during the annual *urs* celebration at his Gulbarga shrine *sama* is organized in accordance with the norms and principles laid down by the saint. Such a *sama* is organized in private, and hence known as *bandh sama*, or closed assembly. This assembly is thus an effort by the descendants and shrine keepers in Gulbarga to conform to the spiritual norms practised by Gisu Daraz around *sama*.[64]

The assembly of *sama* is held behind 'closed' doors probably for two reasons. First, to differentiate it from the more popular *qawwali* that is organized in the shrine complex as a public performance on particular days of the week, like Thursday evenings, and also during *urs* celebrations. Second, *bandh sama* being held in accordance with the rules laid down in the lifetime of the shaykh himself, it naturally becomes an exercise 'closed' to any later day alterations, and at the same time 'closed' for the common devotees. Hence very few are allowed in it, mostly just senior Sufis and members of the family.

The small size of the assembly makes it easy to regulate and creates a conducive ambience for concentration and spiritual contemplation. The sacred *gaddi* (cushion), on which Khwaja Gisu Daraz used to sit, is placed in front of the *sajjada nashin*, who then initiates the assembly. This *sama* is accompanied only by a pair of small tambourines (*duff*), with all other musical instruments strictly excluded, reasons for which will be elaborated later. The couplets are read out in the traditional style, in Hindavi,

---

[64] Syed Shah Khusro Hussaini, 'Bund Sama (or Closed Audition)', *Islamic Culture*, 44 (Jul. 1970), 181.

Figure 3.6 Dargah of Gisu Daraz, Gulbarga

Dakhni, and Persian, as the saint preferred it.[65] Some of them are from his own writings and some are penned by devotees and disciples.

A prolific author in multiple languages, Gisu Daraz in his assembly of *sama* included odes, poems, and hymns in Persian and Hindavi. As regards the language of poetry in *sama*, Gisu Daraz preferred Persian, because for him 'Only in the sweet and tender melody of Persian poetry is it possible to do justice to the feelings and emotions surging in the heart of the singer.'[66] However, the shaykh realized the demands of the age and the social milieu in which he had situated himself. Thus, in spite of characterizing *sama* as a ritual not recommended for the uninitiated, Gisu Daraz took measures to increase its popularity, together with making some verses intelligible for the masses. Towards this end, he encouraged the inclusion of vernacular poetry in *sama*, arguing that 'Hindavi verses are usually soft, sweet and touching. The tunes are also soft and tender like the couplets, which induce humility and submission.'[67] Khwaja Gisu Daraz became one of the earliest among Chishti mystics to use Deccani

---

[65] Ibid., 180.
[66] Samani, *Siyar-i Muhammadi*, 71.
[67] Ibid.

Figure 3.7 Room for *Bandh Sama* (Closed Audition) at the shrine of Gisu Daraz, Gulbarga

vernacular and Hindavi as a medium for communicating and expressing his thoughts and ideas.

In the assembly of *bund sama*, the following couplets written in Dakhni are recited with the accompaniment of the tambourine, invoking the memory of the Chishti saint, while at the same time seeking grace from the Unseen.[68] An analysis of the verses, read out in the closed assembly of *sama*, provides us with some ideas on the spiritual ideals and orientation of the saint:

> *Aj birahe ki aag mujtane laage re*
> *Mu ka dikhlaye kar radi kursi lagaye*
> *Aj birahe ki aag mujtane laage re*
> *Ud batti ka shor mor ujala re*
> *Nisdin jalti mor mashakh mor sala re*
> *Aisi sada saujalti mirch ki khala re*
> *Hal hawala re, aj birahe ki aag mujtane laage re*
> *Han Mohammad Hussaini tu mera lala re*

---

[68] Hussaini, 'Bund Sama', 181.

Nisdin jalti mor mashakh mor sala re
Aisi sada saujalti mirch ki khala re
Hal hawala re, aj birahe ki aag mujtane laage re

The fire of separation has kindled
Today in my body and soul
My Beloved is on the throne
Himself and His splendour on display
I am burning in the fire of love today
Incense burns night and day
Likewise I am being burnt always
By my Beloved, who is more pungent than a chilli
This is the state and condition which I am passing through
The fire of separation has kindled
Today in my body and soul
Yes! You are my beloved, O Muhammad Hussaini!
You are the one, who night and day
Is making me suffer and burn always
You my Beloved, who is more pungent than a chili
This is the state and condition which I am passing through
The fire of separation has kindled
Today in my body and soul

Gisu Daraz remarked that *sama* is a blessing from the Unseen, which affects the heart of the listener, stirring up feelings of separation from, and hence longing for, the Beloved.[69] Music and poetry are meant to facilitate in this direction depending on the spiritual maturity of the listener and the emotions that surge in his heart after the audition of poetry. Under the influence of such emotions, as Baba Farid al-Din rightly remarked, a Sufi lover continues to burn in the fire that separates him from his Beloved.[70] It is this condition of separation that, according to Gisu Daraz, motivates an individual in his journey towards the Beloved, through participation in *sama*. At the end of his spiritual journey, when the Sufi mystic beholds the Lord, he is overcome with emotions of ecstasy. Subsequently nothing

---

[69] Ibid., 178–179.
[70] *Siyar al-awliya*, 535.

of the *self* remains within the mystic, and he completely annihilates himself (*fana*) in the essence of the Lord. Thus for the spiritually mature *sama* provides the most effective means of experiencing emotions of love and longing for the Divine Beloved. For the Sufi lover, *sama* is a means to receive spiritual succour, knowledge of the Unseen and Divine beneficence. It is an exercise of patient contemplation for the Divine Beloved, seeking to witness His glory. Only the spiritually adept are allowed to enter this space and participate in the exercise.

While it is agreed that *sama* facilitates proximity between the Sufi lover and the Divine Beloved, the issue that remains unexplored concerns the *modus operandi* of the exercise. To put it differently, how does an assembly of *sama* function that leads those who are spiritually inclined towards the other realm? Is there any particular method followed in *sama*? How does simple love poetry invoke such strong feelings in the heart for the Divine? Most importantly, what is the key to distancing oneself from worldly thoughts during such an exercise?

Any complete and satisfactory answer to these knotty queries cannot be expected, as *sama* is believed to function through the psychology of experience, which remains largely inexpressible in words. The idea was lucidly explained by Nizam al-Din when he remarked that it was his spiritual disposition that enabled him to extract the maximum benefit from *sama*. However, the most important practice for any participant in *sama* lies in the act of correlation or allegorical interpretation (*tahmil*). It was through the process of *tahmil* that Nizam al-Din was able to relate meanings from verses of simple poetry to the attributes of his master, Baba Farid al-Din.[71]

For Khwaja Gisu Daraz, therefore, the use of terms in an assembly of *sama* signifying the beauty of the Beloved through the cheek, face, and mole etc. was allowed, keeping in mind the important precondition that all such references needed to be spiritually related (*tahmil*) to one's preceptor, or else to God.[72] It is proper *tahmil* which enables the listener to move beyond the apparent literary meaning of the verses towards a deeper understanding of the poetry, thereby allowing emotions to arise within his heart. An analysis of the process of *tahmil* is crucial if one wants to fully comprehend its functioning in an assembly of *sama*.

---

[71] Ibid., 515.
[72] *Khatima*, 26–29.

The verse referred to above begins with a description of the condition of a Sufi participant in *sama*, expressed through feelings of pain and separation that burn the heart of the mystic lover. *Sama* as a spiritual exercise is meant to make the Sufi saint realize the pain of separation from the Divine Beloved, which happens when the heart is stirred in the remembrance of the Lord, stimulated by the poetry heard by the Sufi. Purity of the heart and concentration of the mind are essential conditions for participating in *sama*. In the verse above, it is only after the Sufi lover has endured the fire of separation that the Divine Beloved unveils Himself, in full splendour and magnificence. Beholding the glory of the Lord agitates the heart of the lover mystic.

Waiting for the Beloved, the lover burns incessantly, day and night. A sense of pain pierces the heart of the lover who yearns for the Divine. The breath of the Sufi burns through the heart as feelings of separation rob his soul of all calmness. *Birahe ki aag* (fire of separation) is used in the sense of a metaphor to portray the idea of a lover burning himself in the fire of love that melts his heart as it suffers the pains of separation. It is interesting to note the inclusion of the idea of the body together with the soul. On many occasions, the Sufi saint in a *mehfil i-sama* is not in control of his physical self, which is stirred into movement when agitation affects the heart. Being unable to restrain one's physical movement is the outcome of ecstasy (*wajd*) that enters the heart of a Sufi.

In the above verse, any sense of physical agitation that may arise has been deftly masked by a description of the painful condition of separation from the Divine. As the reputed seventeenth-century poet from the Deccan, Wali Dakhani (1667–1707), expressed so eloquently, 'the best distraction is pursuit of love'. In this spiritual path, deeper spiritual knowledge can only be achieved by surviving moments of separation through longing and pain. This is precisely the condition portrayed in the above verse when it repeats *hal hawala re*. It is meant to emphasize that this state of despair is a direct result of the heart of the Sufi saint burning in the fire of separation.

Variations in *Tahmil*

It may so happen that, in *sama*, what the *qawwal* recites may not address the state (*hal*) of the listener or be in accordance with the spiritual stations (*maqam*) achieved by participants in that assembly. The verses recited can be irrelevant to the spiritual experience of the Sufi listener at that particular moment.

Does such a situation dilute the essence of the assembly? What method should the Sufi listener follow to derive benefits from the verses recited? Gisu Daraz emphasized that for a Sufi to reach the core meaning of the verses recited, the only way is by following the principle of *tahmil*.[73] The primary approach to *tahmil* is through the process of attaching one universal truth (*kulli haqiqat*) to another.[74] In the same way a Sufi mystic can attach a spiritual state (*hal*) to another, an anecdote (*hikayat*) to another, and continue likewise.[75] This process functions when the Sufi participant takes universal truth, a spiritual state, and anecdotes heard in the assembly of *sama* as the metaphor (*majaz*) and then tries to relate it through allegory to the reality (*haqiqat*). It is through such a process that the intention of the Sufi listener is kept pure, and he is able to understand the significance of the verses heard in *sama*, gaining from the process of correlation. This places the Sufi participant among the people of reality (*mardan-i haqiqat*).[76]

Before moving on to the second variety of *tahmil* elaborated by Gisu Daraz, it may be useful to elaborate a bit more on the above discussion. For the first type of *tahmil* to work beneficially for the listener, the basic precondition is his ability to relate it to the correct form of realities (*haqiqat*).[77] In an assembly of *sama*, whenever a Sufi hears poetry it is incumbent upon him to associate it with the attributes of his master (*pir*), as in the instance of Nizam al-Din mentioned above. The master here is the beloved of the listener, and it is only under such circumstances that *sama* is beneficial for the participant. The image of the *pir* should always remain in the mind of the Sufi so that whenever he hears any couplet or verse of spiritual significance, he should remember his master and his qualities.[78] This in turn leads to proper understanding of the verses read out in the assembly, thereby helping the Sufi in his spiritual journey.

---

[73] Ibid., 41.
[74] Ibid., 31.
[75] Ibid., 32.
[76] Ibid.
[77] Ibid.
[78] *Siyar al-awliya*, 515.

In the above-mentioned verse, the poet, probably a disciple of Khwaja Gisu Daraz, placed the master in the position of the beloved. Being the master of the assembly, all disciples of Gisu Daraz when participating in *sama* were meant to focus their attention on him. So charismatic is the power of the beloved's beauty that the lover cannot hold himself back from expressing his joy on beholding it, rising above the pain of separation that burns him incessantly. Such is the passion of the lover that, lost in ecstasy, he calls out to his beloved day and night. In remembering the beloved the emotional turmoil of the lover allows him no peace and calmness in the heart. Rather he pushes himself through the experience of a lover's torment, suffering in the fire of separation from his beloved.

In this poem, a rhythmic style and pattern has been maintained to carry forward the central idea—the complex, yet aesthetic, position of the lover and the Beloved. Every time the cycle of recitation is repeated to strengthen the message of the composition through the interjection of the verse, *aj birahe ki aag mujtane laage re*—the central idea of the poetic composition, that of portraying the lover-beloved relationship, is pushed deeper into the hearts of those present in the assembly. It is the experience of audition that is enriched through the spirit of the poem set to music, together with the complexities of the message it attempts to convey, building up the spiritual mood in *sama*.

The style of measured repetition of verses at times undermines the rhythmic balance of the assembly, yet at the same time upholds a unique approach. It is seen as an attempt at arousing emotions of the heart which lie dormant under normal circumstances. It is only when a verse of high emotional content is read out in *sama* that the heart stirs up to the realization of solitude. The verse when sung in a repetitive loop gradually amplifies the layered meaning of words and phrases, as they merge into the central theme of the composition—'the fire of separation' that burns the lover, making him yearn for that cherished union (*jam*).

Another interesting aspect of such verses, that is often overlooked, lies in the context in which they are sung. The above-mentioned verse is performed exclusively on the occasion of the saint's *urs*, the commemoration of his death anniversary, also celebrated as his union or 'wedding' with God. Such occasions are celebrated in the *dargah*, or the 'royal court', of the saint. Here a latent paradox seems to be at play. While the verse, set in a devotional setting, expresses the pain of separation, yearning, and longing for the Beloved, it is also sung to celebrate the 'union' of the saint with the Lord. Thus it is not the saint's death that is memorialized; rather it is his union with his Divine Beloved which is celebrated over moments of sorrow and pathos, when the assembly immerses into rapture through the performance of *sama* on these poems. Here one also tries to discern a sense of optimism in the verses, where it states 'the beloved is on a throne, himself and his splendour on display.' Many would improvise on the verse to suggest that God's presence is not lost in this moment. It encourages the lover Sufi saint to look beyond the narrowness of conventional meaning, of the verses, in an attempt to unravel the stages of love through beholding of the Beloved.

Moving beyond the multiple layers of meanings within the poem cited above, we now return to our discussion on the second method of *tahmil*, as elaborated by Gisu Daraz. Such an allegorical interpretation is possible only when the individual attending *sama* tries to relate the meaning of the verse (*hamal*) listened to with his own spiritual condition.[79] If an aggrieved person listens to a verse conveying an emotion of intense sadness, then it is natural that he would relate that to his own state of affairs. This in turn would create a sense of agitation within the listener.[80] In conditions of intense spiritual turmoil, the listener after experiencing the verses throws himself into the folds of ecstasy and uncontrollable emotions often resulting in the movement of his limbs—*raqs*, when carried out in the pattern of a dance. In the opinion of Khwaja Gisu Daraz, such is the behaviour of mystics when they listen to poetry, composed in Persian or local Hindavi, describing attributes of coquetry (*karishma*), pride (*nas*), cheek (*khad*), mole (*khal*), separation (*firaaq*), and union (*wisal*), among others.[81]

On which days should *sama* be arranged, or avoided? Once, a few qawwals arrived in the *khanqah* of Gisu Daraz and began to sing for those who had gathered there. At this point the shaykh remarked that since it was the tenth day (*ashura*) of the month of Muharram, and people were busy praying and mourning the death of Hussain, it was not proper to do *sama*. However, if someone is oblivious of the day and the time it is

[79] Ibid., 22.
[80] Ibid., 23.
[81] Ibid., 26–29.

not possible for him to refrain from the exercise. Some Sufis argue that the *sama* should be practiced in moments of trouble. The practice of *sama* also depends on the tradition of one's master and the rules that he set for his disciples for listening to *sama*. Any disciple who is trained by his master in the exercise of *sama* reaches the stage of perfection faster. Therefore if the master is physically absent from the assembly, it is advised by some to mourn one's separation from the master through actions of weeping and loud exclamations.

When having a proper effect on the listener, *sama* creates a sense of exhilaration in the heart which is then manifested through the limbs. Gisu Daraz, while describing the participation of his master Nasir al-Din Mahmud in *sama*, remarked that even when the shaykh had become old and feeble, he would show remarkable bursts of energy on listening to *sama*. As a result, he would move his limbs and do *raqs* for a long time, which even young and energetic disciples in the *khanqah* found difficult to match up to. Later, it so happened that one day when Nasir al-Din Mahmud was doing *raqs* in *sama*, he felt a trembling in his feet and had to sit down. Henceforth he never stood up on his feet when participating in *sama*. If he was overcome with ecstasy he would express it in a seated position, and would only rise up briefly when someone rose from within the assembly. Else he would enter into a state of ecstasy and intoxication while remaining seated. Nasir al-Din enjoyed poetry in Persian and Hindavi more than in any other language. In moments of extreme ecstasy and rapture he would throw his sleeves and prayer cap towards the *qawwal* as a mark of appreciation for the verses sung.

Once Gisu Daraz was asked on the issue of death in *sama*. He narrated how Abu Hasan Nuri died. One day while in an assembly of *sama*, Nuri became intoxicated by a verse and went into a state of ecstasy. Losing control over his self, he left his house, passed by the city centre, and started walking into the wilderness. Along his way lay a tree which was freshly chopped, so that one of its branches from the base stuck out like a sharp protrusion. In a state of ecstasy, when he fell on the branch it pierced from one end of his body, while coming out from the other end. The Shaykh died immediately. At this Gisu Daraz also remarked that it cannot be called death by *sama*, since it is death caused by accidental circumstances, rather than one induced only by *sama*, as in the case of Qutb al-Din Bakhtiyar Kaki discussed earlier.

Qawwal and the Quality of Verse in *Sama*

Poetry that is chosen to be recited in *sama* needs to be suitable for the occasion. Hence the *qawwal* doing the recitation should be a learned one, so that he is able to recite poetry of high quality with great finesse, together with having the ability to explain the meaning of the verses recited. At the same time the *qawwal* should be an individual of clean heart and pure intentions, so that whatever he recites is appropriate for the assembly of *sama*.

Thereafter the meaning and wisdom that emerge from those verses is a benefaction from the Divine that inclines the heart towards listening to more of such verses by creating a strong feeling of receptivity. It is believed that good poetry always originates from the Divine, where the human medium is limited to only being the recipient and the disseminator. Whatever the *qawwal* recites in *sama* is through the will of God, the secret of which is beyond human comprehension.

Since verses sung in *sama* originate from the Unseen, they touch the inner chords within the heart of an individual, creating a beneficial effect on his soul, which is considered an important reason for the suitability of this practice. The inclination of the heart towards the Divine on listening to these verses is considered a gift from the Unseen that is bestowed on whomsoever God wishes. But this grace does not occur continuously, rather only at special moments during deep contemplation. Thus the state of being in the manifestation of the Divine during *sama* is a momentary occurrence that seldom continues over long duration. Its temporality is also subject to the listening to the melodious voice that recites poetry in the assembly of *sama*. Such a voice is considered a boon on the *qawwal*, bestowed from the Unseen.

It is also argued that poetry that deeply affects a listener, leading to thoughts of the Divine within his heart, is much superior in comparison to a good voice. A pleasing sound that induces ecstasy can emerge from any source, including the sweet voices of animals like the singing of birds, or that of musical instruments. However, the poetry that originates from the Unseen is a special gift intended for the listener which can be comprehended only by those whose hearts have attained complete purity. In such a state, verses create a strong sense of urge within the heart of the listener, leading him towards higher spiritual stations.

Participants in *sama* need to grasp the inner meaning of the poetry recited in the assembly. And secondly, the poetry should be pleasing to the ear. The reason being that it is commonly believed that pleasing sounds reach the heart faster through the medium of the ears. A good voice is also considered essential for narrating good poetry, which then increases the listeners' taste and desire for such verses. Such participants are true admirers of *sama*, listening to it in the correct state of mind, with their attention towards God.

At the same time, the content of the poetry must be heard carefully and its meaning understood in a way that creates thoughts for the Divine within one's heart, rather than leading towards worldly desires. It is forbidden to recite such poetry in an assembly of *sama* which dwells on the physical qualities of beautiful women and young boys. On the other hand, if poetry recited in *sama* contains descriptions of the beauty of heaven and its maidens, then it is permissible, as such verses create a sense of urge and yearning in the heart of the believer. Therefore, *ghina*, or singing in itself, is not a forbidden exercise. It becomes forbidden only when it is performed and attended by young boys and beautiful women playing musical instruments. Such circumstances lead to distraction in the assembly of *sama* whereby the mind is fixed on the singers and musicians rather than on the content of the poetry and thoughts of the Divine. If *ghina* is kept away from creating disruptions and encouraging playful thoughts in the minds of the listener, then it is permissible for all.

Some even went to the extent of considering hand-clapping as a permissible act in *sama*. They argue that such an act creates a sense of rhythm alongside recitation, thereby leading to happiness in the heart and mind of the listener. However, beating of the tambourine (*duff*) in a way that leads to feelings of ecstasy within the heart of the listener is a forbidden act.

It is agreed by Sufis that *sama* is permissible only when the exercise is related to one's spiritual state. Else, if it is related to worldly desires and playful thoughts, then it is strictly forbidden. Those who consider *sama* as forbidden do so primarily on three grounds. First, they are unaware of the traditions of the Prophet where he listened to singing accompanied by musical instruments like the tambourine (*duff*). Secondly, they are narrow-minded and focused only on themselves, rather than taking note of other perspectives, on the basis of which *sama* has been argued as permissible. Thirdly, they lack the intellect to understand the value of *sama* as a worthy spiritual exercise for travellers in the Sufi path.

'Tools of Satan': Permissibility of Musical Instruments

It is said that in religious gatherings, if musical instruments are played without any accompanying voice, it is considered permissible. Traditionally, it is forbidden particularly in situations when people play and listen to them under the influence of wine with disreputable companions, which triggers worldly desires and is hence considered unlawful in the eyes of the law. Stringed instruments like the *chang* are included in this category. Singing (*ghina*) with the accompaniment of musical instruments is also considered unlawful in the eyes of the law. If *sama* of the Sufis does not fall within the category of *ghina* that is, free from the combination of singing with instruments, then *sama* is considered permissible (*mubah*).

However, musical instruments are also played on various occasions for a specific purpose, which does not make it forbidden. On occasions of war, drums are beaten to mark the beginning and end of battle. Gongs are used to announce the time for prayer. In *sama*, if musical instruments are used, it is imperative to ensure that the listeners are of a pure heart, purged of greed, jealousy, and selfishness. It is only under such conditions that music turns into food for the soul. The Egyptian mystic Dhun Nun permitted a sweet voice in *sama*, since it is considered a blessing from the Divine.

Contested Hadith traditions are also cited in defence of musical instruments, where it is argued that even Prophet Muhammad allowed the use of *duff* (tambourine) on occasions of celebration and when making announcements. It is said that Ayesha once solemnized a wedding from the Ansar tribe. When the Prophet came to know of this, he enquired with Ayesha whether the marriage ceremony was celebrated with singing and musical instruments, as this was the practice of the Ansar tribe on occasions of happiness. The *duff* was also sounded to gather people when the Prophet would deliver his sermons. One day, Abu Bakr entered the house of Ayesha, and found two Bedouin girls sitting in the courtyard singing while playing the duff. When Abu Bakr reprimanded them for playing the music of Satan, the Prophet allowed the girls to play and sing as it was their day of happiness (*eid*), which justified such actions. What Abu Bakr was probably resentful of was an ancient Arab practice which used singing and musical instruments for purposes of entertainment, often accused of being vulgar in nature.

Thus poetry and music in *sama* depend on the content which allows the heart to remember the Divine. For Sufis orientated towards *sama*, the practice is not restricted to any particular day or time, though certain preferences exist, but whenever the heart of the Sufi is inclined towards remembering God. However, *sama* is not advised as a public performance of singing with instruments. For Sufis, referring to such Hadith traditions is an attempt to uphold the legality of music and poetry as a Sufi practice under regulated circumstances. Some prefer *sama* accompanied by musical instruments, since such sweet sounds allow them to immerse themselves in ecstatic moments.

However, those Sufis who are adepts in the spiritual path are less interested in musical instruments, and focus more on the verses recited by the *qawwal*. Such was the approach of Sufi masters like Nasir al-Din Mahmud Chiragh i Dehli, who strictly disapproved the inclusion of musical instruments in *sama*. It is recorded that early in his spiritual career Gisu Daraz allowed the use of musical instruments in *sama* assemblies, though he personally refrained from using any instruments of music except the *duff*.[82] Once, Gisu Daraz, along with Maulana Sadar al-Din Tabib and Maulana Ala al-Din, decided to organize *sama* with a variety of musical instruments. The arrangements being on a grand scale, Sufis opened their hearts in contemplation of the Divine. Such were the emotions stirred in their hearts that they refused to be distracted for three days, listening with unflagging attention to the verses. When Nasir al-Din Mahmud, the spiritual preceptor of Gisu Daraz, came to know about this he immediately forbade Gisu Daraz to organize *sama* where instruments of music took precedence over emotions of the heart.[83]

Henceforth Gisu Daraz limited the use of any musical instrument in *sama* except the small tambourine (*duff*), though he did not object to

---

[82] Hussaini, *Sayyid Muhammad*, 135.
[83] Samani, *Siyar-i Muhammadi*, 70.

participants bringing their own instruments and playing them during the *sama*.[84] Although Gisu Daraz considered musical instruments to be the tools of Satan, he also argued that instruments of music were not without worth in *sama*.[85] But it is only the 'people of the heart' (*ahl -i dil*) who are aware of the true nature of music as a spiritual enhancer in *sama*. Once, Burhan al-Din Gharib was engaged in *sama* when someone in the assembly started playing a *sarangi*. The shaykh liked the sound of the instrument so much that he pulled it closer to him and urged the musician to continue playing it, while he derived pleasure from its sound.

Since Gisu Daraz could not ignore the instruction and practice of his master, he conceded that it is better for a Sufi (*ahl -i irshad wa da'wat*) in the path of spirituality to avoid the use of musical instruments while participating in *sama*. One of the more important reasons being that the inclusion of instruments in *sama* was forbidden by legists.[86] Thus it was unsuitable for Sufi mystics to indulge themselves in the sound of musical instruments that could be charged in the eyes of the law. However, as the saint went on to argue, *sama* conducted with proper manners and spiritual contemplation does not attract any objection towards the practice. Unfortunately, as he remarked, on many occasions people do not prefer to maintain proper *adab* in *sama*, which subject the practice to sharp criticisms.

Reservation towards the use of musical instruments in *sama* has been the position of Chishti Sufis even during the time of Nizam al-Din. Once some of his disciples shared that a few dervishes in the circle of the shaykh had participated in *sama* where people danced when playing on lutes and other wind instruments. On hearing this Nizam al-Din retorted that it was completely improper for them to join such an assembly, and they were not behaving properly. Since it is forbidden by law, musical instruments should never be indulged in. Later, when the dervishes were asked to clarify their questionable action of participating in an assembly where people danced and rejoiced and listened to wind instruments, they tried to justify this by arguing that they were so engrossed in *sama* that they became completely oblivious of the presence of wind instruments.

---

[84] Ibid., 72.
[85] *Khatima*, 36.
[86] Ibid., 33.

When this response was reported to Nizam al-Din, he said that the justification forwarded by the dervishes was not satisfactory, and that the act will be included in their record of misdeeds.[87] Elaborating further on this, Nizam al-Din remarked that true participants in *sama*, who carry a taste for Divine love, are moved into agitation by a single verse of poetry, irrespective of musical instruments. However, those who are not trained in the spirit of *sama* are unable to concentrate on the proceedings of the assembly.[88] Musical instruments are not little help for those who do not carry feelings of pain and longing for God. For those whose hearts are dead to the remembrance of the Divine, instruments of music are of little worth.

In the Assembly of *Sama*

Different from individual practices of contemplation, *sama* as a spiritual practice is organized as a congregation of Sufi saints who come together to participate in the *mehfil –i sama*, seeking to immerse their hearts in the remembrance of the Divine. Keeping in mind the emphasis of Shaykh Junaid, *sama* is organized at a proper place (*makan*), which is usually the *khanqah* or the shrine of a Sufi saint, it is organized at certain times (*zaman*) of the day, usually after night prayers so that the assembly can continue until late hours, and the people (*ikhwan*) attending the assembly are carefully chosen, so that not anyone can participate in *sama*. In the shrine complex of a Sufi saint, *sama* is a special ritual organized during the celebration of *'urs*. Such a *sama* can be attended by lay devotees, or it can be organized privately, as discussed above.

In the period of our study, we lack any comprehensive description regarding the structure and performance of a *sama* assembly. However, based on our discussion up to now, we can try to reconstruct how an assembly of *sama* functions. In the absence of any normative description across different Sufi *silsilas*, we can observe this exercise primarily through the practices of the Chishti order, who are recognized as the most vocal exponent of *sama* in South Asia. As a spiritual experience the

---

[87] *Fawaid al Fuad*, 189; *Morals for the Heart*, 335.
[88] Ibid.

assembly of *sama* constitutes an ongoing interaction between the performer, who is the *qawwal*, and his companions, the Sufi listener, who is the participant, and the master of the assembly, who is also the senior Sufi saint presiding over the proceedings. In a way, *sama* is a hierarchical assembly of Sufis, starting from the beginner to the senior Sufi master, accompanied by other members of the Sufi fraternity.

Sama usually begins and ends with a recitation of the Quran, followed by the recitations of the *qawwal* whose selection of poetry, along with its rhythmic repetition, much in the style of *zikr*, sets the mood and energy of the assembly. The poetry recited in *sama* is meant to trigger emotions of love and reverence within the Sufi listener as the assembly progresses by reciting verses in praise of the bygone Sufis, Ali, and Prophet Muhammad, and finally explores the various attributes of God. The *qawwal* is responsible for the interplay of words and phrases upon sensing the mood of the assembly and the emotive response of the Sufi listeners. On some occasions this is accompanied by music, which seeks to strengthen and compliment the performance of poetry. Along with verses, music too plays an important role in arousing emotions of ecstatic love, though its use came to be strictly regulated.

Sama is meant to benefit the spiritual condition of the Sufi listener, who in turn seeks to derive spiritual benefits from *sama*. The latter, however, depends on two complimentary conditions—the ability of the Sufi saint to strive in the spiritual path, and to attain certain stations (*maqam*) in his journey. His spiritual state (*hal*), however, is beyond his control, as it descends from the Divine realm for no specific duration. As they realize the arrival of *hal* upon them, Sufis try to hold on to it for as long as they can, without disrupting their emotional response towards such a state. The inner reality of the Sufi listener in *sama* is manifested through his external behaviour too. In this sense *sama* is also a spiritual experience for Sufi saints.

As a religious practice, *sama* is not just a spiritual experience, but a structured performance often guided by detailed rules. The three conditions of *zaman*, *makan*, and *ikhwan* came to be supplemented with further guidelines from the thirteenth century onwards. As a communal assembly of spiritual seekers, *sama* is usually organized in the *khanqah* or the shrine, but also at times as a private gathering or a closed assembly in the meditation cell (*hujra*) of the Sufi master. The Sufi saint who organizes *sama* also assumes the leadership of the assembly, not only as the host, but also as the spiritual leader. In that capacity he guides the proceedings and order of seating, and regulates the conduct of his disciples. Once, Amir Khusrau started doing *raqs* in *sama*, while raising both his hands under the effect of his ecstatic mood. He was gently asked by Nizam al-Din to stop dancing with his hands raised, as he was a worldly individual, and not from the Sufi fraternity.

> If you dance then carry out the dance like the Gnostics,
> Trample the world under your feet,
> And extend your hands towards the other world.

It may so happen that when *sajjada-nashins* of Sufi shrines preside over *sama* in memory of the deceased Sufi saint, they prefer to place the latter's seat (*gaddi*) at the centre of the assembly. If *sama* is performed in a shrine complex, *qawwals* take their seats and perform while facing the tomb of the Sufi master, while the congregation assembles all around.

Though Chishti Sufis allowed novices to participate in *sama*, there was a consensus in not allowing common masses in the assembly. Participants need to be ritually pure (ablution) and clean and in a spiritual state of mind. Their attires should conform to the purpose, usually a cloak or robe with a headgear. It is advised that attires should not be conspicuous so as to distract the attention of other participants. Those who are distracted in worldly affairs are discouraged to participate. Similarly, women and young boys are not allowed in *sama* as onlookers and participants, to avoid distraction in the assembly. Unless overcome with uncontrollable emotion, participants are advised not to move around within the assembly, disturbing others who may have attained spiritual states.

As an exercise aimed towards a spontaneous remembrance of the Divine, *sama* can be organized whenever there is an urge for it among the Sufi seekers. However, there are certain customary norms that are adhered to when organizing *sama*. It is advisable to have *sama* at a time when there are no immediate worldly engagements to attend to. And prayer times also need to be avoided. The preferred time for organizing *sama* is after the last prayer has been completed, so that Sufis can continue to participate in the assembly until late at night. In case of the latter, the duration of *sama* on many occasions can be extended to cover the whole night until the early hours of dawn, before the morning prayer. At other times, the duration of *sama* is regulated as per the schedule of ritual prayers.

In defence of *sama* as a permissible religious practice, Sufis advised beginning and ending *sama* with a recitation of the Quran—through select chapters and verses, followed by intercessory prayer (*dua*). Also recited as part of the proceedings is the spiritual genealogy (*shajrah*) of the Sufi order, like the Chishti, which connects the current Sufi saint through his master and mentors, and bygone saints of the order, to reputed Sufi masters like Junaid and Hasan Basri, linking further back to Ali, and finally reaching the Prophet Muhammad. This often constitutes an important ritual during *sama*, seeking blessings through remembering and recollecting the spiritual genealogy in the form of *zikr*. Songs and poetry recited in *sama* follow a definite order of hierarchy, starting with the praise of God and His creation (*hamd*), followed by the praise of Prophet Muhammad (*naat*), who is recognized as the fountainhead of the Sufi tradition, and from whom Islamic spirituality is believed to have assumed a philosophical frame and structure. This is followed by the praise of Ali, and the reputed Sufis (*manqabat*), both belonging to the order, as well as reputed masters from the earlier generations. Specific verses could also be addressed to the founding saint of the order, like Muin al-Din Chishti, as the spiritual apex.

Emotions that are explored in *sama* through the recitation of poetry usually invoke love, separation, and union, whose feelings are at times enhanced through the use of musical instruments. There is no fixed order or formulae in which these themes are engaged with, as it constitutes the choice of the *qawwal*. Through a process of measured engagement with the mood of the assembly, the *qawwal* uses his repertoire of poetry in *sama*, gradually intensifying the response from Sufi participants. The intention at all times is to seek a spiritual experience through Divine blessing. Rather than formal structures of recitation, it is the emotion and pathos of the *qawwal*, combined with the inner message of the verses, which set the mood for the listeners, occasionally leading to ecstatic behaviour in some Sufis. And the message conveyed through the verses could range from expressions of love and longing for the Sufi master and God, remembrance of famous Sufi saints, love for and devotion to the saint at whose shrine the *sama* is organized, or the promise of union for lovers of God. The experience of the *qawwal* in such an assembly becomes critical in making a fine distinction between the idea of human love (*ishq –i majazi*) and spiritual love (*ishq –i haqiqi*), all the while being careful not to turn it into a popular performance. *Sama* for the *qawwal* is not an occasion to stage his performance, but instead to facilitate the spiritual advancement of the assembly of Sufis. Theatrical performance and vocal display are not expected from him, apart from a sincere effort to improve his singing, at times through the use of classical musical notes (*raga*) appropriate for the occasion. The senior Sufi master who presides over the assembly is careful that the performance of the *qawwal*, along with his content, does not create any undesired impact on the listener.

For novices, participating in *sama* requires rigorous spiritual training, as well as sitting in the assembly under the careful guidance of one's spiritual guide. In order to experience spiritual delight in *sama*, which can gradually lead to ecstatic emotions, the beginner needs to graduate to the status of a spiritually advanced Sufi. As the Moroccan Sufi saint Abu Madyan (d. 1198) warned, a 'beginner should not be present at ecstatic sessions until he has mortified his carnal soul' through rigorous fasting, prayer, and meditation.

In the same way as preference for *sama* varies from one Sufi order to another, there are differences in opinion with regard to ecstatic behaviour, and the extent to which Sufis should be allowed to manifest ecstasy physically. Sufis agree that moments of intense internal ecstasy will manifest themselves, even though in varying degrees, through physical behaviour. Complete restraint is impossible, similar to someone who tries hard not to sneeze but fails to control it. However, conspicuous behaviour expressing emotional ecstasy is usually frowned upon in Sufi circles. There is no given form in which *sama* effects the Sufi listener. His spiritual state (*hal*) is an outcome of the content recited at the assembly, combined with the grace from the Unseen. Such a state could be initially expressed through tears, as well as restlessness and verbal exclamations. When emotions of the heart do not subside, but continue to surge, it can make the Sufi stand up on his feet and start doing *raqs*, a rhythmic movement of dance in response to the poetry and the inner emotions. In extreme cases the Sufi may not be able to stand, but falls on the ground. Rending the patched cloak and throwing the prayer cap towards the *qawwal* express various degrees of ecstasy in a Sufi, as well as appreciation for the *qawwal*.

The latter responds to such ecstatic emotional behaviour by continuing to repeat the verse, or a particular couplet, in order to sustain the spiritual state, thereby allowing divine grace to continue on the gathering. In Chishti *sama,* participants who are yet to experience ecstasy are nonetheless expected to rise up and give company to a Sufi who has reached the point of ecstasy by conforming to his movements, thereby engaging in empathetic ecstasy (*tawajud*).

Sama is practiced primarily as an oral tradition by Sufis of the Chishti order in South Asia. Its written record is available from the oral discourses of eminent Chishti Sufis as recorded in writing by their disciples from time to time, as well as in the biographical literature that concern saints from the Chishti order. As a religious exercise, organized privately in a Sufi *khanqah, sama* is meant to facilitate a spiritual dialogue between the Sufi lover and the Divine beloved, in the company (*suhbat*) of other Sufi saints as well as disciples. The gathering is focused on seeking Divine grace that connects the saints of that Sufi order, through a spiritual lineage and genealogy, with Prophet Muhammad. As an assembly of poetry and music, *sama* is also dependent on the availability of well-versed *qawwals* who are selected on certain criteria. Sufis are meant to be the listeners of what the *qawwals* recite, keeping in mind the spiritual goals of the assembly. So *sama* cannot be organized on many instances due to the absence of *qawwals.* Special compositions of poetry, in Persian or the regional vernacular, are preserved for *sama* assemblies held on memorable occasions like 'urs, and attended by a close group of Sufi saints and shrine-keepers. Such *sama* are closed assemblies held at Sufi shrines to commemorate special memories related to the Sufi master. By preserving the content that is recited in *sama*, and by adhering to parameters of performance laid down during the lifetime of the saint, such *sama* assemblies preserve a historical tradition, along with the historicity of the Sufi ritual, ensured through temporal continuity.

.

4

Sufi Rituals across Orders

Sama and *Zikr* as Shared Practices

On a certain Sunday morning in the summer of 1309, the *jamaat khana* of Nizam al-Din buzzed with activity as numerous disciples, visitors, common people, other mystics, and scholars gathered to benefit from the blessings and company of Delhi's most revered Sufi master. As discussions veered through diverse topics on spiritual and everyday concerns, the issue of *sama* came to the fore. The discussion turned towards the Suhrawardi Sufi saint, Shihab al-Din Suhrawardi, and his practice of *sama*. Nizam al-Din remarked that his predecessor and the renowned Sufi saint Najm al-Din Kubra (d. 1221) often used to say that the Most Merciful has bestowed Shihab al-Din with the best possible grace, except the taste (*zawq*) for music (*sama*).[1]

The above observation may convince many that Suhrawardi Sufis were particularly disinterested towards assemblies of audition (*sama*). Emanating from and attested through the person of two distinguished Sufi masters, Najm al-Din and Nizam al-Din, the Suhrawardi position on *sama* can to a certain extent be considered unfavourable. And here lies the problem. We may want to remember that the Suhrawardi disinterest towards *sama* referred to by contemporary and later Sufis is a normative position. This reflects the general sentiment of the order towards the practice of *sama*, to which Suhrawardi Sufis attached less importance when compared to the practice of *zikr* (remembrance). The problem lies in accepting such a normative position as a fixed and non-negotiable spiritual preference. In Sufi practices, we are drawn into a similar trap by adopting a rigid approach that rejects any possibility for exceptions. Perhaps we can understand Sufi rituals better by following a model where a particular spiritual exercise like *sama* is not given an inalienable status

---

[1] *Fawaid al Fuad*, 84; *Morals for the Heart*, 118.

Sufi Rituals and Practices. Kashshaf Ghani, Oxford University Press. © Kashshaf Ghani 2024.
DOI: 10.1093/oso/9780192889225.003.0005

vis-à-vis the Chishti order. Though *sama* came to be recognized as the defining spiritual practice of the Chishti Sufis, exceptions were not altogether absent; some Suhrawardi Sufi saints too appreciated the efficacy of the ritual and engaged with it, both in theory and practice. After discussing the participation of the Suhrawardi saint of Delhi Qazi Hamid al-Din Nagauri's participation in *sama* in an earlier chapter, we can elaborate on the Suhrawardi position on *sama* through the writings of Suhrawardi masters. The later part of the chapter will argue against considering *zikr* to be an exclusively Suhrawardi practice, by exploring the position of the Chishti Sufis on the spiritual exercise. By adopting an approach that attempts to delimit our understanding of Sufi rituals along narrow confines of specific Sufi orders, we can argue for a shared space for spiritual practices created by the participation of two premier Sufi orders from South Asia—the Chishti and the Suhrawardi.

Commenting on the preference of spiritual practices by Shihab al-Din, Nizam al-Din mentioned that Awhad Kirmani (d. 1238) once visited the *khanqah* of the Suhrawardi master in Baghdad. Upon his arrival, Shihab al-Din immediately folded his prayer carpet and placed it under his knees, in a gesture of extreme reverence for the visitor. Awhad Kirmani carried a reputation as a master of spiritual contemplation, and developed his own style of *shahid bazi* that involved the contemplation of Divine beauty through beautiful human faces, particularly beardless young youths, often accompanied by musical gatherings of *sama*, which were used to induce spiritual ecstasy. It is not surprising, then, that as the evening melted into the night Kirmani requested his Suhrawardi host for an assembly of *sama*. Shihab al-Din immediately called for some musicians and arranged for *sama*. He restrained himself from participation, but for the sake of social courtesy (*adab*) stayed close to the physical space of the *mehfil*, while retiring to a corner. As the *mehfil* raged in full fervour, Shihab al-Din quietly immersed himself in contemplation of the Almighty through *zikr*.[2]

Next morning at dawn, one of the attendants of the *khanqah* enquired with Shihab al-Din Suhrawardi about the previous night; while Awhad Kirmani and other saints were completely absorbed in *sama*, they were at the same time also apprehensive about whether their music and emotional

---

[2] Ibid.

outbursts had interrupted the contemplation of the Suhrawardi master. On hearing this Shihab al-Din replied with much surprise, 'Was there music?'. When the attendant replied in the affirmative, Shihab al-Din further remarked, 'I was not aware of it'.[3]

Nizam al-Din marvelled at the degree of concentration with which Shihab al-Din Suhrawardi immersed himself in spiritual contemplation. Nizam al-Din went on to add further that every time a *mehfil* was held at the *khanqah* of Shihab al-Din Suhrawardi, the latter would only participate until the verses of the Holy Quran were being read before the proceedings of *sama* began. After which, during the actual exercise of *sama* with poetry and musical accompaniments, the shaykh would retire and immerse himself in deep contemplation of the Lord through *zikr*.[4] Such was his spiritual maturity that even while the rest of the assembly was emotionally agitated by the overpowering effect of *sama*, he would remain oblivious to those proceedings.

The above incident is instructional in certain ways. It clearly brings out the differences in the Chishti and Suhrawardi attitude as far as the defining spiritual exercises of the individual orders are concerned. However, this difference in attitude towards spiritual practices cannot be considered to be indicative of disrespect towards each other. Sufi masters, irrespective of the order they belonged to, were inclusive in their practice of spiritual harmony, in order to be able to acknowledge the preferences of shaykhs from orders different to theirs. Hence, disrespect towards another order for being dispassionate towards a particular spiritual exercise, be it *sama* or *zikr*, is not something we see either from the Chishti or Suhrawardi Sufis. It is only while trying to read from a modern-day perspective that we tend to imagine, perhaps mistakenly, thirteenth-century Sufi orders to be akin to competing missionary brotherhoods or political groups operating within walled-up social spaces, at times even critical of each other's approaches. What we find, rather, in contemporary sources on Sufism, is a sense of deep respect and compassion among masters of different orders, acknowledging each other's spiritual training as well as devotional practices.

---

[3] *Fawaid al Fuad*, 84; *Morals for the Heart*, 119.
[4] Ibid.

A similar attitude of mutual respect is strikingly visible when we closely examine interactions between Sufi orders in medieval India. Although Shihab al-Din Suhrawardi restrained himself from participating in *sama*, he was courteous and welcoming to eminent shaykhs who carried a taste for the exercise. Alluding to his wishes, Awhad Kirmani was honoured with a full scale *mehfil-i sama*. Even though Shihab al-Din chose not to participate in it, he displayed great etiquette (*adab*) by sharing the physical space where *sama* was held. He chose not to leave the space, but retired to the corner, allowing himself to concentrate on the remembrance of God (*zikr*). This not only indicates important gestures of social hospitality, but spiritual hospitality as well, on the part of Shihab al-Din towards the visitor Awhad Kirmani, even if that meant organizing an exercise that did not hold primacy for Suhrawardi Sufis. It can be taken as the spiritual maturity of someone in the stature of Shihab al-Din Suhrawardi that despite sitting close to an emphatic gathering of Sufis immersed in poetry and music, the Suhrawardi master was successful in transferring himself to a completely different plane of spiritual realization, where even eloquent recitation and musical instruments failed to disrupt his concentration.

The general indifference of Suhrawardi Sufis towards *sama* was balanced by their preference for the exercise of silent recollection (*zikr*) of God's names and attributes. As a spiritual order, Suhrawardis preferred to avoid practices that involved poetry and musical instruments, which could potentially agitate the heart of the listener, leading to *raqs*. Suhrawardi Sufis were critical about physical agitation while in contemplation as well. Though they never preferred *sama* as their core spiritual exercise, Suhrawardi *khanqahs* were not unfamiliar with the practice of *sama*, as noted from the above incident. Probably, *sama* would be organized for saints visiting a Suhrawardi *khanqah* and having a taste for the particular ritual, like in the case of Kirmani. Hence *sama* was duly recognized by Suhrawardi saints as a means of enhancing one's spiritual maturity.[5] At the level of defining the core practice of their order, Suhrawardi saints sought to derive from *zikr* as much spiritual succour as probably the Chishtis did from the assembly of audition.

Returning to the idea of a shared spiritual space, it can be better grasped perhaps by exploring the position of the Suhrawardi order with regard to

---

[5] Ibid.

an exercise like *sama*, so that we gain another perspective on the possible argument that Sufi rituals like *sama* and *zikr* were not practices limited to a particular order, and hence out of bounds for others. In this regard, no work is more illustrative of the Suhrawardi point of view on various spiritual practices than the *Awarif al- Maarif* (Knowledge of the Learned). While Shihab al-Din Suhrawardi wrote many treatises on the tradition of *tasawwuf*, none reached the heights of popularity of the *Awarif*. To contemporaries and later generations of Sufis, spanning across orders (*silsila*) and geographical regions, this manual became the most closely studied text on spiritual training. Therefore, in order to garner a precise idea as to the Suhrawardi disposition towards *sama*, it is important that views stated in the *Awarif* are studied closely.

Being the polestar of the Suhrawardi order and a leading Sufi master of his age, Shihab al-Din was well aware of the controversy around *sama*. Thus it is of little surprise that he opens the discussion on *sama* with the remark 'Of the number of most laudable Sufi mysteries, denied by outward *ulama*, one is the assembly for: (a) the *sama* (hearing) of the *ghina* (song) and *ilhan* (lilt); and, (b) the summoning of the *qawwal* (singer)'.[6]

Depending on the level of spiritual maturity, Shihab al-Din Suhrawardi, borrowing from the model of Sarraj, divides men of *sama* (*ahl-i sama*) into three categories. In descending order of adeptness, first are those who are the men of Truth (*ahl-i haqq*), for they are blessed with the ability to hear directly from the words of God, His voice and His creations. Whatever they hear they attribute to God (*haqq*). Second are those who are the devout attendants of *sama*. They take the proceedings of the assembly to their heart and apply every verse that they hear from the mouth of the *qawwal* to their spiritual condition (*hal*) and station (*maqam*). They are men of *alim* and *fazil*, and the most sincere in the assembly. Thus whatever they ascribe to God is in the true spirit of the exercise, rather than in worldly thought. Lastly are the *fakirs* and celibate ascetics who have rejected the bindings of the material world in every possible manner. They turn their hearts and minds perpetually towards the service of God. For them *sama* is nothing but to seek joy for the pure heart carrying them closer to the presence of the Lord.[7] *Sama* as a Sufi

---

[6] Wilberforce Clarke, Eng. trans., *The Awarif ul Maarif by Shaikh Shahabuddin Umar b. Muhammad Suhrawardi* (Delhi: Taj Company, 1984), 49.

[7] Ibid.

practice is most appropriate for this group, as they are individuals closest to God and farthest from lust and desire. However, for those whose hearts are drawn more towards worldly desires, *sama* is a futile exercise.[8]

Shihab al-Din Suhrawardi argues that the reason *sama* was abhorred by the contemporary *ulama* and legists lies in its tradition of innovation.[9] This is because such an exercise for spiritual advancement has little or no historical evidence from the time of the Prophet, his Companions, the Followers, and the first generation of Sufi mystics. Such a practice was the innovation of later-day Sufi saints, who took to *sama* and established its veracity according to debated Hadith traditions attributed to the Prophet and his Companions.[10]

In spite of the uncertainty regarding the historical origins of *sama* from the time of the Prophet, Shihab al-Din Suhrawardi does not deny the importance of *sama* as a spiritual practice, nor the benefits Sufis claim to derive from it. Rather he recognizes *sama* as an exercise of audition whose value is not doubted even by men of faith. People who listen to *sama* are men of intellect who follow the right path. Thereafter Shihab al-Din goes on to list the benefits from *sama* as being of three kinds.

First, he considers *sama* to be appropriate only for those who follow austerity and spiritual rigour, striving against material attractions. For such individuals *sama* is a spiritual composition of sweet and melodious sounds, poetic verses, and lilt, aimed at arousing emotions of the heart towards remembering the Divine and His attributes. Shihab al-Din argues that such a practice basically acts as a powerful medium for stirring up the heart when at times it suffers from spiritual enervation.[11]

For Shihab al-Din Suhrawardi, the longing for *sama* arises from the calmness and certainty of one's faith, expressed through emotions of passionate love for the Divine. Such a feeling is evident from the tears that result from a heart which is agitated, washing away all impurities while flowing through the eyes. Agitation in the limbs of the body arises from passionate yearning and deep longing for the Divine. Such conditions are meant to affect the heart of the listener in two forms: if the revelation is

---

[8] Clarke, *Awarif ul Maarif* (Eng.), 56; Shihab al-Din Suhrawardi, *Awarif ul Maarif*, Urdu trans. Shams Barelwi (Lahore: Progressive Books, 1998), 351–352.
[9] Ibid.
[10] Ibid.
[11] Ibid.

of wrath the effect is seen on the body through sadness; if the emotional upsurge is severe, it can affect the mind. Such revelations also have an impact on the soul of the listener. When the impact is severe it can lead to a feeling of the soul being released from the body. In such states of agitation, cries are heard and bodily movements increase, indicating severity. Problems arise when individuals try to imitate ecstasy, in order to benefit from it. For Suhrawardi Sufis, empathetic ecstasy results from the influence of the lower self (*nafs*) that tempts the listener to imitate other people's ecstatic behaviour.[12]

Suhrawardi Sufis consider such ecstatic behaviour in *sama* as a blessing from the Divine that affects various listeners differently. In some it results in agitation leading to cries and lament. While these are believed to emanate from Divine wrath, those who are drowned in the emotion of passionate love for the Divine receive *sama* calmly.[13]

According to Shihab al-Din Suhrawardi, the lasting contribution of *sama* is that it helps the Sufi listener travel, through those moments of participation, the distance which he could not have travelled in years without the help of audition.[14]

Secondly, on occasions when the lower self (*nafs*) of a Sufi dominates, it blocks the heart from receiving blessings from the Divine. On such occasions a veil (*hijab*) descends between the Lord and his creation, separating the listener from the Lord.[15] This separation has a demoralizing effect on the spiritual condition (*hal*) of the Sufi. Under such conditions, *sama*, through harmonious sounds, and reference to love and union, reinvigorates within the heart a remembrance of the Divine Beloved. It helps pierce the veil that separates the Sufi from his Lord.

The third and most significant achievement derived from *sama* is with regard to the blessing the listener derives from such an exercise.[16] To men of the spiritual path, who move from one spiritual station to another, *sama* aids in opening up the ear of the heart so that it stirs up to Divine revelations, reminding him of the secret of creation and the primordial

---

[12] Ibid., 338–339.
[13] Ibid., 364.
[14] Ibid.
[15] Clarke, *Awarif ul Maarif* (Eng.), 50.
[16] Ibid.

covenant between man and God. This guides the mystic towards the realm of the Unseen, beyond the attractions of the material world.

In the *Awarif*, Shihab al-Din Suhrawardi categorizes lamentation (*buka*) that arises within a Sufi into two kinds: *buka* of joy and *buka* of ecstasy (*wajd*).[17] While the first type is associated with worldly expressions of joy, fear, and desire, the second type is concerned with ecstasy.[18] When the mystic beholds the manifestation (*tajalli*) of the Divine, he finds himself in the presence of the Almighty, where the truth of certainty (*haqq al yaqin*) increases. The enraptured one (*wajid*) is left under the influence of the Unseen. In such a situation the state of the Sufi saint is partially understandable through his external demeanour. For the lovers of God, *sama* increases their tryst with the Beloved, which makes itself known through external manifestations like the movement of limbs and shedding of tears. *Sama* is the medium through which Sufis realize the love of God, and it is only through such a realization that one's heart is orientated towards spiritual perfection. This perfect spiritual state of the mystic attracts blessings from the Divine.[19]

For those in the spiritual path, *wajd* or ecstasy is experienced from *sama*. However, Suhrawardi Sufis differ on *wajd* being a higher state of realizing the Divine. While agreeing that feelings of ecstasy in an assembly of *sama* signify the perfection of the Sufi spiritual state (*hal*), for Suhrawardi Sufis it is also a mark of regression in an adept.[20] For an experienced Sufi saint who has progressed sufficiently on the spiritual path, depending on *wajd* need not be the only means of attaining his spiritual state. Rather his maturity in the path should be sufficient to aid him in the act of witnessing (*shahada*).[21] Therefore, longing for *wajd* as a specific aid with which to arrive at the state of *shahada* signifies a weakness in the spiritual rigour of the adept.[22] In an assembly of *sama*, as Shihab al-Din would remark, an adept loses himself to ecstasy (*wajd*) and thereby becomes the *wajid*, but at the same time also loses out on the continuity of his spiritual state. And the primary reason for the loss of *hal* lies in

---

[17] Ibid., 53.
[18] Ibid.
[19] Ibid.
[20] Ibid.
[21] Ibid.
[22] Ibid.

the qualities of existence (*wujud*) gaining prominence in the heart of the mystic.[23]

It can be argued that the realm of existence is omnipresent. It never escapes the world of the Sufi saint, for the Sufi himself is a reality due to the principles of existence. However hard he may try, and whatever spiritual station he may achieve, he cannot completely free himself from the shackles of worldly existence. It envelops his material self in the same way that piety does his spiritual self. But at the same time it is undeniable that a Sufi is a traveller in the spiritual path primarily because of his ability to control his material emotions and worldly desires. Even though the material world exists in and around his spiritual existence, his spiritual training equips him to control such an influence only for his material existence, rather than allowing it to seep into his heart.

Here Shihab al-Din Suhrawardi spells out in clear terms the characteristics of existence (*wujud*) and the ways in which it tends to intrude upon the spiritual realm of the mystic. The primary source of worldliness within the heart of an individual in the spiritual path is his deviation from self-discipline and piety. A simultaneous cause is the presence of lust and material desires within a heart that is thus veiled from the Unseen.[24] When such tendencies of worldliness arise, it is natural that the individual will be led astray from the spiritual path, for it leaves no space for the remembrance of the Lord.[25]

Experiencing ecstasy (*wajd*) as a Divine benefaction is a preserve of the pure heart, and does not descend in a heart influenced by worldly traits. Shihab al-Din Suhrawardi argues that *wajd* can be achieved in *sama* either through the pure sweetness of melodies, or through the audition of poetry and verses that stir the heart towards the realization of God.[26] A proper interpretation (*tahmil*) of the verses of poetry can be undertaken only by a heart that is blessed by the Divine.[27] Only when the heart is emptied from worldly thoughts will it be able to withstand the ultimate experience of witnessing (*shahada*), for witnessing the Lord is a perpetual act and should not be limited to participation in *sama*. For adepts

---

[23] Ibid., 54.
[24] Ibid.
[25] Ibid.
[26] Ibid.
[27] Ibid.

the constant experience of witnessing remains at the root of all spiritual achievements.[28]

The audition of melodious sounds creates within the heart a sense of agitation only when it is blessed by the Divine. Shihab al-Din Suhrawardi argues that the hearing of sweet sounds stirs the soul rather than the heart, which becomes agitated only when it experiences the presence of Truth within it.[29] So *sama* is beneficial only for the pure heart, whereas the heart which is dominated by the lower self is veiled from receiving Divine beneficence.[30] For a spiritually mature Sufi saint, freed from the shackles of material existence, the state (*hal*) of witnessing is a perpetual blessing. Such an individual therefore benefits little from an assembly of *sama*. To him, *sama* is no more an exercise to be pursued for achieving higher spiritual states. Rather it becomes a spiritual burden, and as a result verses recited by the *qawwal* sound nothing more than the 'croaking of the ravens'.[31]

Sufi theorists, developing a point already made by Shihab al-Din, and on the basis of the above-mentioned conditions, argue that a mystic who is in a state of perpetual witnessing (*shahada*) of the Divine needs no *sama* to induce ecstasy. He remains as much blessed by the Divine during the course of the assembly as he was before it. Thus his spiritual progress is no longer dependent on participation in *sama*, and what he hears is no more than mere sound, music, and verses of poetry.[32] Rather he hears through the ear of his heart. Whatever he hears is in accordance with the attributes of the Divine, and the thought of the Divine never escapes his heart, which is cleansed of worldly desires. The heart that is ever present with God hears directly from Him, so that irrespective of whether he is in *sama*, every sound and word reaches his ears, as the voice of God and His creations.[33]

---

[28] Ibid., 55.
[29] Ibid.
[30] Ibid.
[31] I borrow this phrase from the famous mystical treatise of Uthman al-Hujwiri, *Kashf ul-Mahjub*, where the author states that once when he was deeply agitated by the spiritual effect of music, a mystic named Abu Ahmad al-Muzaffar remarked quite prophetically, 'A day will come when the music will be no more to you than the croaking of a raven. The influence of music only lasts so long as there is no contemplation'. For the complete account, see *Kashf ul-Mahjub*, 170–171.
[32] *Awarif ul Maarif* (Eng.), 55.
[33] Ibid.

Shihab al-Din Suhrawardi is also emphatic while enumerating the dangers attached to *sama*. In spite of being the spiritual succour for Sufis, *sama* also carries elements that may spell disaster—both for the assembly and the individual listener.[34] If an assembly of *sama* is organized with the intention of encouraging one's passion for lust and sensuality, it steers the listener away from the spiritual path. On such occasions *sama* is a harmful deterrent on the Sufi way. Assemblies of *sama* where poetry is read describing the face, cheek, and mole of the female beloved, together with her physical beauty, should not be arranged and attended by people of true faith. In the same way, when poetry is recited in *sama* sessions by beardless and handsome youths, or by a woman, without being accompanied by a *mehram*, looking at them causes the danger of lustful desires; it is not the singing and the voice, but the desires of lust that make such *sama* assemblies forbidden.[35]

After detailing the ill-effects brought about when *sama* is arranged in the manner mentioned above, Shihab al-Din Suhrawardi states that one may visit an assembly of *sama* with the intention of gathering material provisions that are at times distributed before or after the assembly. *Sama* for the immature and the lay individual then turns into a pastime, and an occasion for enjoying oneself in laughter, frivolity, and enjoyment through dancing. Singing and dancing, with the occasional playing of the flute, which is meant to bring pleasure to the passions, is strictly forbidden by Sufis.[36] Even if one does not voluntarily participate in such acts, he amuses himself by witnessing such activities, which the common masses are forbidden to indulge in. Individuals arrive in *sama* with the sole intention of witnessing manifestations of ecstasy (*wajd*) and spiritual states (*hal*) in others. Being a popular practice for Sufis across orders, the practice of *sama* is often pursued by those who wish to be counted as Sufi shaykhs. On such occasions *sama* is less a spiritual practice, and more an instrument for inciting desire.[37] In such an assembly, if worldly passions are aroused it completely defeats the purpose of *sama*. As a result, it becomes difficult for the Sufi saint to attain the spiritual state (*hal*) he seeks.[38]

---

[34] Ibid., 51.
[35] *Awarif ul Maarif* (Urdu), 349, 358.
[36] Ibid., 349, 355, 358.
[37] Ibid.
[38] Ibid.

Participating in an assembly of *sama* is intended to help Sufis in the spiritual path. *Sama* is meant to arouse the dormant emotions of the heart that give rise to an urge for spiritual union.[39] For Sufis with a pure heart, *sama* is an exercise for seeking the Divine Beloved, and at the same time expressing sympathy for travellers on the path. Hence, a Sufi who is trained to participate in *sama* should focus his thoughts on paradise and hell, on the Day of Judgement, praise of the Lord, Divine contemplation, and charity in the name of the Lord. Verses that orientate the mind of the listener towards such thoughts should be allowed in *sama*. When the Sufi listener attaches such meaning to his Lord, his heart is agitated, and loses itself in the remembrance of the Divine.[40]

Thus any improper application of *sama* could lead to disastrous consequences. Spiritual practices if not applied properly under the capable supervision of the Sufi master can lead to complete destruction of spiritual states. Thus *sama* as a Sufi practice needs to be carefully pursued with *adab* in order to serve the goal of spiritual perfection.

Shaykh Baha al-Din Zakariyya of Multan

The Suhrawardi order in South Asia was established by Baha al-Din Zakariyya, one of the foremost disciples of Shihab al-Din Suhrawardi. He played a major role in upholding the ideals of the newly established order in this region. His *khanqah* in Multan symbolizes the foundation and early history of the *silsila*. Inhabitants of Multan, together with the surrounding areas, regard his hospice as the source of spiritual and religious inspiration. Such was the social influence and spiritual charisma of Baha al-Din that even sultans of Delhi honoured his decisions and chose not to get involved in any direct confrontation with the shaykh.[41] Due to the aversion of Chishti Sufis to government positions, the post of *Shaykh-ul Islam* came to be occupied by one Suhrawardi saint or another. Nur al-Din Mubarak Ghaznavi (d. 1234) held the post in Delhi, Baha al-Din Zakariyya held it in Multan. Maulana Majid al-Din Haji held the position

---

[39] Ibid.
[40] Ibid., 340–341, 347–349.
[41] Qamar-ul Huda, *Striving for Divine Union: Spiritual Exercises for Suhrawardi Sufis* (London: RoutledgeCurzon, 2003), 138–146.

of *sadr*—all of them were disciples of Shihab al-Din Suhrawardi. The acceptability of Suhrawardi Sufis at the court of Delhi made the position of *Shaykh-ul Islam* hereditary for the descendants of Baha al-Din.

With regard to *sama*, the earliest Chishti *malfuzat*, like the *Fawaid-al Fuad*, mentions two incidents from where it is evident that Baha al-Din Zakariyya took part in the exercise. The first record says that, once, Nizam al-Din recalled that one day Baha al-Din Zakariyya was visited by an individual who introduced himself as Abd Allah Rumi. The latter confessed that he had had the good fortune to perform *sama* in the august presence of the great Sufi master, Shihab al-Din Suhrawardi. On hearing this, Baha al-Din Zakariyya, overcome by a deep sense of love and remembrance for his master, thought it incumbent that since his master participated in *sama*, he too should do the same. With this the shaykh instructed one of his aides to take Abd Allah Rumi and his friend to a cell and keep them there till he arrived. As the evening advanced and the late-night prayers were completed, the shaykh finished his invocatory (*awrad*) prayers and proceeded towards the cell where the *qawwal* was kept waiting. Thereafter, as Rumi narrates, 'The shaykh sat down and immersed himself in invocations. He also recited half a section of the Quran. Then he rose and closed the door of the cell and asked "Say something", to which I started doing *sama*. After some time agitation and movement gradually appeared in the shaykh who went up and extinguished the lamp. The cell became dark and I kept performing *sama* in the dark. I only knew what I could feel and every time the shaykh came near only his skirt would become visible, so that I knew that it was he who had become agitated and was moving. But since the cell was dark I did not know whether the shaykh was moving to the beat of the music or not. In short when *sama* was over the shaykh opened the door and returned to his own place.'[42]

Nizam al-Din further narrated that when he was a disciple under the tutelage of Baba Farid al-Din at Ajodhan, he heard the above incident from Abd Allah himself when he came to Ajodhan to visit Baba Farid al-Din.[43] This is reflective of the congenial ambience in which early Sufi orders flourished in South Asia, where mutual respect and compassion is visible rather than any imagined sense of intense spiritual animosity

---

[42] *Fawaid al Fuad*, 135–136; *Morals for the Heart*, 238–239.
[43] *Fawaid al Fuad*, 142; *Morals for the Heart*, 239.

laced with disrespect. When an ordinary *qawwal* like Abd Allah shared his experience with the spiritual master of a different, albeit equally important Sufi order like the Suhrawardi, to a Chishti Sufi saint like Baba Farid al-Din, he witnessed the great degree of respect Sufi masters in South Asia showed towards each other.

Important issues can be deduced from the incident narrated above. If Abd Allah Rumi's travels are mapped from the above description, then he performed *sama* in Baghdad in the *khanqah* of Shihab al-Din Suhrawardi, and thereafter came down to Multan to the *khanqah* of his disciple Baha al-Din Zakariyya. This not only gives us an interesting insight into the networks that connected important centres of Sufi activity like Baghdad (Iraq), Multan, and Ajodhan (Punjab), but it also reinforces the idea of Sufi spirituality being connected beyond territorial and political borders. Contemporary men of learning, piety, and arts like music and poetry, engaged in an itinerant way of life that took them to important centres of the Islamic east. Baghdad was the cultural and intellectual capital of the Islamic world, both as the seat of the Abbasid Caliphate and also due to its rich traditions of learning—spiritual, religious, and legal—that saw men of diverse backgrounds converge within the limits of the city. But the Islamic east at that time was also experiencing tumult, largely due to the dark clouds of Mongol invasions from the steppe regions. Baghdad was not spared either. As a result, Sufis, scholars, and men of letters were forced to leave for safer havens in the east across the Indus River, and into the areas beyond. Thus major trading centres and administrative outposts like Multan, and villages, remote and unheard of, like Ajodhan, became seats of Sufi activities occupied by major orders like the Suhrawardi and Chishti. The visit of Abd Allah Rumi to the *jamaat khanah* of Baba Farid al-Din in Ajodhan pushes us to look beyond territorial boundaries into ideas of transregional mobility and interaction among scholars and men of letters, including important Sufi saints.

The other important fact to be noted here concerns an essential criterion of spiritual training, the master-disciple relation. The *murshid-murid* relation is considered as the foundation of the spiritual path, leading the Sufi novice towards the larger goal of an eventual realization of the Divine. Interestingly, this relation is not limited to the period of actual training under the Sufi master, but continues even after the disciple has been granted the permission to train his own disciples. In spite of being a non-enthusiast for *sama*, Baha al-Din Zakariyya readily agreed to engage in *sama*, since his master, the great Shihab al-Din Suhrawardi, practiced the same. It becomes highly evident that the practice of the *pir-murid* relationship reigned supreme in Sufi orders, reminding us of a famous saying that the *murid* should place himself at the feet of this *pir* just as a corpse is placed in the hands of the washerman. The hidden implication being that, similar to the corpse which has no wish of his own and does not question or behave except in the manner treated by the washerman, the *murid* too should give up all his wishes, and should be completely dependent on his *pir* for guiding him in the spiritual path. Baha al-Din Zakariyya was respecting this very *adab* of spiritual training when he engaged himself in the exercise of *sama*.

The most visible influence of *sama* on the spiritual state of Baha al-Din Zakariyya was manifested through limb movements (*raqs*). The recitation of poetry in the course of *sama* had its effect on the spiritual state of the Suhrawardi saint, who could not restrain himself from *raqs*. While participating in *sama*, Baha al-Din Zakariyya could not ignore the effect poetry brought into the exercise, for verses have a lasting impact on men of the spiritual Path (*ahl-i tasawwuf*). When *sama* had the desired effect on Baha al-Din, his agitated emotions created a stir in the limbs. Hence he could not restrain himself from rising up in response to the impact of ecstasy.

On the issue of *raqs* in *sama*, it may be relevant to elaborate on the Suhrawardi position regarding 'limb movements' when aroused in ecstasy. These insights can be gathered from the famous Suhrawardi manual of etiquette (*adab*) *Adab-al Muridin* (Manners for Disciples), written by Abu Najib Suhrawardi, founder of the Suhrawardi order and uncle of Shihab al-Din Suhrawardi. Abu Najib was himself a mystic of great repute. In his *Kitab*, Abu Najib includes among the many dispensations (*rukhsa*) regulating the quest for spirituality (*tasawwuf*) a section on the manners of Sufi dancing. While commenting on the subject, Abu Najib at the very outset rejects the application of the word *raqs* to Sufi dance on the premise that *raqs* signifies the form of dance we usually recognize as popular and gaudy, and thereby reprehensible in any spiritual assembly.[44]

---

[44] Abu al-Najib al-Suhrawardi, *Kitab Adab al-Muridin,* trans. Menahem Milson, *A Sufi Rule for Novices: Kitab Adab al-Muridin* (Cambridge: Harvard University Press, 1975), 75. Henceforth *Kitab Adab al-Muridin.*

Thereafter Abu Najib argues that while one may surely rise up and move his limbs in *sama*, it is prescribed that the matter be conducted in accordance with the spirit of the assembly. On such occasions it is advised that one should avoid limb movements as much as possible, even if it is participation by his own effort and done completely out of empathy.[45] Only the ones who are in ecstasy should engage in limb movement. However, it may sometimes happen that in an assembly of *sama* listeners are allowed to rise up in *raqs* as a gesture of support to other participants of the assembly. On such occasions it is permissible that an individual not in ecstasy may take part in dance, but under no circumstances should he feign ecstasy.[46]

From the above discussion it thus becomes evident that, contrary to the Chishti practice, Suhrawadi norms did not, under any circumstances, allow the practice of *tawajud* or empathetic ecstasy in *sama* to encourage novices and other participants. This brings into focus the differences in the spiritual approach and training of the two dominant Sufi orders in South Asia. It is incorrect, however, to read into such differences through an 'inferior-superior' binary. Instead, one needs to appreciate the dynamicity these Sufi orders brought into Sufi practices in South Asia through their various ways of training and practice.

In the *Fawaid al Fuad*, Nizam al-Din mentions another incident. When he was twelve years old and engaged one day in the recitation of the Quran, a person called Abu Bakr Kharrat, also known as Abu Bakr Qawwal, came to the presence of his teacher. Abu Bakr said that he had just returned from Multan and had had the good fortune to perform *sama* in the assembly of the renowned master, Baha al-Din Zakariyya.[47] Abu Bakr also recited the verses he had read in the assembly of the Suhrawardi saint:

> Each morning, and again, each evening
> My eyes, due to love of you, keep weeping
> My liver, bitten by the snake of desire
> No doctor nor charmer has the means of curing

---

[45] Ibid.
[46] Ibid.
[47] *Fawaid al Fuad*, 142; *Morals for the Heart*, 251.

The *qawwal* failed to remember the rest of the verse which was added as:

> For none but he who inflames me with desire
> Can, if he chooses, quench that raging fire

Thus, when the verse was completed it came to represent a quartet:

> My liver is pinched by a serpent's deadly bite
> Which no spell, however potent, can hope to right
> Only that one whose love distracts and destroys me
> Can cast a healing spell; who but he knows my plight?[48]

The above verses portray emotions of intense love and pangs of separation, a common theme in *sama* assemblies. It is known that Baha al-Din Zakariyya showed little interest in *sama* as a spiritual exercise. Rather, he considered invocations and remembrance of God (*zikr*) to be the primary way towards spiritual perfection, so that even the common masses of Multan became used to the practice of *zikr* and supererogatory prayers.[49]

However, one should not accept Baha al-Din Zakariyya's approach to *sama* as reflecting the normative position of the Suhrawardi order. Interestingly, later generations of Suhrawardi Sufis did appreciate *sama* as a spiritual exercise. Chishti master Qazi Hamid al-Din Nagauri was recognized in Chishti circles, as well as in court chronicles, as an emphatic supporter of *sama*. Being close to Qutb al-Din Bakhtiyar Kaki, Hamid al-Din Nagauri spent many evenings in Chishti *jamaat khanas*, participating in *sama* with rapt attention. Qazi Hamid al-Din liked *sama* accompanied by stringed instruments like *chang*, stating that he had heard *sama* with musical instruments many times and would continue to listen in the same manner whenever it was organized. So close was Hamid al-Din to his Chishti contemporary that he chose to be buried in the same premises that housed the shrine of Bakhtiyar Kaki.[50]

---

[48] *Fawaid al Fuad*, 143; *Morals for the Heart*, 251.

[49] Huda, *Spiritual Exercises*, 147.

[50] The *dargah* of Qazi Hamid al-Din Nagauri, in the interior of the Mehrauli area in modern-day New Delhi, overlooks the spacious open courtyard containing the tomb of Shaykh Qutb al-Din Bakhtiyar Kaki. It is perhaps the only instance where two leading Sufi masters of different orders (*silsila*) share their last resting place within the same *dargah* complex. The marble epitaph of the Suhrawardi master reads: *Mazar Mubarak. Hazrat Qazi Bandagi Shaykh Hamid al-Din*

Such was Hamid al-Din's love for *sama* that on many occasions as he immersed himself in the exercise his critics would issue *fatwas* against him, insisting that *sama* was forbidden. Once there was a jurist (*faqih*) who frequently visited Hamid al-Din. However, the jurist too issued a fatwa that *sama* was a forbidden exercise. When Qazi Hamid al-Din came to know of this he called the jurist and enquired about the legal ruling (*fatwa*) he had passed. The *faqih* became embarrassed in front of Hamid al-Din, and gently nodded his head in affirmation. Qazi Hamid al-Din replied that those who have decreed *sama* as forbidden are, in his eyes, still in their mother's womb—that is, they lack the requisite spiritual maturity to understand an issue as serious as *sama*. Then, looking at the jurist, Hamid al-Din stated that though he considered him out of his mother's womb, he was yet too young to deliberate on issues like *sama*.

What is striking is that despite being a Suhrawardi saint and at the same time a *qazi*, Hamid al-Din Nagauri whole-heartedly supported the exercise of *sama*. So much so that it irked the *ulama*, who, led by the notorious Qadi Sad and Qadi Imad, approached the then Sultan of Delhi, Iltutmish, to arbitrate on the issue and deliver judgement. They raised the issue of religious mockery and brought to the attention of the Sultan that as a result of Qazi Hamid al-Din's support of *sama*, together with his elaborate *sama* parties, the 'entire city has fallen victim to this mischief'. The Sultan, while keeping with the arguments forwarded by his *qazis*, called an arbitration council (*mahzar*) to decide on the issue. When Qazi Hamid al-Din Nagauri entered the assembly, the Sultan received him with utmost respect and seated the Sufi master by his side. While arguing in favour of *sama*, Hamid al-Din Nagauri stated that *sama* is for the spiritually adept, who find themselves closer to the realm of the Divine. In the same breath it is prohibited for worldly individuals who seek nothing but material pleasures from such an assembly. It ought to be noted that although he did not clarify the category of 'worldly individuals', he was perhaps including lay participants, and critics like the *ulama*. Going further, he stated that it was Iltutmish's participation, as a young slave boy, in the *sama* assemblies of Baghdad that earned him the blessings of the leading Sufis of the time, which in turn proved instrumental in his rise as the Sultan of Hindustan.[51]

Though the veracity of the incident, together with Iltutmish's spiritual inclination, needs further investigation, it goes without saying that Hamid al-Din Nagauri was able to undermine all voices that were raised against his practice of *sama*. By invoking the memories of spiritual blessings received by the young Iltutmish from Sufis in Baghdad, the shaykh at once ruled out any chances of a royal judgement against *sama*. It therefore ably demonstrates the authority of the Suhrawardi shaykh. His excellent skills in defending the exercise of *sama* made the most powerful political authority of the day remain silent in the face of spirited criticism from the *ulama* and religious scholars.[52] This is highly significant and illustrative of the position and authority Suhrawardi Sufis wielded in the Delhi Sultanate. In spite of the ambiguity over the validity of the action, that matters could be resolved so swiftly and with such dignity showed the spiritual influence of the Suhrawardi *silsila* to mould royal opinion in their favour.

The above discussion shows *sama* as a spiritual exercise acceptable to Suhrawardi saints in South Asia and beyond, though they showed little spiritual and emotional attachment towards the practice, unlike their Chishti contemporaries. Shihab al-Din Suhrawardi's disposition towards *sama* may have been influenced by his great predecessor, Junaid of Baghdad. The *Awarif* is replete with Junaid's teachings and remarks, including his position on *sama*—that of indifference and aloofness, if not outright dismissal of the ritual.

Most importantly, the Suhrawardi position on *sama* brings forth the plurality of South Asia's socio-cultural milieu, reflected, among other things, through Sufi masters and their practices in this region. The arrival of the earliest Sufi orders like the Chishti and Suhrawardi, and their influences on each other as far as spiritual practices were concerned, reveals an important dimension of Sufism in South Asia. We now turn towards exploring the remaining part of these shared spiritual practices, through the Chishti engagement with the exercise of *zikr*.

---

[51] Maulana Isami, *Futuh al-salatin ya shahnama-i Hind* (Agra: The Educational Press, 1938), 119.

[52] Huda, *Spiritual Exercises*, 121.

Chishti Approach to *Zikr*

It is interesting that the participation of Suhrawardis in *sama*, and the Chishti engagement with *zikr*, came to be witnessed in regions where these two orders started their careers in South Asia—Multan for the Suhrawardi, and Ajmer for the Chishti. Suhrawardi saints in Delhi enjoyed the company of their Chishti counterparts in assemblies of *sama*. In the Deccan, Chishti Sufis like Gisu Daraz regularized the practice of *zikr*, while writing on it.[53]

Chishti Sufis believed that there exists a hidden (*ghaib*) relation between man and God that forms the basis of the path (*tariqa*) that leads the Sufi saint closer to God. The stages of spiritual progress elaborated by Chishti Sufis included one's approach to life, the surrounding world, and religion, apart from spiritual beliefs. The first stage consisted of the *shariah*, or law, that was seen as the foundation for all spiritual training. This stage not only involved the study of religious law, but also of Islamic sciences, jurisprudence, and traditions of the Prophet. The second stage constituted the *tariqa*, or the path a Sufi had to follow towards his spiritual goal, which passed through his initial training on the principles of the spiritual path, and the particular Sufi order into which he was initiated. Only when the disciple interiorizes this initial training is he led to the stage of *marifat*. In the last stage of *haqiqat*, the complete realization of the Divine occurs through esoteric knowledge when the Sufi reaches the final stages of the spiritual journey and is a witness to Divine revelation. While the above-mentioned four stages remain the classic framework for spiritual training, some Chishti Sufis, mostly from the Deccan, add the stage of nearness (*maqam-e qurb*). They argue that when the Sufi reaches the stage of being under the complete protection of God, then all his actions are by Divine consent. The Sufi seeker is allowed a greater degree of proximity through the stage of nearness. This stage is probably achieved by Sufis in the course of the state of permanence (*baqa*), after he has annihilated his 'self' in God.[54]

For the Chishti practice of *zikr* we turn towards Deccan, where the leading disciple of the north Indian Sufi master Nasir al-Din

---

[53] Richard Eaton, *Sufis of Bijapur* (Princeton: Princeton University Press, 1978), 144.
[54] Ibid., 146.

Mahmud—Muhammad Husayni Gisu Daraz—arrived in the early fif-
teenth century. Gisu Daraz left behind in his works a rich collection of
zikr practices that he prescribed for attaining a variety of spiritual benefits. The description of individual *zikr* exercises is available to us in great
detail through the various works written by this Chishti master during
his days in the Deccan. In the following section we turn to a discussion of
these *zikr* practices, which constituted an important spiritual practice for
Chishti Sufis. Gisu Daraz emphasized the importance of *zikr* as a mandatory spiritual exercise, so that later Sufi masters considered it to be a
beneficial way of engaging their disciples on the path towards spiritual
progress. An elaboration of the various *zikr* practices will provide us with
a comprehensive idea as to how this ritual came to occupy a place of importance within a Sufi order that considered *sama* to be their spiritual
sine qua non.

The perfect way of performing *zikr,* according to Khwaja Gisu Daraz, is
when the seeker of the Divine sits alone in a dark room before the break of
dawn or between the evening (*maghrib*) and night (*isha*) prayers. He has
to sit cross-legged, with a straight back, placing his hands on the thighs.
Sitting in this position, he should use the big toe and the one next to it
of the right foot to firmly press the sciatic nerve (*rag-i kimas*) that runs
behind the left knee. While doing this he should gradually relieve himself of all worldly shackles that bind his heart, and at the same time continue to repeat *La Ilaha* (no God) in specific beats. When repeating this
negation his eyes should remain open, and while verifying the truth *Ila
'llah* (but Allah) the individual has to be aware of the reality that none except God exists. After ten beats (*zarb*) he should recite *Muhammad Rasul
Allah* (Muhammad, the Prophet of Allah). Following this schedule, the
Sufi should practice *zikr* as frequently as he can.[55]

In *zikr*, the beats should be strong and done in a loud voice. The individual doing *zikr* should make an effort to show that this voice originates
from within the heart. While doing *zikr* it is important for the practitioner (*zakir*) to always keep in mind that he is witnessing God. In such
a condition one should not be forgetful (*gafil*) of God, or else there will
be no benefits coming forth from the exercise. When *zikr* is undertaken

---

[55] *Khatima*, 158–159; Scott Kugle, ed., *Sufi Meditation and Contemplation: Timeless Wisdom from Mughal India* (New York: Omega Publications, 2012), 57–58.

in this manner, Gisu Daraz remarks that, together with *zikr*, meditation (*muraqaba*) is also practiced. Thus it brings dual benefits for the *zakir*. It should also be remembered that while doing *zikr*, if one is mindful of the suspension of breath (*habs-i dam*), it diminishes the impact of danger.[56]

This kind of *zikr* can be done in two ways. The first way is that in which the beats are done in a high-pitched and loud voice. This is called *zikr-i jali*. The second is that in which the beats are done with the hand (*ba hastgi*). This is called *zikr-i khafi*.

If *zikr* is practiced by the tongue then it is called *ta'alluqa*, and if it is done from the heart then it is called *susa*. *Zikr* of the heart is popularly called *zikr-i khafi*. This *zikr* takes place within the heart, where it is applied according to the beat of the heart. Two ways are suggested for undertaking this *zikr*. The first one involves guarding/taking care of the external being. In this method, although the *zikr* takes place within the heart, the body receives some agitation externally as well. In the second form there is no guarding/taking care of the external being. That is, the external body receives no agitation while doing *zikr*, which is applied simply to the beats of the heart. The second process of doing *zikr* is believed to bring great benefit to the practitioner who shows greater restraint by maintaining his external calmness while continuing to perform *zikr* internally.

The individual who undertakes *zikr-i khafi* loses himself completely in the contemplation of the Unseen. The *zakir* reaches a stage where no object disturbs his spiritual state and the quality of his meditation. Gradually the *zakir* is annihilated in the essence of the God, losing his own being (*wujud*). There is nothing worldly left in him, and he is enveloped in the Divine light that surrounds him. No grief or fear remains in him. This state is achieved only through the quality of his *zikr*.

When the stage of Divine witnessing is reached, the *zakir* is prepared for performing the *zikr-i ruhi* (meditation of the soul), which is also known by its quality of witnessing (*mushahada*). When doing this *zikr*, the individual reaches the stage where he imagines a state in the presence of God, sitting in front of him and witnessing His glory. This is called *zikr-i ruhi*, because the soul (*ruh*) witnesses the Divine splendour, and together with the *zakir* his soul does *zikr* as well. This is understandably

---

[56] *Khatima*, 167–168.

a higher stage of practicing *zikr*, where the *zakir* progresses from vocal repetition through the tongue to silent repetition through the soul.

Apart from the above two types of *zikr*, Gisu Daraz mentions a third type, called *zikr-i sar*, and this is also known as the act of survey (*mo'ayana*). When the difference between the two acts of *mo'ayana* and *mushahada* is elaborated, it can be argued that *zikr-i sar* lies somewhere between *zikr-i khafi* and *zikr-i ruhi,* where the latter is the highest form of *zikr* practice. In these practices of recollection, *mushahada* is compared to the act of beholding in broad sunlight where no ambiguity remains. Whatever was hidden is unveiled without any trace of opaqueness in it. *Mo'ayana* has been compared to the act of seeing during dawn, when sunlight is yet to reach its full brightness. Hence some amount of darkness remains. The act of witnessing does not happen clearly, since a light veil continues to hang, creating a sense of opaqueness. Thus, in *zikr*, only when an individual reaches the stage of *mushahada* is the truth unveiled to him. This experience during *zikr-i ruhi* is known as *kashf-i haqiqat* (unveiling of truth).[57]

The *Khatima* lists three ways of doing *zikr* of the essential divine names of Allah (*ism-i zat*). First, while suspending the breath (*habs-i dam*) and keeping eyes open, one should repeat 'Allah Allah' to such an extent that darkness descends in front of the eyes and the tongue becomes numb. By doing this *zikr*, the heart involuntarily begins to remember and praise God. After a certain period of rigorous striving with this *zikr*, all the limbs and vital organs of the body appear to be remembering God. After some time, the Sufi achieves the state of annihilation in God (*fana fillah*) and permanence in God (*baqa billah*).[58]

The second method of *zikr* is by observing the breath (*pas anfas*). While releasing the breath one should say 'no God' (*la ilaha*), and when drawing in breath one should say 'but Allah' (*ila 'llah*). Or else one should continuously repeat 'you ... you' (*hu hu*) and engage himself deeply in the exercise.

The third *zikr* involves repeating 'ha ... hu'. This *zikr* is called *Zikr-i Award wa Burd*, and is supposedly from the established custom of

---

[57] S. S. K. Hussaini, ed., *Fawaid az Maktubat* (Gulbarga: All India Sayyid Muhammad Gisu Daraz Research Academy, 2014), 44–46.
[58] *Khatima*, 160; Kugle, *Sufi Meditation*, 67.

Ghaus-al Azam Abdul Qadir Gilani. To perform this *zikr*, one has to sit cross-legged and bend his head forward towards the belly. Then, turning his head towards the right shoulder he should say '*ha*' (He), and turning his head towards the left shoulder he should say '*hu*' (You). One should apply the beat while keeping the head low.

The other way of doing *zikr* by observing the breath (*pas anfas*) is to visualize 'no God' (*la ilaha*) while exhaling. While doing this *zikr* through inhaling and exhaling, the focus should be on the navel 'as it is drawn in and extended out during breathing'.[59]

Meditation on the essential divine names of Allah can be done through multiple beats. For one beat (*zikr-i yek zarbi*) the individual has to sit in the aforementioned manner, on both knees, and focus gradually on the right shoulder. Then, repeating *Allahu Akbar*, one should apply one beat on the left side. This process has to be repeated continuously. Once familiar with this *zikr*, one may keep their eyes open and, in a pure body, picture to oneself the image of God.

For doing this same *zikr* in another manner, the individual should keep both hands on his thigh. Then, while repeating *Allahu Akbar*, one should firmly pull the stomach upwards. Repeating *Allahu Akbar* for the second time, he should direct the beat below the navel. Following one step at a time, the *zakir* should continue doing *zikr* in this way.

Seated on the knees in a well-attended assembly, the above *zikr* should be done by starting to repeat *Allah* from the side of the right shoulder and ending by directing it towards the left side. From this point one should start repeating '*hu*', and turn the head towards the right shoulder. This cycle of doing *zikr* should be continuously followed.[60]

While doing 'Meditation of two beats' (*zikr-i do zarbi*), the phrase 'no God' (*la ilaha*) is recited in one beat towards the right shoulder. And the second phrase, 'but Allah' (*ila 'llah*), is recited towards the left shoulder. After the third or fifth or seventh or ninth repetition of this phrase, one should say '*Muhammad rasul Allah*' (Muhammad is the Prophet of Allah).[61]

---

[59] *Khatima*, 160.
[60] Ibid., 163.
[61] Ibid., 161.

When doing the 'Meditation of three beats' (*zikr-i se zarbi*), the first beat should be applied on the right side, the second beat on the left side, and the final third beat should be directed towards the heart.

'Meditation of four beats' (*zikr-i chahar zarbi*) is done in four beats. While sitting on the knees, one should drag 'la' from between the two knees towards the left knee. And '*ila*' should be recited towards the right shoulder. Then '*ha*' should be recited towards the left knee and arm, and the fourth beat of '*ila 'llah*' should be placed on the heart.

'Meditation of five beats' (*zikr-i panj zarbi*) is done in five beats. In this *zikr*, starting from the left side, the recitation of '*la ilaha*' should be done towards the right shoulder. And the beat of '*ila 'llah*' should be repeated after raising the bone of the right shoulder. Then, after taking the head towards the back, it should be brought towards the left shoulder and the phrase repeated once again. Then, bringing the head halfway down to the back, the phrase should be repeated once. Then bringing both shoulders closer to the ears, the phrase should be repeated once. Then one rises up from the ground on one's knees and repeats the phrase five times. After this the entire cycle should be started again from the beginning. In this *zikr* the suspension of breath (*habs-i dam*) is considered important and should be always remembered by the *zakir*.

In 'Meditation of seven beats' (*zikr-i haft zarbi*) the head should be lowered towards the ground, and while repeating '*la ilaha*' the head should be raised slowly. Then, while looking at the sky, '*ila 'llah*' should be repeated. Again, the head should be bowed towards the ground and the phrase repeated. The phrase should be repeated again, once towards the left, once towards the right, once at the front, and once bending towards the back. At the end all seven repetitions should be done in one's heart while sitting straight and keeping the head high.

When these recitations are directed towards the heart, the benefit is that the heat produced by the heart from such deep meditation melts away the impurities that accumulate around one's heart. Through the practice of this *zikr*, the *zakir* is secured from misfortunes.

In 'Meditation of sixteen beats' (*zikr-i shanzdah zarbi*), one should sit on both knees and keep the hands on the thigh. After this one should spin the head three times. During this *la ilaha* has to be repeated with the suspension of breath (*habs-i dam*). Then, keeping one's focus on the belly, *ila 'llah* should be repeated thrice while drawing the breath from deep below.

Then *ila 'llah* should be repeated again. One repetition should be done towards the left knee, one towards the right knee, and one repetition should be done between the two knees.[62]

A beginner who seeks benefits from such complex litanies of *nafi wa asbat* (negation and proof) requires the supervision of and instruction from an adept Sufi master. When the master explains the significance of repeating *la ilaha ila 'llah* to the disciple, then the latter is secured from any dangers that could result from possible mistakes while doing *zikr*. At the same time, the disciple continues to derive benefits from this *zikr*. While repeating *ila 'llah* externally (*zahir*) through the mouth, the disciple should also repeat *maujud ila 'llah* (there is none present but he) within himself (*batin*). In this case, therefore, the practice of *zikr* happens simultaneously—vocally through the mouth and silently within the heart. When repeating *ila 'llah*, the disciple should bow his head close to the ground, then raise it again. After this he should bow his head again towards the ground on the right side then lift it up. This exercise should be repeated continuously.[63]

When 'Meditation of affirmation' (*zikr-i isbat*) is done in one beat at a well-attended assembly, the *zakir* should sit silently on his knees and repeat *ila 'llah* from the tongue. Externally he should keep in mind that there is none other than Allah (*la maujud ila 'llah*). When this same *zikr* is done in two beats (*do zarbi*), the disciple has to repeat one beat on the knee, and for the second beat he has to bend slightly towards the front and repeat the phrase directed at the left elbow. While repeating *ila 'llah*, the head should be bent closer to the ground and lifted. Again, while repeating the phrase the head should be bent towards the ground on the right and lifted back. In this way repetitions should continue. When this same *zikr* is done in three beats (*se zarbi*), one beat has to be applied while sitting on the knees, the other beat has to be applied between the shoulders, and the third beat between the thighs. All the while *ila 'llah* should be continuously recited and applied towards the heart. One step at a time, the *zakir* should continue to do *zikr* in this way.[64]

---

[62] Ibid., 161–162.
[63] Ibid., 162.
[64] Ibid.

In the 'Meditation of non-termination' (*zikr-i mutanahi*), one should sit on his knees. Then, starting from the left knee, one should repeat *hu* in one breath and direct it towards the right knee.[65]

Some miscellaneous *zikr* practices pertain to various realms of the Divine. The benefits that are obtained from such recollections originate from that particular realm after which these meditations are named. The first of these is 'Meditation from the Realm of Divinity' (*zikr-i lahut*). In this *zikr* the head should be moved towards the left shoulder blade and bent towards the back, while repeating *hu* continuously. During this repetition one beat should be directed towards oneself. The focus should be on the same position. Then the head should be moved again towards the left shoulder blade while repeating *hu* continuously. One beat should now be directed towards the right side. After this, two beats should be applied on the left knee and two between the two knees, and one beat should be directed to oneself. Thereafter, two beats should be directed at the right knee and one towards the left side.

The head should be taken closer to the right shoulder blade, repeating *hu*. One beat should be applied to the left side. Then, placing the hips on the ground, the body should be straightened in small measures. Thereafter one should sit on both knees and apply three beats. Then one should again move from the left towards the right and begin all over again from the first position.

After this is the 'Meditation from the Realm of Omnipotence' (*Zikr-i Jabrut*). In this *zikr,* the head needs to be lowered close to the ground between the knees while repeating '*ya ahad*' (O! One). Thereafter, one beat should be applied after repeating *ya wahid*. Then *ya ahad* and *ya wahid* should be repeated together, continuously for ten times. And seven beats should be applied while repeating *Allah*. Then one should again begin from the first position.

Next is the 'Meditation from the Realm of Angels' (*zikr-i Malkut*). In this *zikr* one beat should be applied towards the left knee while repeating *ya hadiya*. One beat should be applied towards the right side while repeating *ya bais*. One beat should be applied towards the right knee while

[65] Ibid., 163.

repeating *ya nur.* One beat should be applied towards the left side of the body while repeating *ya samir.* Then one beat should be applied repeating *Allah.* Then one should again begin from the first position.

Finally is the 'Meditation of the Realm of Material World' (*zikr-i Nasut*). In this *zikr* the head should be placed between the knees thrice, and while raising the head one has to repeat *Allah.* The beat of *ya Allah* should be applied towards oneself. Then the head should be placed back in the previous position and the beat of *ya Allah* should be directed towards the left knee. The head should again be placed in the position between the two knees, and the beat of *ya Allah* should now be directed towards the right knee, following the previous method.

Nasir al-Din Mahmud, the principal disciple of Nizam al-Din in Delhi, prescribed a *zikr* where the head should be turned from the left shoulder blade towards the right shoulder blade while repeating *la ilaha.* From there one should apply the beat of *ila 'llah* towards the left knee, and remain continuously engaged in repeating this process.

Being located in the region of Punjab, Baba Farid al-Din's contribution to the local vernacular of Punjabi is well recorded. It is not surprising therefore that Baba Farid al-Din, the spiritual mentor of Nizam al-Din, and one of the premier Sufi masters of the Chishti order, prescribed a *zikr* in the local vernacular. In this *zikr* the disciple, while looking at the sky, has to repeat '*Aho Tu*' (Bless me O Lord!) while continuing to look at the sky for some time. Then, while looking towards the ground, he should repeat *Aho Tu* and continue looking towards the ground for some time. In between these two repetitions he should continuously say '*Haan Hain Tu*' three to seven times. After this he should again start from the beginning. This *zikr* is useful for removing the veil of separation and attaining closeness to Beloved God.[66]

Gisu Daraz recommended that after an individual finishes meditation in a loud voice (*zikr-i jali*) and the meditation of negation and affirmation (*zikr-i nafy o isbat*), the light of Divine grace (*nur inayat*) begins to shine brightly within his heart. At this moment he should deeply engage in the meditation of the hidden (*zikr-i khafi*). There are three types of *zikr-i khafi*:

---

[66] Ibid., 164.

1. Pas Anfas (observing the breath): while engaged in continuous and deep meditation, one should say 'no God' (*la ilaha*) when releasing the breath, and when drawing in the breath one should say 'but Allah' (*ila 'llah*).

2. Zikr Qalb: with strong determination one should practice suspension of the breath (*habs-i dam*) and create an image before oneself of the essential divine names of Allah (*ism-i zat*) to shake up the heart. While breathing the belly should be firmly pulled upwards, and then released downwards. This action should be repeated. When one feels suffocated, he should release his breath. After a while the exercise should be repeated.

3. Zikr Istila: it is important for the traveller on the Sufi Path to always remember the *Kalima Taiyyaba*. When reciting the *kalima* the tongue should touch the palate. Then, while suspending the breath, one should begin with *lam* from the right shoulder blade. *Alif* following *lam* should be dragged to the left shoulder. *Ila* should be recited between *alif* and *lam*, and *illa 'llah* should be directed towards the heart.[67]

The benefits accrued from *zikr* are believed to cleanse the heart and remove all veils that separate it from the Divine, so that the Sufi experiences states of unveiling (*mukashifa*) and witnessing (*mushahada*).

The 'meditation of fana wa baqa' (*zikr-i fana wa baqa*) is also called *nafy o isbat award wa burd*. While doing this *zikr* the first beat should be applied to the heart. The second beat has to be directed either towards the heart while bowing the head down towards the ground or towards the left side and the heart or the right side and the heart. All those who perform this *zikr* place both their knees on the ground while holding them with their hands. While doing this *zikr* one has to visualize God in front of their eyes through the recitation of any of the following phrases. The unveiling of the Divine secrets is supposed to occur according to the attribute of the litany on which *zikr* is done:

1. *la mabud ila 'llah*
2. *la maujud ila 'llah*

---

[67] Ibid., 165.

3. *la matlub ila 'llah*
4. *la mashud ila 'llah*

There are multiple ways of doing the above *zikr*:

1. One has to keep the right knee erect, and place the left knee in a flat position. Then he should sit on the left leg in a manner done during prayers. The chest has to be stretched towards the heart. In this position one beat of *la ilaha* should be applied on the knee that is erect. The second beat of *ila 'llah* should be directed towards the heart.
2. One should stand on both knees and the chest should be tightly stretched towards the heart. One beat should be on the right side and one towards the heart.
3. While balancing on one knee one has to bow the body forward (*ruku*) like in prayer. The other knee should be left lying. *Zikr* should be continued in this posture.
4. Another way of doing this *zikr* is while standing one should put the right foot forward by one step and with great resolve repeat *la ilaha*. And *ila 'llah* should be directed towards the heart while pulling the step back.
5. In a position of lying flat, the first beat should be directed towards the right side and the second beat on the left side.
6. While holding a crutch handle (*zafar takiya*) to the chest, one beat should be applied upwards while looking up, and the other beat has to be applied downwards while looking down.
7. While sitting on the knees one should hold the big toe of the right foot with the right hand, and do similarly for the left foot. Then one beat of *la ilaha* should be applied on the right shoulder and *ila 'llah* should be directed towards the heart.
8. The last method of doing this *zikr* is that while lowering the head close to the navel the individual should recite *la ilaha* and stretch it towards the right shoulder, then *ila 'llah* should be directed towards the heart.[68]

[68] Ibid., 167–171.

It is also recommended that the practice of *zikr* is done with the Quran so that the individual beholds the manifestation of Divine glory. This exercise of recollection is known as 'Meditation of the revelation of Quran' (*zikr kashf-i Quran*). Four copies of the Quran have to be placed—one each in front, on the left, and on the right, and the fourth copy on the lap. The first beat has to be directed towards the Quran on the right, the second to the Quran on one's lap. In the second round the first beat should be directed towards the Quran on the left, and the second directed towards the Quran on the front. In the benefit of this *zikr* the doer is believed to receive the manifestation (*tajalli*) of the Quran from God. In the second method, after placing a Quran in front one beat should be directed towards it. The second beat should be directed towards the heart. In the benefit of this *zikr* the manifestation of God's glory is received by the *zakir*.[69]

Zikr-i nuri is prescribed for those who desire the divine light of God. This meditation is done while sitting in front of a burning fireplace. The first beat in this *zikr* should be directed towards the fire, signifying the burning of any distraction in the way of remembering Allah. The second beat is to be directed towards the heart, keeping the essence of Oneness (*wahid*) alive. By the beneficence of this *zikr*, Divine light (*anwar*) is revealed in the heart and mind of the individual doing this exercise.[70]

Zikr-i abdal is recommended for those who have experienced Divine light. In this *zikr* both hands should be stretched upwards towards the sky in a manner as if light from the Divine realm is being received. Then both hands should be brought close to the mouth and *ila 'llah* be recited. Through this practice Divine light is captured. In this *zikr* one should rush forward with the first beat, and during the second beat one should sit firmly in one's place. This *zikr* can also be done in a standing position.

Another way of doing this *zikr* is that *la ilaha* should be directed towards the heart while taking both hands close to it. Then, after closing the fists, the hands should be pointed upwards, indicating that all distractions are thrown out from the heart. Thereafter the fists should be released. After this one has to visualize that Divine light is descending upon him and at the same time close the fists. While reciting *ila 'llah* one

[69] Ibid., 170.
[70] Ibid.

beat should be applied to the heart. Then, bringing the hands closer to the heart, the fists should be opened.

In this particular *zikr*, both methods carry great merit. When someone does this *zikr*, the *abdals* come closer to him and participate in this exercise as well.[71]

Illumination of the heart also takes place through the practice of *zikr-i nur*. In this *zikr* one beat should be applied towards the heart. Then, turning towards the right side, one should say *ya nur*. Then turning towards the left one has to say *ya nur al-nur*. While reciting *ya munawwar al-nur*, one strong beat should be applied to the heart. If this *zikr* can be done regularly without fail, then soon the heart will be illuminated.[72]

Many *zikr* exercises are prescribed in order to aid Sufis realize the unveiling (*kashf*) of various states. These include *zikr kashf-i arwah*, *zikr kashf-i qubur*, *zikr kashf-i haqaiq*, and *zikr kashf-i malakut*.

Through the practice of *zikr kashf-i arwah*, the condition of any soul is revealed in any place. One should sit in the normal position of *zikr*. Then *ya rab* has to be recited twenty-one times. Then, raising the head towards the sky, one should say *ya ruh*. After this, *ya ruh al-ruh* has to be recited once, with force upon the heart. One will meet the soul, and can ask for anything. Nasir al-Din Mahmud Chiragh-i Dehli taught this meditation to Gisu Daraz.

Zikr kashf-i qubur is the method that can be used to discover the state of those in graves, whether they are in *sawab* or *aazab*, or if any other issue needs to be known. The method is to sit close to the grave facing towards the face of the deceased. Then lifting the head high, one has to say *ya nur*. Then in a strong beat towards the heart one should say *akshif li*. Then with a strong beat towards the deceased person one should say *an halihi*. The soul will appear and the complete state will be known. When this *zikr* is practiced thoroughly, it is no longer required to physically visit the grave. One can practice *kashf al-arwah* from home or from anywhere else in a state of purity.[73]

---

[71] Ibid., 171.
[72] Ibid., 174.
[73] Ibid., 173.

To practice *zikr kashf-i haqaiq*, one has to turn the face towards the sky and say *ya ahad*, then *ya samad*. One beat should be applied on the heart. These two beats can also be applied to the left and the right side.

In *zikr kashf-i malakut* the unveiling occurs and angels can be seen. They talk to the individual undertaking the *zikr*. On the left side one should say *sabukh* and on the right side one should say *quddus*. Then, facing the heart, one should say *rabbul malaekat wa al-ruh*.[74]

For one's prayers to be answered the *zikr ijabat dawat* has to be practiced. The individual should turn the face towards his right side and say *ya kareeb*, and after turning on the left side he should say *ya raqeeb*. While maintaining focus on the heart one should say *ya muhito*, then raising the head upwards one should say *ya mujeeb*. It is recommended that this meditation is practiced regularly. When the individual stands on his knees, opens his hands towards the sky, and prays while visualizing his master, then all his prayers will be answered. Also, from the tradition of the great master Ibn al-Arabi it is known that *ya rabb* has to be said on the right side, and also on the left side and within the heart. Then turning the face towards the sky, one should say *ya rabbi*.[75]

A number of smaller *zikr* litanies are prescribed that may not be as efficacious as ones detailed above, but are nonetheless suggested for the various kinds of hidden benefits that they may bring about in the spiritual career of the Sufi practitioner. In *zikr -i hawashi*, one should place all five fingers of the right hand on the forehead, then it should be placed on the right shoulder, then on the left shoulder, and finally on the heart.[76]

Zikr ya hu should be recited first on the right side, then on the left side, then moving forward it should be recited again, and on the fourth time it should be directed towards the heart. In *zikr-i hu* one should turn the mouth towards the right side and say *hu*, then the same is to be repeated on the left side, then a strong beat should be applied to the heart after saying *hu*.[77]

In *zikr la hu ila hu* the head should be lowered towards the heart, and while reciting *la hu* the head should be taken towards the right shoulder. One should imagine that all that distracts him from God has been thrown

---

[74] Ibid., 175.
[75] Ibid., 173–174.
[76] Ibid., 171.
[77] Ibid., 172.

out of the heart, behind him. Then while reciting *ila hu* one beat should be applied on the heart. The passion for the One should be firmly confirmed within the heart. While doing *zikr tajalli zaat*, the face should be turned towards the right side with the recitation of *illa hae*, and while turning to the left side *Allah hae* should be repeated. Finally, one beat should be applied on the heart.[78]

Zikr-i haqq is practiced in pursuit of divine beneficence. In the first three beats the individual should recite *haqq* and the fourth beat should be applied strongly to the heart. In the course of this *zikr* many fearful things are revealed to the *zakir*. If this can be withstood and tolerated, then the individual will be prepared for great things ahead.

While doing *zikr-i hindi* one needs to sit in the posture of yogis. Then while turning the face towards the sky, he should say *wahi hain*. This should be repeated a minimum of 1,000 times.

Zikr-i ism shaykh requires continuous repetition of the name of the Sufi master. In this *zikr* one should turn the face towards the sky and direct a beat at the heart. This should be repeated 1,000 times. When done diligently, this *zikr* can prove very beneficial for the *zakir*.[79]

In *zikr dafa imraz wa askam* one should recite *ya ahad* on the right side, and *ya samad* on the left side, and *ya farid* towards the heart. *Zikr mashi iqdam* is done when walking briskly, lifting every step and placing it on the ground while repeating *ila 'llah*. When walking leisurely *ila* should be recited on placing one step, and on placing the other step *'llah* should be said. If one is walking silently then he should say *la* when placing the right foot, and *'llah* when placing the left foot. In doing *zikr-i aruz* one beat should be placed on the left side, the right side, above the head, and towards the heart, while repeating *ali ya rafi.*[80]

Chishti Etiquette (*Adab*) in *Zikr*

Similar to the spiritual exercise of *sama*, the practice of *zikr* needs to be combined with strict discipline and proper conduct, irrespective of the

---

[78] Ibid., 173.
[79] Ibid., 174.
[80] Ibid., 175.

spiritual maturity of the Sufi participant. In the Chishti practice of *zikr*, as elaborated above, the earliest instructions on etiquette and conduct in the assembly can be traced to the writings of Khwaja Gisu Daraz in Deccan. He mentions in the *Khatima* that the inspiration for enumerating the details of rules and manners during the exercise of *zikr* was derived from a work entitled *Minhaj al-Salik ila Ashraf al-Masalik* (The Spiritual Seeker's Method to Reach the Noblest of Goals).[81] He goes on to remark that the *Minhaj* lists twenty rules to be followed during the exercise of *zikr*. Of these five should be adhered to before starting *zikr*, twelve should be followed during the practice of *zikr*, and the remaining three after the exercise is over.

The following manners are advised to be followed prior to beginning the exercise of *zikr*:

1. *Tauba* (Repentance)

Before beginning the exercise of *zikr*, it is mandatory for the participant to seek repentance for all his misdeeds that he may have committed knowingly or unknowingly. This is the primary moral responsibility emphasized in the Holy Quran for all those who desire to tread on the spiritual path towards the Divine. Mere training in the principles of the path does not place a Sufi in the 'station of nearness' (*maqam-i qurb*) to God. Rather, it is imperative that he must purify himself from within by repenting for his mistakes and wrongful actions before surrendering to the will of God.

2. Eitmenan (Calmness/Tranquility)

For a Sufi, the state of calmness within the heart is considered one of the most important preconditions for the exercise of *zikr*. If the heart of the Sufi is crowded by affairs of the material world, the mind then will be distracted by thoughts that take him away from the spiritual path. Thus, to engage in the exercise of *zikr* without proper resolve of the heart turns it into a futile effort.

---

[81] Ibid., 157; Kugle, *Sufi Meditation*, 41–43.

3. Taharat (Purity/Cleanliness)

The quality of purity is not attained only by conforming to it by words of the mouth. Pure are those who do not deter from the path of God, irrespective of the outcome. It is therefore important that those who travel on the spiritual path should purify their hearts of all insidious tendencies so that the light of the Divine (nur) can penetrate and illumine the heart. On the contrary, if the heart is occupied with thoughts of an impure and worldly nature, then it is impossible for Divine light to penetrate it, since it is well known that purity and malaise cannot reside together in the heart of any spiritual seeker.

4. Seek help from the spiritual master (istimdad)

Advice from Nizam al-Din Awliya describes best the action of seeking help by the disciple from his master (shaykh) during spiritual exercises. Although Nizam al-Din mentioned this with regard to the practice of sama, it can nonetheless be applied to the practice of zikr as well. When queried as to the reason for his success in spiritual exercises, the Chishti Sufi master from Delhi replied that whatever he heard from the qawwal during sama he attributed to his master Baba Farid al-Din. Here in the exercise of zikr it is similarly advised to pray for help from one's shaykh when repeating the litanies of zikr, be it names of God, or verses from the Holy Quran.

Khwaja Gisu Daraz once remarked that it is important for the seeker that he remains focused on his master. While doing zikr, and any other spiritual exercise, the disciple must visualize his master in front of him and trust that whatever beneficence arrives from the Unseen is due to the spiritual stature and intercession of his master.[82]

5. In the ritual of zikr, the disciple should seek help only from his master

And seeking any help from the Sufi master should be considered similar to seeking for help from the Prophet himself. It is through the person of

---

[82] Ibid., 167–168.

the shaykh that the disciple seeks blessings from the Prophet. When the Sufi seeker receives beneficence from Muhammad, he should trust and thus visualize as if he is being blessed by the Almighty. It is through the person of Muhammad that the Sufi seeker can hope to reach the threshold of the Divine, when there remains no veil separating him from the Lord.

The following manners need to be observed during the exercise of *zikr*:[83]

1. The individual at the time of *zikr* should sit in a cross-legged position on his knees (*char zanu*), or kneel. It should be similar to the posture followed during prayers (*salat*).
2. While sitting in this position both hands should rest on the knees.
3. The Sufi saint should apply fragrance, or the place of *zikr* should be fragrant with incense.
4. Clothes worn during *zikr* must be clean and pure.
5. The meditation cell (*hujra*) should be dark or dimly lit.
6. During *zikr* both eyes should be closed.
7. During *zikr* both ears should be sealed.
8. The Sufi saint should visualize his spiritual master or his form in front of him during the exercise.
9. The participant should be truthful and sincere both inwardly (*batin*) and outwardly (*zahir*) and should not exaggerate his efforts and behave like a hypocrite.
10. The Sufi should do a *zikr* of *kalima* Tauhid, saying *la ilaha illa 'llah*, emphasizing on the Oneness of God which helps to keep him away from vain thoughts.

The following manners must be maintained after the exercise of *zikr*:[84]

1. After completing *zikr*, one should remain silent for a long period of time.
2. The Sufi should practice the suspension of breath (*habs-i nafas*).
3. Every time when *zikr* is performed one should try to decipher the meaning of the litany within the heart.

---

[83] Ibid., 157; Kugle, *Sufi Meditation*, 41–43.
[84] *Khatima*, 158, 169.

4. After the completion of *zikr*, one should refrain from coming into contact with cold wind or using cold water.

5. Immediately after finishing *zikr*, one should refrain from breathing fast. Ideally, the individual needs to hold back the breath and release it slowly and gradually so that the fervour and passion gathered from *zikr* does not dissipate. When releasing this breath, one needs to be careful not to open the mouth, perhaps to stop cold air from entering and diluting the heat gathered within one's body.

6. It is said that at the time of performing vocal *zikr*, the heart too becomes pure. So it is mandatory for mystics engaging in vocal *zikr* to place their tongue and heart in conformity to each other.

Benefits Accrued from *Zikr*

Khwaja Gisu Daraz, while enumerating the benefits of *zikr*, borrows from the authority of *Miftah al-Falah wa Misbah al-Arwah* (The Key to Salvation) by Shaykh Ibn Ataullah al-Iskandari Shadhili (d. 1309). When a Sufi repeats the litany *la ilaha illa 'llah Muhammad ur-Rasul Allah* (There is no God but Allah and Muhammad is his Prophet), also known as the *Kalima-i Tayyab*, during *zikr*, he attracts blessings from the Unseen. Anyone who repeats the litany,[85] known as the *Kalima-i Tauhid*, every morning after ablutions will be blessed by God with means of sustenance that could be material as well as spiritual.[86] For an individual who recites the *Kalima-i Tauhid* 1,000 times before sleep, his soul, during sleep, will rest under the Divine throne and 'grow in strength'.[87] Any Sufi who does a *zikr* of *Kalima-i Tauhid* 1,000 times during noon will be freed from the ill-effects of temptation and the carnal self (*nafs*) within him. One who recites the *Kalima-i Tayyab* on the new moon will be protected by Allah from all forms of illness. An individual who enters and leaves a city after reciting the *Kalima-i Tayyab* 1,000 times will be protected by the Lord from all dangers and things that scare him. Similarly, any individual who

---

[85] 'There is none worthy of worship but Allah, He is alone and (He) has no partners, to Him belong the world and for Him is all the praise, He gives life and causes death, in His hand is all good, and He has the power over everything'.

[86] *Khatima*, 158; Kugle, *Sufi Meditation*, 43.

[87] Kugle, *Sufi Meditation*, 43.

SUFI RITUALS ACROSS ORDERS 205

faces a tyrant after reciting the *Kalima-i Tayyab* 1,000 times will witness the destruction of the oppressor in the hands of the Almighty.[88] If one recites the *Kalima* 1,000 times with the intention to spiritually witness Unseen things (*kashf-i ghuyub*), those secrets of material and spiritual realms will be unveiled to him. Anyone who recites the *Kalima* 70,000 times will be welcomed into paradise. Some Sufi saints have remarked that *zikr* of the tongue also leads to *zikr* of the heart. Thus, while doing *zikr*, it is extremely beneficial if one can keep the tongue and the heart in union so that the exercise moves towards perfection.[89] There are countless ways of doing *zikr* and contemplation.

The above discussion is strongly indicative that both Suhrawardi and Chishti Sufi saints did not limit themselves to following a single spiritual exercise. In spite of *sama* being the core spiritual practice of the Chishtis, and *zikr* holding similar importance for Suhrawardi Sufis, saints from both these orders refused to confine their ideology and practice of spirituality to being narrow and mutually opposed. Rather they showed an inclusive spiritual behaviour by recognizing spiritual exercises from other Sufi orders, and occasionally engaging in them. This not only builds a case for a broader vision of Sufi ethics in medieval South Asia, but more importantly allows us to understand the creation of a dynamic spiritual environment in this region. This dynamicity would only be enhanced in the coming generations through various acts of spiritual training and meditative collaboration, with Indian mystic groups as well, like the yogis and mendicants in north India.

Such practices of spiritual inclusivity stand in contrast to the relations Sufis shared with the ruling elite, the *ulama*, and religious scholars. In earlier chapters we explored some dimensions of this lukewarm relation with regard to the spiritual practice of *sama*. The cultural canvas of South Asia was enriched by the spiritual endeavours of its earliest Sufi orders—Chishti and Suhrawardi—who readily borrowed from each other many of their defining elements. This inclusivity went on to serve multiple purposes—disciples who initiated themselves in either of these orders did not feel isolated and compartmentalized, as they could always seek cross-order training and spiritual guidance. A brilliant example of

---

[88] *Khatima*, 158.
[89] Ibid.; Kugle, *Sufi Meditation*, 44.

this trend is Shah Mina (d. 1465), who traced his ancestry to the Chishti lineage through Ibrahim ibn Adham and also to the Suhrawardi lineage going back to Junaid.[90] Another prominent Chishti Sufi, Shaykh Ashraf Jahangir Simnani (d. 1405), claimed initiation to fourteen different orders, including the Suhrawardi.[91] Thus when these saints went on to pen their experiences on spiritual exercises, they found it justified to include both the practices of *sama* and *zikr*.

This idea of a shared spiritual realm found perfect expression through the enumeration of the variety of spiritual practices considered a preserve of either the Chishti or the Suhrawardi. Secondly, unlike *sama*, which was centred on strict spiritual and textual training, *zikr* was believed to be a more receptive spiritual practice, which could be undertaken even by the common masses, a trend we see later with regard to the *chakkinama* and *charkhanama* traditions practiced even by the rural womenfolk of the Deccan.[92] In this sense, Sufis of the Chishti order were perhaps offering a direct challenge to the *ulama* and clerics by prescribing a pliant litany of exercises, which being spiritual in nature also conformed to the essential parameters of Islam. Incorporating the traditions of Islam, such as the *Kalima,* the names of God, in the practice of *zikr* was intended to serve as an easy alternative to the rigid formalization of religion as propounded by religious scholars. Thus while the practice of *sama* among the Suhrawardi saints sent a message of acceptance of the core Chishti spiritual practice, the incorporation of *zikr* in the litany of Chishti spiritual exercises, also in the age of Chishti revival, was significant enough to strengthen the spiritual terrain of Islam in the subcontinent in the face of continued opposition and intolerance from the *ulama.*

---

[90] Carl Ernst and Bruce B. Lawrence, *Sufi Martyrs of Love: The Chishti Order in South Asia and Beyond* (London: Palgrave Macmillan, 2002), 51–52.
[91] Ibid., 28.
[92] Richard M. Eaton, 'Sufi Folk Literature and the Expansion of Indian Islam', *History of Religions*, 14/2 (1974), 117–127.

5

Etiquette is the Key

Adab as a Sufi Practice

One day the famous Sufi master from Baghdad, Shaykh Junaid, was participating in *sama*. When the spirit of the assembly reached a crescendo and participants went into rapture while listening to poetry and music in praise of the Divine, Junaid's sober state and external calmness amazed his ecstatic companion Abul Husayn al-Nuri. The latter could not resist asking Shaykh Junaid how he could practice such restrain when other Sufis in the same assembly whirled in *raqs*, responding to the agitation within their hearts. Junaid replied, 'You see the mountains—you think they are firm, yet they move like clouds'.[1] This statement of Shaykh Junaid is immortalized in the annals of Sufism, not only because it is derived from the Holy Quran, but more importantly because it contains one of the greatest truths of *tasawwuf*. For Sufis, seeking proximity to God is the ultimate goal, as well as the ultimate reward, for their spiritual toils. So much so that in assemblies of *sama* Sufis readily pour out their ecstatic emotions brought about under the effect of poetry and music, and many times lose control over their limbs.

On many occasions *sama* affects the listener strongly, even if the individual is an adept in the spiritual path, to such an extent that Sufis who participate in it become oblivious to feelings of bodily pain and pleasure. Sufis listen to *sama* in three ways—with love, with fear, and with hope. These emotions descend on the Sufi listener depending on the meaning and interpretation of the poetry that is listened to. If the assembly experiences Divine grace, it also creates hope for Divine proximity, and hence is believed to be the source of ecstasy (*wajd*) in *sama*. Enraptured by the poetry, accompanied on many occasions by musical instruments, Sufis exhibit limb movements in the form of whirling, and in extreme

---

[1] *Kashf al Mahjub*, 415; Quran 27:90.

Sufi Rituals and Practices. Kashshaf Ghani, Oxford University Press. © Kashshaf Ghani 2024.
DOI: 10.1093/oso/9780192889225.003.0006

conditions of self-effacement even fall down on the ground, or rend their robes. While there are recorded instances of death in the course of *sama*, some lose self-control, and at times even disappear into thin air. Similarly, a dark complexion listener turning white under the effect of such ecstatic states is the stuff of legends. At the same time, an indication of Divine wrath in *sama* leads to bodily expression of fear, which manifests itself on the facial contours and external behaviour of the participant.[2]

Such uncontrolled and seemingly unreal behaviour arising from ecstatic experiences were criticized, and discouraged. Sufis like Junaid strongly advised against such behaviour in spiritual assemblies, particularly for novices, realizing the dangers hidden in such dramatic expressions of ecstasy. Sufi masters who were contemporaries of Junaid, and also from later generations, realized the necessity of restrained behaviour by Sufis in spiritual exercises, particularly *sama* which led to ecstatic behaviour. The question remained as to whether a listener in *sama*, occupied in the thought of the Lord, needs to restrain his emotions, or whether should he be allowed to show ecstatic behaviour under the effect of music and poetry. In other words, the debate centred around whether a Sufi is required to hold onto his sober self while approaching the state of Divine experience. Sufis like Junaid vehemently argued for a sober state of composure (*sahw*) rather than intoxicated behaviour.[3]

Junaid spoke on the quality of perfection of the spiritual state, where every thought, every love, every inclination, every fear, and every hope concerning the Divine occurred under a state of perfect realization by the mystic, and not under any form of spirited intoxication.[4] According to Junaid, it was this state of 'perfect concentration' that ensured success for the Sufi in his spiritual efforts—moving towards the experience of increasing awareness of existence in God, where the being of the Sufi is lost in the essence of the Lord—the station of *baqa* being achieved. However, if we move beyond such intricate spiritual language, then we realize two crucial things: that the reason behind advocating soberness in practices like *sama* has multiple layers of interpretations, and that Junaid had a far deeper understanding of the problem than what was apparent.

---

[2] Annemarie Schimmel, *Mystical Dimensions of Islam* (Chapell Hill: University of North Carolina Press, 1975), 181.
[3] Ibid.
[4] Ibid., 182.

At a time when Junaid lived and spoke on such intensely debatable issues concerning spiritual practice, the institutionalization of the Islamic spiritual tradition was yet to achieve concrete form. In the absence of well-elaborated doctrines on spiritual practices, the display of ecstatic behaviour resulting from mystical experiences became a contentious subject of public discussion. With the public execution of Hallaj (d. 922) due to his ecstatic utterance of 'I am the Truth' (*ana al-Haq*), Sufi activities came to be viewed with a degree of scepticism, to the extent of bordering on blasphemy, by the conservative religious elite, together with the political authority of the day. It would have been disastrous therefore if such intensely esoteric realities of the spiritual journey, and the experience of Divine union, began to be discussed, as well as displayed, in public.[5]

Keeping such issues in mind, it became imperative for Sufi masters like Junaid to emphasize strict regulation of Sufi rituals and practices. Even though he supported the exercise of *sama* in his early days of Sufi training, Junaid became more and more sceptic of the efficacy of *sama* as a spiritual practice as he progressed along the Sufi path and gained deeper knowledge of the intricate spiritual realities.[6] Thus in the generations after Junaid, Sufi saints and scholars worked hard to advocate multiple layers of regulations for those participating in spiritual exercises. All this was done with the express intention of limiting its unseen dangers for the initiated, but more importantly for the uninitiated.

Adab as Spiritual Aid

Is there a model of ideal behaviour among Sufis? Sufi orders, along with antinomian sects like qalandars, malamatis, and hydaris, differ in their understanding of ideal spiritual conduct. However, it is accepted that ideal behaviour equips the spiritual seeker to reach an emotional and spiritual stage where he is concerned with the pursuit of *tasawwuf*. The organization of a Sufi order depends on the ability of the Sufi master to create a conducive spiritual environment which helps seekers and fellow

[5] Ibid., 181–182.
[6] Ibid.

mystics to train themselves in the Sufi path towards Divine proximity.[7] How, then, should such a goal be pursued? And what should be the spiritual foundation on which this aim should rest?

According to Shihab al-Din Suhrawardi, Sufis of the Suhrawardi order were attempting a larger goal rather than limiting themselves merely to the tenets of doctrinal religion—in a sense they were, as mentioned above, contemplating and moving towards the aim of achieving union with the Creator.[8] A spiritual exercise that leads a Sufi towards a goal of such magnitude requires complete control over one's inner self, thoughts, and actions, at every moment, and at all times. In order to command such a degree of spiritual control, it is absolutely essential for the Sufi seeker to adhere to proper etiquette (*adab*) in spiritual practice.[9] This idea is central to the Suhrawardi insistence on the norms of *adab* in worship, Sufi rituals, and *zikr* sessions. It is through a detailed understanding of the idea of *adab* that one can fully appreciate the spiritual position of Suhrawardi Sufis, together with its practical application during their everyday spiritual pursuits.

The emphasis on proper *adab* was the foundational, and the most essential, rule to which Suhrawardi Sufis adhered in their journey on the spiritual path. Since the spiritual approach of Suhrawardi Sufis, unlike the Chishtis, did not require a strict separation of the spiritual and the material worlds, rather considering them to be intertwined, it was important for Suhrawardi saints to perfect their spiritual approach while balancing their spiritual engagement with worldly responsibilities. Their adherence to *adab* thus meant perfecting their spiritual position, but at the same time it was integral for developing a strong sense of internal and external discipline.

Suhrawardi Sufis spoke on the centrality of *adab* in spiritual training primarily as a means to ensure that the flow of spiritual knowledge from the master to the disciple was not disrupted or threatened.[10] This was ensured through a process whereby the disciple took a pledge to follow his master in deep obedience so that the disciple would be trained in

[7] Qamar ul Huda, *Spiritual Exercises for Suhrawardi Sufis* (London: Routledge Curzon, 2003), 62.

[8] Ibid.

[9] Ibid.

[10] Ibid.

the goals of the Sufi tradition. And for the realization of this objective it is necessary that one's thoughts and beliefs be in complete control—at every moment. Such control allows Sufis to balance their inner and outer realms of conduct, which if disturbed through improper influence could deprive the Sufi of his spiritual goal.[11]

Sufis of the Suhrawardi order trace the root of *adab* from traditions going back to the Prophet Muhammad, where he states that God taught him good etiquette (*adab*) so that he could be closer to His knowledge. As the 'perfect being' (*insan-ikamil*) who brought God's final message of guidance to humanity, for proper understanding of the various aspects of worldly life and hereafter, the Prophet is said to have repeatedly emphasized that acquiring proper *adab* is essential for travelling on the path that leads a believer closer to his Lord.[12] By tracing the origin of their understanding of *adab* to the Prophet, who as the messenger of God received it as a direct beneficence from the Almighty, Suhrawardi Sufis created a genealogy of spiritual conduct that was traced back to the Prophet as the model.

The adherence to *adab* being central to any spiritual practice foregrounds two important aspects of the Sufi path. First, it upholds the *sunnah* of the Prophet as the model for the practice of *adab,* essential for both material and spiritual pursuits. Over generations Sufi shaykhs came to conceive the practice of *adab* through such a genealogy of knowledge transmission that connected them to the traditions of Prophet Muhammad. Thereafter, *adab* came to be handed down through the medium of personalized training which disciples received from their master—on many occasions multiple Sufi masters across orders—upholding the importance of the master-disciple relationship within the Sufi tradition.

Secondly, like all creation Sufis consider that the origin of *adab* is also from God. It was bestowed on the Prophet as a gift for mankind so that later generations could continue to seek the right path. For Sufis, then, *adab* becomes a mandatory practice received from the Prophet, as a means to express their love for the Divine Beloved, and in turn witness (*shahada*) His manifestation.

[11] Ibid.
[12] Ibid., 63.

Suhrawardis understood the practice of *adab* as a cardinal feature of their spiritual pursuit, and at the same time an essential means for achieving perfection of inner and outer qualities within a spiritual seeker, which include the use of reason, intellectual enquiry, and proper exchange of ideas.[13] The practice of proper *adab* leads to correct behaviour in an individual, guiding him towards the purity of thought and action.[14] In the quality of *adab* is hidden God's own will for purging human beings of immoral influences, leading him towards the Divine.[15]

For Suhrawardis as much as for any Sufi order which functioned through training promising disciples in the spiritual path by shaykhs who in turn were themselves trained and perfected by earlier generations of shaykhs, spiritual knowledge and guidance arrived from the Unseen whose successful transfer to deserving disciples was an essential component of Sufi training.[16] The practice of *adab* became important and instructional for securing this master-disciple relationship, thereby ensuring the easy transfer of knowledge, which the Sufi masters were bestowed with from the Unseen, to their disciples in the process of training them in the ways of the *tariqa*.[17] This spiritual knowledge subsequently strengthened the foundation of the *tariqa*, leading the disciple towards the pursuit of the Divine.[18]

Adab constituted an indispensable part of the spiritual regime that successfully combined multiple knowledge traditions—the *sunnah* of the Prophet, Quranic doctrines, Islamic law (*shariah*)—together with the body of spiritual knowledge left behind by Sufi masters.[19] Thus a complete understanding of the practice of *adab* is in accordance with the Prophet's *sunnah* and upholds the sanctity of the Quranic instructions.[20]

It is emphasized that *tasawwuf* without the practice of *adab* loses its worth, since for every stage of *tasawwuf* there is a corresponding idea of *adab*. Individuals who remain steadfast on the spiritual path do so by

---

[13] Huda, *Spiritual Exercises*, 63.
[14] Wilberforce Clarke, Eng. trans., *The Awarif ul Maarif by Shaikh Shahabuddin Umar b. Muhammad Suhrawardi* (Delhi: Taj Company, 1984), 261.
[15] Ibid.
[16] Huda, *Spiritual Exercises*, 64.
[17] Ibid.
[18] Ibid.
[19] Ibid., 65.
[20] Ibid.

strict adherence to the tenets of *adab*. Those who neglect the pursuit of *adab* are deprived of the experience of higher spiritual states.[21] When Sufi masters impart spiritual training to their disciples, it is combined with the pursuit of proper *adab*. The same conduct is expected from disciples, not only towards the shaykh, but also towards the entire process of learning and knowledge transmission. And this process of learning the subtleties of gnosis (*irfan*) from a Sufi master is similar in spirit to how companions of the Prophet learnt the essentials of the Islamic faith and its practice from the messenger of God.[22]

According to Shihab al-Din Suhrawardi, the concept of *adab* encompasses both the words and actions of the Sufi shaykh. Words signify the knowledge disciples gain from their Sufi shaykh, while actions signify the practices they adhere to based on that knowledge.[23] In the course of such training any individual who adheres to *adab* in his spiritual practice moves 'closer to God, by being a part of the love in His heart'.[24] It is important for Sufis and their disciples alike to cultivate proper *adab*, since all spiritual knowledge is wasted if it is pursued without the practice of *adab* which constitutes understanding, compassion, concentration, and sincerity.[25] Thus the knowledge of *tasawwuf*, as mentioned earlier, remains incomplete without adherence to *adab*.[26] The light of gnosis (*nur-i irfan*) never descends on an ignorant heart, a heart that is hardened towards emotions of love and devotion, and most importantly the realization of *adab*.

Adab towards the Sufi Shaykh

The primary task for a seeker on the spiritual path is to search for a suitable master (*shaykh*). Upon finding one, the disciple should surrender himself at the feet of the shaykh, and take the oath of discipleship (*bayat*), which includes a pledge to obey all instructions. If a disciple refuses to

---

[21] Ibid., 66.
[22] Ibid.
[23] Ibid., 71.
[24] Ibid., 72.
[25] Ibid.
[26] Ibid.

acknowledge his discipleship under a particular master, he loses the spiritual resolve.[27] Gisu Daraz remarked that in the Chishti tradition disciples who are committed to the Sufi path never consider any other individual equal in stature to their master, let alone considering him superior, even if he be Junaid Baghdadi or Bayazid Bistami.

It is not advisable for the disciple to leave the protection of his master. For a Sufi shaykh carries the ability to protect his disciples from the dangers and pitfalls of the material world and the spiritual, as well as the ability to guide the disciple through dreams and visions, even from the afterlife. Such lessons through dreams at times concerned issues of conduct and behavioural courtesy, being acceptable references to *adab*. It is recalled by Amir Hasan Sijzi that one day a visitor arrived at the gates of Nizam al-Din's *khanqah* while the shaykh was taking his midday rest. One of the inmates of the *khanqah*, Akhi Mubarak, sent him away. At that very moment, Baba Farid al-Din appeared in the dreams of Nizam al-Din, with the advice 'If you have nothing to give to a visitor, at least receive him cordially'. On enquiring about the incident, Nizam al-Din gave instructions to wake him whenever any visitor arrived.[28]

A Sufi master should ideally be seen on the same plane as Prophet Muhammad and God. For the disciple, the love for his master should be more than the love for his wife, children, life, and material possessions. The Sufi master is the keeper of the treasure received from the Unseen, and whatever the disciple receives from God is through the grace of his master. Therefore it is advised as good practice for a disciple to recite the name of the master during his last moments.[29]

Respect and *adab* towards a Sufi shaykh are considered the most important element of conduct by a devotee. In a different context *adab* is a key component of the relation that binds a disciple to his Sufi master. This relation survives the full length of the disciple's spiritual training, or even more, until the time he is permitted to admit his own disciples. The practice of *adab* between a disciple and his master manifests itself in various ways that may range from everyday tasks and activities in the *khanqah*, to general interaction between the shaykh and the disciple, and

---

[27] *Khatima*, 73.
[28] *Siyar al-awliya*, 129.
[29] *Khatima*, 65, 77.

how the disciple in course of his training interacts with the world outside the *khanqah*.

Once the disciple is initiated in the spiritual path, it is expected as standard practice that the disciple must serve his master with all heart and soul. Even the limbs of his body need to be in the service of his master. If a disciple is asked by the shaykh to do any of his personal work, the former should consider it an opportunity to acquire Divine beneficence. The work should be completed at the earliest, even if that means joining the congregation late for prayer. A second congregation can be found, but it is not possible to rectify the disobedience shown towards the shaykh by not completing his order. Even if the shaykh asks for something impossible, the disciple should try to arrange it from somewhere. Therefore, it is argued that it is not wise to incur the displeasure of the shaykh, and the disciple needs to fear the wrath of his master more than the wrath from the Unseen.[30]

On the issue of incurring the displeasure of one's master, an incident from the days of Nizam al-Din's discipleship is pertinent. As an essential component of spiritual training among Suhrawardis and Chishtis, reading the text of *Awarif ul Maarif* was part of the curriculum. Baba Farid al-Din was once teaching from a copy whose transcription was imperfect. While he proceeded slowly, correcting the errors, Nizam al-Din remarked that Najib al-Din Mutawakkil had a better copy of the work. Annoyed and irritated at this remark, Baba Farid exclaimed, 'Has this dervish no capacity to correct a defective manuscript?'. Nizam al-Din, eventually realizing his misconduct, fell at the feet of his master to seek forgiveness, but the shaykh refused to oblige. Distressed and overcome with remorse, Nizam al-Din went to the wilderness, even thinking of committing suicide. Finally it was through the intercession of Baba Farid's son, Shihab al-Din, who was also a friend of Nizam al-Din, that the latter was forgiven. When Nizam al-Din arrived in the presence of his master, the latter remarked 'All this I have done for your perfection'.[31] Nizam al-Din's remark at the training session may not seem disrespectful, but to the seasoned eyes of Baba Farid it was unacceptable behaviour to

---

[30] Ibid., 60–63, 76.
[31] *Fawaid al Fuad*, 43–44; *Morals for the Heart*, 109–110.

carry the arrogance of scholarship within the Sufi fraternity, particularly in respect to the bond a disciple shared with his shaykh.

When arriving in the service of his master, the disciple should bow his head before the shaykh, touching the ground with his forehead in respect. However, it is to be remembered that such an act of bowing is not similar to prostration (*sijda*) done during prayer. Gisu Daraz once remarked that when presenting himself in front of his master, Nasir al-Din Mahmud, only the plait of Gisu Daraz's turban touched the ground, instead of the entire forehead.[32]

In the presence of his shaykh a disciple is required to follow certain norms of behaviour that begin from standing in front of the master. The disciple has to remain standing in proper *adab*, focusing his mind on the charisma and beauty of his master, while watching him all the while just as a lover watches the beloved. Gisu Daraz remarked that disciples are lovers while the master is the beloved. However, it is forbidden for the disciple to look straight into the eyes of the shaykh, as this is considered an expression of arrogance. Rather the disciple needs to keep his eyes lowered and fixed towards his own feet, even when the master is looking at him. Only when he is asked to sit, he should do so with legs folded and eyes fixed on the heart of the master. If people in the assembly insist on making him sit in the first row, he should accept without any objection. Their insistence is indication of the worth of the disciple. The disciple should not get distracted and should sit calmly without moving frequently or rising up suddenly to leave the assembly. Words and comments that incite anger and jealousy should not be spoken in an assembly. While sitting in this posture the disciple should not show signs of sleepiness. If he is overcome by slumber, then he should retire to one corner of the room.[33]

The disciple should refrain from consuming food in the presence of the shaykh that is served in the assembly, thereby following the path of poverty. Sufis argue that it is through poverty and fasting that desires of the lower self (*nafs*) can be successfully controlled. Consuming food is permissible only when the master himself is eating and asks his disciples to join him. Even when asked, the food must be consumed with extreme

[32] *Khatima*, 59.
[33] Ibid.

adab, only in small morsels. At the end of the meal the disciple should not chew betel leaf in front of the master.

It is forbidden for the disciple to consume food from any source but a legal (*halal*) one. Not only should he abstain from having food from someone else's share, but such kinds of food must never be brought to the *khanqah* in the presence of the shaykh. Anything that is presented to the service of the shaykh must be from a legitimate source and placed in front of him with proper *adab*.[34]

It is considered a good practice of emulation if the style of clothing worn by the disciple resembles that of his master. However, when presenting himself to his shaykh he should be careful not to wear clothes like a *mashaikh*, and avoid wearing such dresses whose ends drag on the ground. Appearing in such a manner will trend to create hatred in the heart of the master for the disciple. Thus without being very particular about his attire the disciple should wear whatever is available to him.[35]

When excusing himself from his shaykh, the disciple must not show his back. Like his heart, his face should also be orientated towards the shaykh. However, Gisu Daraz noted that such courtesy may not be possible every time for a disciple who is continuously in the service of the Sufi master. Such individuals should retrace the first few steps facing the master, before turning their back towards him. While walking back a disciple should not run in front of the shaykh, neither should he move very slowly, but rather in a graceful manner. When the shaykh enters the cell or rises up to leave any gathering, disciples should rise with him in proper *adab*. It is improper to frequently come and leave in the presence of the shaykh without any reason.[36]

In the course of his spiritual training, listening carefully to and interiorizing what the Sufi master says carries great benefit for the disciple. A Sufi master is the seeker of Truth and has deeper experience of the Way. Hence he can enlighten the disciple on a problem through a single sentence, which the disciple without proper guidance may not be able to understand even after years of effort. Since the Sufi master is well aware of the path towards spiritual progress, its distance, dangers, loftiness,

---

[34] Ibid., 59, 76.
[35] Ibid., 77–78.
[36] Ibid., 59–60.

and means of access, it is repeatedly advised to listen carefully to what one's shaykh has to say, rather than be engrossed in *zikr* and prayers in his presence.[37]

Listening to the words and advice of one's shaykh must be done in the manner in which Moses listened to the revelations of God on Mount Sinai. Whatever is being said by the shaykh must be heard with great attention without any stray thoughts of ascertaining the truth behind those sayings. If the truth of such statements needs to be ascertained, that will be done by the master himself. A Sufi shaykh listens from the authority of God and is witness to the Divine Truth before speaking about it to his disciples.[38]

When the master imparts lessons and advice, it is not advisable for the disciple to look for its explanation from other people. If the lesson requires explanation, the master himself will do the needful.[39] Leaving his master, the disciple must not share the truth of his spiritual state and experiences with any lay individual. Neither should the disciple approach anyone else to pray for him. Whatever the disciple intends to seek from God he should rather seek from his master, and whatever he receives from the Unseen he should consider it as arriving from his master.[40] A Sufi master is enlightened from the realm of the Unseen and has knowledge of affairs whose significance only he is capable of understanding. Therefore, the disciple should visualize the master as his life, and if he experiences something he does not know about, then he should immediately share it with his master. Rather than performing *zikr*, and immersing himself in deep contemplation, a disciple should listen carefully to whatever the shaykh has to instruct, and learn from those teachings.[41]

As an expression of obedience, the name of the shaykh must be recited continuously by the disciple while keeping his mind occupied in thoughts of the master. The image of the master has to be in front of his eyes (*tasawwur-i shaykh*) whenever the disciple thinks about him. For this exercise no particular time of the day is allotted. The disciple should remember that his master is witness to many things from the Unseen.

[37] Ibid.
[38] Ibid., 64.
[39] Ibid., 65.
[40] Ibid., 73.
[41] Ibid., 60.

Hence while contemplating the shaykh the disciple should remember the grace and splendour (*tajalli*) his master is bestowed from the Unseen.

Contemplating the Sufi master can be done when sitting right in front of him in the assembly. However, this practice should never be considered as worshipping the master, but rather as worshipping the Lord. When the shaykh is visually absent it is advised that the disciple imagines him within the heart, or imagines himself as being one with the shaykh. This act of contemplating the saint by the disciple is categorized not as *muraqaba*, nor as *mushahada* or *makashifa*, but as *muayina*. While participating in the assembly of *sama*, it is advisable for the disciple to attribute experiences of union, separation, pain, and quest to his shaykh. Nizam al-Din once mentioned that whatever he heard from the *qawwal* in assemblies of *sama* he used to attribute to the pious personality of his master, Baba Farid al-Din. This proves that even in deep contemplation during *sama*, Nizam al-Din was never forgetful of his master.

Through such continuous contemplation a time will arrive when the disciple will be able to visualize the Sufi master in front of him whenever he retires for privacy (*khalwat*) during meditation. The heart of the disciple will become a mirror through which he will be able to witness the reflection of the splendour (*tajalli*) that is bestowed on his master from the Unseen, similar to the manner in which the reflection of the sun becomes visible in water. When the disciple is yet to reach spiritual maturity, it is advisable for him not to contemplate the Divine, but to turn his face towards his shaykh so that he may benefit from the abundant grace bestowed on his master.[42]

For disciples therefore, the countenance of the master becomes a way for visualizing God Himself, since whatever the Sufi master does is under direct guidance from the Unseen, which illumines the heart of the Sufi. This exercise takes the disciple to the station of annihilation in his master (*fana fil shaykh*). It is only after this stage is reached that the disciple moves towards the stage of contemplating the Lord, which should be done in such earnest that the disciple loses his state of calmness. He should focus his mind on the litany of *hua al-awwal hua al-akhir hua al-zahir hua al-batin* (He is first, He is last, He is the beginning, He is the end). The focus of the master will also be on the heart of the disciple.[43]

[42] Ibid., 61.
[43] Ibid.

In the eyes of the disciple there is no shaykh greater than his master. Even if the master of his immediate shaykh is present in the same space, it is advisable for the disciple to believe that the abundant grace (*faiz*) he receives from his master cannot possibly be received from the master of his shaykh. If the faith of the disciple is firmly in his master, then blessings and grace from the master of his shaykh will flow towards him voluntarily. Gisu Daraz remarked that such was the tradition of benevolence and blessings that flowed from Khwaja Muin al-Din Chishti to Qutb al-Din Bakhtiyar Kaki and finally to Baba Farid al-Din.[44]

In continuity with the above, Gisu Daraz mentioned that in the famous Sufi treatise of *Awarif ul Maarif*, it is prescribed that whatever a disciple desires he should pray for from his master. Blessings from the Divine will descend on the disciple through the countenance of his shaykh. Whatever attributes of God are unveiled to a disciple, in the form of subtleties, benefaction, wrath, beauty, majesty, it is through the medium of his master.

While undergoing training it is possible that a disciple may not be able to comprehend his spiritual station. Such was the case for Gisu Daraz himself, when one day he narrated to his master Nasir al-Din Mahmud a dream where he saw people coming to him, asking him to wear and take off a series of robes—the robe of Dominion, the robe of Prophethood, the robe of Unity, and the robe of Divine Essence. Nasir al-Din could immediately read the hidden indication in the dream, and handed over to Gisu Daraz his prayer carpet, signifying spiritual succession.[45]

Whatever dreams a disciple experiences, he should share it with his master. However, he must not seek an interpretation. If the shaykh explains it to him voluntarily, the disciple should listen to it carefully. If not shared voluntarily with the disciple, it is not wise, particularly for intermediaries and adepts, to request the master to explain spiritual secrets. This is because there are many forms of hidden knowledge, the significance of which the disciple may not be mature enough to grasp while he is still a beginner. It is also not proper for a disciple to ask anything from his master, except *dua*. He should also not express his state of seizure to

---

[44] Ibid.

[45] Ali Samani, *Siyar e Muhammadi*, in Richard M. Eaton, *A Social History of the Deccan, 1300–1761: Eight Indian Lives* (New York: Cambridge University Press, 2005), 36.

his master. But it is good if the master comes to know of it by himself, through intuition from God.[46]

It is a good sign, however, to see one's master in dream. If a disciple sees himself visiting (*ziyarat*) the tombs of prophets and saints, he should know that visiting the shrine of his master is a better practice. Even when a disciple experiences a dream where wrong things are being said about his master, it is not advisable for the disciple to lose faith in the shaykh. Every disciple should believe that although there are numerous Sufi shaykhs who are masters of the spiritual path, his master is on the path of Truth and hence the best knower of them all.[47]

If the disciple sees his master in the image of the Prophet in a dream, then he should realize that the stature of his master is elevated and closer to the Prophet. This should be seen as an indication from the Prophet on the proximity of the Sufi master to the former. If a disciple on seeing his master in a dream equates him with God, then it is meant that the Sufi master is the manifestation of God, and the splendour (*tajalli*) of God is bestowed on the master as well.[48]

If it is revealed to the disciple that a second shaykh is more learned and spiritually adept than his master, even then it is not advisable for him to leave his shaykh. The intellectual and spiritual upbringing of a disciple is best done by his shaykh under whom he took initiation, and not by some other Sufi saint. The disciple is believed to be the intellectual off-spring of his master. In the early days the mind of disciple is strengthened through rigorous training in law (*fiqh*), traditions of the Prophet (Hadith), and Quranic commentaries (*tafsir*) that whet his appetite for greater knowledge.

In the *Khatima*, Gisu Daraz advises that irrespective of the spiritual station a disciple achieves through his training, he should remain under the supervision of his shaykh for as long as possible. Even when the disciple reaches the state of perfection, he should present and conduct himself in front of his master with the same humility that he showed at the time of initiation. The disciple must also share every event of his life with the master. There are numerous intricacies and nuances on the path

---

[46] *Khatima*, 60, 77.
[47] Ibid., 65, 70.
[48] Ibid., 76.

towards spiritual progress which can only be understood correctly with help of the master, who is experienced enough to understand indications from the Unseen. If the disciple is the physical body, he should consider his shaykh as the soul. Until the disciple surrenders himself to the shaykh in the above manner, he will not be able to imbibe the qualities of his master.

Recalling his own personal experience, Gisu Daraz mentioned that he remained under the feet of his master for seventeen long years. On many matters he held a high opinion of himself and the knowledge he had acquired under his shaykh. However, when Nasir al-Din Mahmud passed away, Gisu Daraz slowly came to realize that there were many things that should have been done only in the presence of his shaykh. But, as Gisu Daraz recalled, such was his devotion and attachment towards his master that he continued to receive help and guidance from Nasir al-Din whenever he needed it. Nasir al-Din Mahmud remained with him even after departing from his worldly presence. Thus Gisu Daraz advised that irrespective of the station a disciple reaches, he must never dissociate himself from the love and care of his master, as there are subtle signs hidden in that relation which not all can understand.[49]

In course of his spiritual training, it is desired from a disciple that he should model himself on his master, and be grateful to the master for accepting him, and at the same time be thankful for the services he can offer to his shaykh. Gisu Daraz once remarked that a master can be seen as a wine cup bearer (saqi), and the disciple should be assured that the wine of gnosis will be available to him through the master. To taste the wine of gnosis, the disciple has to surrender himself completely to his shaykh. He must share all his feelings and thoughts with his master, provided the latter can spare that amount of time. It is mandatory for the disciple to recognize his spiritual goal clearly, which is achievable only through his master. The Sufi master therefore becomes the 'desire' (murad) for the disciple (murid), who should open his heart so that his wellness is assured by the grace of the shaykh. When a disciple, even if mistakenly, refuses to acknowledge his master, he immediately loses his goal. One who disobeys the master, does not love him, and follows the path of worldly desires is

[49] Ibid., 68.

doomed in both the worlds.[50] Thereafter no amount of faith in the shaykh will be of any use.[51]

It is improper for any disciple to have a false sense of dignity and high stature in his heart, considering himself as a perfect shaykh. He then disrespects his master and holds the master-disciple relationship to be superfluous. Such a disciple does not taste Divine beneficence. In the desire for Divine beauty, he pays little attention to the commands of his shaykh that would eventually lead him towards his goal. Therefore, unless a disciple is clearly instructed by his master, he should not venture into spiritual practices on his own. Rather seeking any spiritual station on his own can be dangerous for a novice who is unaware of the pitfalls in the spiritual path. He should rather stick to whatever his master instructs, following this carefully. If a disciple is not beautiful to look at and lacks a charming behaviour, it is good for him, since it creates distraction within him.[52]

It is improper for any disciple to leave his master and take initiation under a different shaykh. The disciple then becomes a turncoat (*murtad*) and a sinner in the eyes of God. Also, one who is already being trained by a shaykh will not be initiated into the path by any other Sufi master. Thus the disciple will end up losing his way even further. Even if he comes across an *abdal* (considered the lieutenants of God through whom He rules the earth), it is advisable not to take discipleship under him, but to remain attached to his original master. Out of increased expectation a disciple must not demand anything from his shaykh, like a miracle, which is not required in the spiritual path. A disciple who brings faith in his master only after seeing a miracle being performed by the latter does not have the resolute character to walk the spiritual path. Such should be the faith in his master that no miracles are required to ascertain it. A devoted disciple is one who strongly believes that secrets from the Unseen are unveiled on his master.[53]

In the absence of the shaykh it is usually one among his disciples who takes up the mantle of succession (*khilafat*). The *khilafat* is handed over through the transfer of a few items like the cloak, prayer carpet, and at

[50] Ibid., 65–66.
[51] Ibid., 73.
[52] Ibid., 60, 68.
[53] Ibid., 69–70.

times the walking stick. These are believed to carry the spiritual grace and intercessory qualities of the deceased master. If a master gifts his cloak to a disciple, it should be accepted with great humility and gratitude and preserved with special care. In the absence of the shaykh the cloak may be considered as the intercessor for the disciple. Since the soul of the shaykh rests at a higher spiritual station, it can be present in multiple places at any given time. The same is said with regard to the cot on which the shaykh slept. Disciples are instructed not to sit, but to stand in front of it, with proper *adab*. Just like in the presence of the living master, disciples must not turn their back to it. Rather they should retrace their steps with proper humility.[54]

However, in the lifetime of his master it is improper for a disciple to behave as spiritual successor, sit on the prayer carpet, and make servants (*khadim*) work for him. When *sama* is organized in the *khanqah*, it is not befitting for a disciple to go around the assembly like a master and then return to his designated sitting place. Rather he should retire to one corner of the *khanqah* and engage in *zikr* (repeating litanies and names of God), in complete comfort and freedom of mind. However, it is possible that at the time of *sama*, when the disciple is overcome by emotion of deep love for the Divine, he may end up doing limb movements and turning in circles. When that happens in front of the shaykh the disciple need not be ashamed and repent, since such states are blessings from the Unseen which do not require chastisement. These sudden overwhelming emotions arriving from the Unseen reflect the deep bond that a disciple shares with his shaykh.[55]

After the master has passed away it may so happen that the disciple may meet a shaykh who in his eyes has greater spiritual knowledge and has been bestowed with many more secrets from the Unseen. Even in such a situation it is unfair on part of the disciple to lose faith in his deceased master. It is said that in the lifetime of a disciple it is not possible for him to know the spiritual depth of his master completely. Thus it may have so happened that the deceased shaykh may have acquired more spiritual progress and received greater secrets from the Unseen, all of which his disciple may have been unaware of. Rather if a disciple receives any

---

[54] Ibid., 63–64.
[55] Ibid., 77.

important lessons or knowledge from another shaykh, he should attribute it to the mercy of his master.

It is important for a disciple to realize the stature of his master. It is not proper for a disciple to question any activity of his shaykh. Such behaviour could prove detrimental for the disciple. He should always keep in mind that a Sufi master is guided by the Unseen and acts only under the command of God. There is no greater friend than one's master. Therefore, even if he participates in an assembly of *ghina*, listening to songs sung by a beautiful lady, his action must not be questioned. Sufi shaykhs are considered friends of God, and remembered as *Shaykh-ul Islam*. Such acts are believed to be matters between the Sufi saint and his God, which humans are incapable of comprehending. It is important for any disciple to remember that his master and all other Sufi shaykhs are men of firm character and great foresight, achieved through rigorous spiritual efforts. If the disciple is oblivious of such truths regarding Sufi shaykhs, then he will not benefit from their company. In the path of God, Sufi masters achieve a spiritual station where the Truth is unfolded before them, and the Sufi shaykh conducts himself according to the pleasure of God. Thus the Sufi master is capable of doing things and having control over them in a way that may not be possible for the disciple.[56]

When a disciple sees his shaykh enamoured by a beautiful male or female face, it is improper for the disciple to lose faith in the master. Rather he should reason that the shaykh must have witnessed the face of God in their beautiful faces, which resulted in the distraction. In the spiritual path Sufis attain such proximity to the Divine Beloved that in every beautiful face he witnesses the face of God, though to men of the material world these faces appear with human features. The disciple being unaware of this understanding must not think his master as blameworthy. However, without proper training in self-control, if the disciple tries to emulate his shaykh by similar acts he will lose himself in the web of lust and sensual desires, thereby destroying his spiritual gains. In such a state the disciple needs to be handled with care so that he can regain his spiritual station.[57]

---

[56] Ibid., 64, 70.
[57] Ibid., 74.

Therefore, it is strictly prescribed that a disciple who is yet to gain full training in the nuances of the spiritual path should avoid the company of young males, particularly those who are beautiful and sweet talkers. Disciples should also avoid visiting any gathering where such young men are present. If he ends up in such an assembly he should return quickly. If he cannot return he should sit in the assembly with his head lowered so that he is protected from seeing these beautiful young faces. Those disciples who end up in such company are rejected from the Sufi path.

An obedient disciple is one who is pious and perfect in his thoughts and actions, leading to a positive impression from his master. If the disciple shows disobedience, he may invite a negative impression from his master. In order to cultivate perfect thoughts, a disciple should refrain from following general discourses that his master delivers on different spiritual stations and the path. Rather he should focus on lessons by the shaykh that only concern him. Whatever advice a shaykh gives to his disciple through the form of a story, even if there are some visible contradictions in the narrative, it is not proper to pick up an argument with the master. It is considered a sign of disobedience towards the shaykh.[58]

It is important for the disciple to keep in mind that the opportunity he has received to serve a Sufi master is out of the grace and kindness of the shaykh. Therefore the disciple should remain grateful for this opportunity, and as an expression of gratitude he should pray for his masters' long life and proximity to God. This is considered an expression of sincerity and love from the disciple towards his master.[59] Similarly, whatever the disciple receives after the death of his master, he should realize that it is through the agency of his master.[60]

However, when a disciple completes his training under a Sufi master and is bestowed with the mantle of succession (*khilafat*), it is not advisable for him to start taking disciples immediately and consider himself as a Sufi master. Even if he admits some disciples under his supervision, he should remember that this responsibility has been loaned out to him. He needs to walk along the principles laid down by his master. It is only after he has done these properly and come to know his shaykh's consent that

[58] Ibid., 70.
[59] Ibid., 71–72.
[60] Ibid., 75.

he may proceed with his duties.[61] When a shaykh passes away from this world it is the duty of a disciple to keep his soul happy by bestowing it with the benefits accrued from performing virtuous deeds (*Isaal-e Sawaab*).[62]

Adab in *Sama* among Chishtis of North India

In the early thirteenth century, with the arrival of the Chishti *silsila* in north India, we see *sama* being introduced as the core spiritual exercise of the Chishti Sufis. A detailed discussion on the antecedents of this Sufi ritual, along with its spiritual genealogy, has been discussed in previous chapters. The following sections focus on the norms of *adab* set forth by Chishti masters in their practice of *sama*.

Once in an assembly of *sama* at the *khanqah* of Hamid al-DinNagauri, a dervish lost his outer demeanour. Aides (*khadim*) of the shaykh took him by the hand and helped him out of the *khanqah*. After the assembly was over and the dervish regained his soberness, he returned and complained to Hamid al-Din that his aide pulled him out of *sama* at a time when the dervish had already placed one of his legs inside the gates of heaven, and was lifting the other leg in that direction. Hamid al-Din called his aide and asked the reason for pulling the dervish out of the assembly and the *khanqah*. The aide replied that it was the order of the shaykh that whoever behaved against the etiquette of the assembly should be pulled out. He just obeyed the order. Hamid al-Din smiled and replied that it is impossible for someone going against the *adab* and harmony of *majlis-e sama* to enter heaven.

The period of Nizam al-Din Awliya witnessed the popularity of *sama* reach a crescendo in Chishti circles, and at the same time severe controversies arose around this core spiritual practice of Chishti Sufis. *Sama* was at the centre of much debate between Sufis and religious scholars at the royal court.

Time and again the *ulama* would allege that Nizam al-Din's lack of reverence for *shariah* led him to practice such rituals in the name of Sufism that had no approval in Islamic canons. Throughout his life Nizam al-Din

[61] Ibid., 78.
[62] Ibid., 72.

was patient enough to face all criticisms with a certain degree of calmness and resolve, rare among his aggressive opponents. Once he remarked, in reply to a remark in coarse language in support of the prohibition of *sama*, that 'God Almighty has declared His enmity to "he who is extremely violent in quarrelling", since the one who is extremely violent in quarrelling referred to the one who takes recourse to abusive language to strengthen his position'.[63] Whenever questioned, Nizam al-Din would strongly emphasize, as recorded in his discourses, that *sama* is nothing but a stable touchstone of piety, and assemblies of *sama*, if conducted with proper *adab*, are blessed with Divine mercy.

What did Nizam al-Din imply when he emphasized this adherence to proper *adab*? What are the norms of *adab* in an assembly of audition, and how can they be upheld? The answer can be largely located in the pages of the *Fawaid* itself, where the shaykh extensively discussed various aspects of Sufism. Nizam al-Din Awliya, considered by his contemporaries and later generations as a major enthusiast of *sama* among Chishtis, set forth a number of conditions and regulations in his lifetime. The latter, according to the shaykh, needed to be adhered to with precision if the assembly of *sama* was to maintain its sanctity as a practice seeking the Divine.

He remarked that an assembly of *sama* rests on four pillars: the *qawwal*, the content of the assembly (*masmu*), the listener (*mustami*), and instruments of music (*lahw-i sama*).[64] While elaborating on each of these aspects, Nizam al-Din stated that in the assembly the *qawwal* must be a matured individual, and not a young boy. Neither should a woman be made *qawwal*.[65] The reason for this could be that Nizam al-Din was apprehensive of the spiritual maturity of a young boy in managing the affairs of an intensely spiritual gathering. Also, hearts of young boys take time to get hardened to the desires of the material world, so that if he participates in an assembly where verses read out indicate love and passion, it is possible that he may misinterpret those verses according to his worldly dispositions, hence committing himself to serious immoral behaviour. Regarding the prohibition of women, it is argued that presence

[63] *Fawaid al Fuad*, 190; *Morals for the Heart*, 355.
[64] *Fawaid al Fuad*, 201; *Morals for the Heart*, 356.
[65] Ibid.

of women in *sama* becomes more of a distraction than a spiritual catalyst. Verses recited in *sama* carry ideas and imageries that convey descriptions of beauty, love, desire, separation, and similar emotions. The presence of a woman as a *qawwal* on such an occasion may distract listeners, turning the assembly into a self-satisfying and frivolous exercise.

Regarding the second regulation, Nizam al-Din remarked that the content of *sama* must not contain anything lewd and obscene.[66] It is usually normal that verses read in *sama* carry imageries of love and separation, but the *qawwal* needs to be careful so that the poetry recited does not cross limits of decency. The verses read out in the assembly, therefore, must not convey ideas of debauchery, frivolity, distrust, perversion, and lustful desires, etc. Although essentially constituting love poetry with interjections of separation, it should conform to the spirit of the assembly.[67]

In the third condition, the listener should participate in *sama* with a pure heart that is free of all material desires, and filled with the remembrance of God.[68] Since *sama* is an exercise of listening to poetry and music 'with an attempt to participate in a dynamic dialogue between the human lover and the Divine Beloved', it is mandatory that the participant behaves in accordance with the spirit of the assembly. *Sama* being essentially a 'movement of the heart', it is natural that the participant should attend the gathering with a pure heart so that it is receptive to the Divine mercy that descends upon such an assembly.

As for the last condition on musical instruments, it is advised that stringed instruments like the *chang, rabab, flute*, and other similar instruments must not be used in *sama*, as it ruins the spiritual ambience of the assembly. Rather it is permitted that the *tambourine* and *dholak* can be used as accompaniments to the poetry read in the gathering.[69] As discussed previously, Chishti Sufis usually discouraged the use of musical instruments in the assembly of *sama*. However, on certain special occasions, even if the use of musical instruments was permitted it was limited to non-stringed ones like the *duff* and *tambourine*.

---

[66] Ibid.
[67] Ibid.
[68] Ibid.
[69] Ibid.

In the *Siyar al Awliya*—one of the major biographical treatises on early Chishti saints—Mir Khurd dedicates an entire chapter to the various aspects of *sama*,[70] including a section on proper etiquette (*adab*) one needs to follow during the exercise. Mir Khurd mostly cites Nizam al-Din as his primary authority, where the shaykh clarifies certain conditions which need to be kept in mind when organizing *sama*, for example that it should be held at such an hour when the heart is completely immersed in the thought of the Divine and no distractions lead it towards worldly thoughts.[71] Secondly, the place chosen for the assembly should also be pleasing so that on seeing the same the heart is filled with a sense of pleasure and satisfaction.[72] The participants should also belong to a similar spiritual state, that is to say that all members of the assembly are focused towards the exercise of *sama*.[73] It is important to note that together with stressing the necessity of spiritual purity in *sama*, the shaykh emphasized the aspect of physical purity as well. He remarked that while participating in the assembly of *sama*, one should be completely clean and bathed and apply fragrance.[74]

Maulana Fakhr al-Din Zarradi, a disciple of Nizam al-Din, in his treatise states that an important precondition for participating in *sama* is that the individual must be in complete control of his senses while listening to the verses recited. At the same time, it should seem that he is completely absorbed in his own thoughts, contemplating the Lord, without any heed to what his fellow mystics are doing.[75] If the participant is more interested in the affairs of his fellow participants rather than taking care of his own spiritual state, then he is sure to lose the benefits of the assembly. It is strictly instructed that no participant should interfere with or show interest in the spiritual condition of his fellow participant. This way he not only harms his own self, but also others, and at the same time disrupts the proceedings of the assembly.[76]

Zarradi further states that the participant should remain seated in his original place as far as possible, and try not to rise from it.[77] If it be so

---

[70] Ch. 9.
[71] *Siyar al-awliya*, 513.
[72] Ibid.
[73] Ibid.
[74] Ibid.
[75] Ibid.
[76] Ibid.
[77] Fakhr al-Din Zarradi, *Risala-i Usul al-Sama*, in *Siyar al-awliya*, 513.

that emotions of the heart are too heavy for the Sufi to bear, then he may break into tears. Even during such a state of rapture, it is advisable that the Sufi does not raise his voice over that of the assembly. It is important for the Sufi to remain seated in his place where benefaction from the Divine would descend on him in response to the emotions arising within his heart.[78] In the assembly of *sama* it may so happen that another Sufi saint experiences agitation within his heart and hence rises up to perform *raqs*. It can also be that the participant rises up only to express his state of ecstasy (*hal e wajd*), without any limb movements. On both occasions it is advised that Sufis yet to experience such a state should empathize (*tawajud*) by standing up in conformity to the particular spiritual state of the fellow participant, and should not let him feel that others are not experiencing a similar state. However, if a certain verse creates agitation in a listener and leaves others unmoved, then the agitated listener should control his feelings.[79]

Our raconteur narrates an incident which upholds the veracity of the above regulation. A few days after the demise of Badr al-Din Samarqandi,[80] an assembly of *sama* was organized at his place where, along with others, Nizam al-Din was also present. Since the shaykh arrived late, he took his place in the second row of the *majlis*. In the course of *sama*, when participants who arrived early rose up in response to their states of ecstasy, Nizam al-Din also followed suit. Many in the assembly were surprised and asked him to return to his place since he joined late and was yet to reach the desired state of ecstasy. To this Nizam al-Din replied that they were right in their reasoning, but it was mandatory for participants in the assembly of *sama* to conform (*muwafeqat*) and hence stand up in support of those who had already reached their ecstatic states

---

[78] *Siyar al-awliya*, 513.

[79] Ibid.;Sayyid Muhammad Husayni Gisu Daraz, *Khatima Sharif: Ikhtisar*, ed. and trans. Khusro Hussaini (Gulbarga: All India Sayyid Muhammad Gisu Daraz Research Academy, 2014), 5.

[80] Shaykh Badr al-Din Samarqandi was a famous mystic of his age, and was the deputy (*khalifa*) of another renowned Sufi, Shaykh Saif al-Din Bakharzi. He was well acquainted with Shaykh Najib al-Din Kubrawi. Shaykh Samarqandi was not only well versed in the Holy Quran (*hafiz i- Quran*), but at the same time was a master of *tasawwuf*. He was a great lover of *sama* and never participated in the same without the company of Shaykh Nizam al-Din Awliya. It is hence quite evident why Nizam al-Din took the effort of being present at the *sama* assembly held in the memory of Shaykh Samarqandi. The latter was a man of emotions, and at the slightest trigger he would engage in *raqs*, seeing which all those present in the assembly would derive much pleasure and satisfaction within their hearts.

and hence stood up.[81] Thus, through such conduct, Chishti Sufis approved the practice of *tawajud* or empathetic ecstasy.

Adab in *Sama* among Deccani Chishtis

Burhan al-Din Gharib, a senior disciple of Nizam al-Din, was given the responsibility of the Chishti order in the Deccan. Chishti records credit him as instrumental in single-handedly establishing the order on a strong foundation in the little-known town of Khuldabad, away from the political and social epicentre in Daulatabad—the southern capital of the Tughluqs. In the following section we explore the practice of *adab* among the early Chishti Sufis of Deccan. The practice of *adab*, particularly with regard to *sama*, was meant to attract Divine benefaction on Sufi participants who gathered to benefit from the assembly of *sama*.[82] In the Deccan, as in the north, the practice of *adab* formed an intrinsic part of the Chishti spiritual life, ably reflected in their actions and words.

Hammad al-Din Kashani, a disciple of Burhan al-Din, gives a vivid picture of *sama* as it was practiced in the Chishti *jamaat khana*. He mentions that each assembly of *sama* in the circle of Burhan al-Din started and ended with the recitation of the Holy Quran.[83] That Chishti Sufis considered *sama* as much a sacred and pious exercise as the daily prayers (*salat*) is clearly evident from their emphasis on purity. Burhan al-Din made it mandatory on every participant in the assembly to perform ablutions (*wazu*) before entering the *majlis*.[84] At the same time the listener holding a reverence for the exercise should abstain from chewing betel leaf.

Speaking about the traits of *sama*, Burhan al-Din once remarked that *sama* as an exercise for meditating on the Divine constitutes recollection (*zikr*), reflection (*fikr*), and weeping (*girya*). Any other emotion arising from the assembly should be seen as disruption (*fitna*). Some Sufis argue that *sama* is an exercise that stirs the heart through tenderness

---

[81] *Siyar al-awliya*, 513.

[82] Carl Ernst, *Eternal Garden: Mysticism, History, and Politics at a South Asian Sufi Center* (New Delhi: Oxford University Press, 1992), 153.

[83] Hammad al-Din Kashani, *Ahsan al-aqwal* (Khuldabad, 1718), 129, Urdu trans. Farheen Banu (Aurangabad: Welldone Graphics, 2013), Henceforth *Ahsan al-aqwal*; Ernst, *Eternal Garden*, 153.

[84] *Ahsan al-aqwal*, 129; Ernst, *Eternal Garden*, 153.

and compassion. As a result, whatever a Sufi listens to in the assembly of *sama* he relates to the Divine Truth, provided he is an individual inclined to ecstasy. Attributing to the Divine whatever one hears in *sama* is the key towards attaining *wajd* in the assembly. Men of words are incapable of understanding the source of ecstasy, since it is impossible to explain *wajd* through words and discourses. If the listener is a person of worldly thoughts, he will always relate verses of *sama* to worldly contexts. Therefore it is important for the listener to correctly comprehend whatever he listens to in *sama*.[85]

It is recommended that *sama* must not degenerate into an everyday exercise, making it mechanical in nature.[86] Rather it should be organized as and when there is a deep desire for it among Sufi participants.[87] The secret behind the success of this exercise lies in the fact that it completely depends on the spiritual state of the mystic, and by making it a habit or stressing unduly on its performance the Sufi loses out on Divine benefaction that descends voluntarily, irrespective of time and place.[88] Thus, in a way it is recommended that the Sufi listener should concentrate more on interpreting the verses of the *qawwal* than measuring the spiritual adeptness of his fellow mystics.[89]

The Sufi listener will be able to understand what is being revealed from the Unseen only when he trains his attention towards the *qawwal* and tries to understand the words and verses being recited. It is important for Sufis to remain seated calmly, avoid agitating movements as much as possible and listen carefully to the recitation of the *qawwal*. Only then he can realize the inner meaning of the poetry within his heart, stirring it towards an intense love for God.[90]

On occasions when Sufis get overpowered by ecstatic experiences in *sama*, emotional restraint was strongly recommended by Burhan al-Din. The shaykh once remarked that if any Sufi raised his hand in *sama* without proper reason, his participation would no longer be allowed. It

---

[85] *Ahsan al-aqwal*, 134–135; *Ahsan al-aqwal* (Urdu), 100.
[86] Ibid.
[87] Ibid.
[88] *Ahsan ul-Aqwal*, 135; Ernst, *Eternal Garden*, 153.
[89] Ibid.
[90] *Ahsan al-aqwal*, 128–135; *Ahsan al-aqwal* (Urdu), 101–103; Ernst, *Eternal Garden*, 154.

was also strictly instructed that no Sufi participating in *sama* should interrupt the assembly, asking for water or going out for fresh air.[91]

It is also advised that a Sufi in *sama* should prevent himself from getting distracted as much as possible, to the extent that he should not offer *salam* (salute), nor should he respond to one, since, according to Burhan al-Din, Sufis do not offer or respond to *salam* in the middle of *sama*. It is not advisable to create noise and disturbance during *sama*, since it is possible that someone's contemplation might be disturbed by it and he may resent such an action, to an extent that the Sufi who is disturbed may end up doing great harm to the person creating disturbance.[92]

Thus it is ironic when novices in assemblies of *sama* search for physical comfort. Once when a disciple committed such an offence by offering sherbet, he was sharply rebuked by the Chishti master Nizam al-Din, 'Dervishes consume their blood, what I have to do with sherbet?'. On another occasion, when *sama* was being held in the *khanqah* of Burhan al-Din, one of his disciples came out to the door to take some fresh air. When Burhan al-Din noticed this, he remarked that dervishes in *sama* are engaged in contemplating the beauty of the Divine, while disciples who are devoid of such taste must not seek physical comfort like taking fresh air.

If it so happens that a particular verse arouses a sense of agitation in the heart of a Sufi listener, it is not forbidden for him to request the *qawwal* to repeat the verse. Interestingly, 'if in spite of his desire' the Sufi refrains from requesting a repetition of the verse, then 'God inspires the reciter' to repeat the same so that the Sufi can extend his state of rapture and remain immersed in his love for the Divine.[93]

In the opinion of Burhan al-Din, a Sufi shaykh in an assembly of *sama*, when overcome with tender-heartedness and blessings from the Unseen, should not rise first. Any of his disciples or other shaykhs should rise before him, which he should then imitate. Once when Burhan al-Din was overcome by an urge to rise up in a state of ecstasy in *sama*, he instructed his disciple Mubarak Maruf to rise first, after which he followed. Similarly, once, when Baba Farid went into ecstasy he said to one of his

---

[91] Ibid.
[92] Ibid.
[93] Ernst, *Eternal Garden*, 153.

disciples seated next to him, 'Mahmud, you are still alive', indicating that the disciple should rise up, after which Farid al-Din followed.[94] Later in the writings of Gisu Daraz we find his observation that in any assembly of *sama* the individual who rises first displaying symptoms of ecstasy (*wajd*) can bring either grace (*khayr*) or falsehood (*shirk*) for the entire assembly. However, one who rises under the impact of pure ecstasy bestows the entire assembly with happiness and passion.[95]

Under the impact of ecstatic limb movement, if the fold of the turban of the individual who stands up first in the assembly of *sama* unfolds, he should tie it and then continue with his *raqs*. In assemblies of *sama* it is advised that none should participate with an uncovered head. If someone leaves the assembly with his head uncovered, then it is not considered auspicious for the master of the assembly.[96]

In the above regulations concerning *adab* in *sama*, there is a clear influence of Hujwiri's *Kashf al Mahjub*. A detailed analysis of Burhan al-Din's instructions on *sama* can help us achieve a better understanding of this influence. It is forbidden in an assembly of *sama* to question each other's spiritual feelings, so that Sufi participants refrain from interfering in the affairs of their fellow listeners during *sama*.[97] Putting forward inquisitive queries reflects the ego of the enquirer, as he tries to show off his superior knowledge in spiritual affairs. Such actions completely destroy the spiritual ambience of the gathering and therefore distract other Sufis from the real goal of audition—concentrating on the thoughts of the Divine.[98]

Since the *qawwal* forms the focus in the assembly of *sama*, it is recommended that the actions and words of the *qawwal* should not be questioned, since the *qawwal* speaks words inspired by the Truth.[99] This follows a similar precondition where it is stressed that the *qawwal* must be a knowledgeable person adept in the ways of spirituality. If this clause is fulfilled, then it is improper on the part of participants to question the style of recitation of the *qawwal*. One should not pass remarks such as 'sing loudly', or 'I wish your voice was more sweet'—as this reduces the

[94] *Ahsan al-aqwal*, 130; *Ahsan al-aqwal* (Urdu), 101.
[95] Gisu Daraz, *Khatima Sharif*, 6.
[96] *Ahsan al-aqwal*, 131; *Ahsan al-aqwal* (Urdu), 103.
[97] Ernst, *Eternal Garden*, 153.
[98] Ibid.
[99] Kashani, *Shamail al-ataqiya*, 361, in Ernst, *Eternal Garden*, 153.

sanctity of the assembly into a more mundane occasion.[100] Rather, the participant should sit quietly and listen to the *qawwal*. Once the verses have been read, the Sufi listener can start his *wajd*. In assemblies of *sama*, as Chishtis emphasize, importance must be given not to the quality of the voice, but to the ability of the *qawwal* to inspire the assembly through his skills of recitation, thereby facilitating the progress of the assembly towards the experience of rapture and ecstasy.[101]

Control of the human ego is important for any participant in *sama*. Burhan al-Din once elaborated on this aspect by stating that the physical behaviour of participants should be regulated as a precondition to controlling one's ego.[102] Towards this end the dervish should practice physical restrain and should be sober in his actions. If he accidentally raises his hand when in *sama*, then the exercise is no longer allowable for him. The Sufi participant should be extremely careful never to allow his hands or feet touch another shaykh in the assembly.[103] If it so happens, then the Sufi should immediately withdraw himself to the ground. Once, in an assembly of *sama*, Burhan al-Din felt someone's hand touching his head. His heart became happy, through which he came to realize that the individual was moving under the impact of genuine ecstasy. When another individual's hand touched his head, Burhan al-Din did not feel the same degree of happiness in his heart, which made him realize that this person was doing movements under the influence of his lower self and demonstrating false ecstasy. Happiness or displeasure that arises in an assembly of *sama* emanates from the first person who rises up in the assembly under a feeling of ecstasy.[104]

Zain al-Din Shirazi, the spiritual successor of Burhan al-Din, when emphasizing this aspect of proper physical conduct in *sama* remarked that 'If a hundred Sufis are in *sama*, one walks so that one's skirt does not touch the skirt of another'. He further elaborated that there are some Sufis who remain seated in their position and do not bother others even when they are overcome with ecstasy. Others lose control over their self, make noises like weeping loudly and moving from one place to another.

---

[100] Ibid.
[101] Ibid.
[102] *Ahsan al-aqwal*, 129–135; Ernst, *Eternal Garden*, 153.
[103] Ibid.
[104] *Ahsan al-aqwal* (Urdu), 101–102.

However, on most occasions Sufis participate in *sama* with such controlled behaviour that even in a small space in which twenty to thirty Sufis are emotionally overcome by ecstasy and do limb movements, none is disturbed by the other.[105] But at the same time it is quite probable on the part of humans to commit mistakes, and slips do occur, most of the time unintentionally. On such occasions if someone behaves in an ecstatic state, unmindful of *adab*, then it is advised that fellow Sufis should help the person regain his sober state, without ever handling him roughly, or publicly rebuking his coarse actions.[106] Crawling on the ground under the impulse of overwhelming emotions is considered an expression that lacks physical sobriety. Once Burhan al-Din himself was imposed with a fine when he lost control over his sober self while attending *sama*.[107]

It is strongly advised that no participant in *sama* should drink or eat anything during the proceedings or should look for physical comfort, specifically fanning oneself for air, as discussed above.[108] Considering the warm and inclement climate of north India and the Deccan, the reason for imposing such a regulation is understandable. *Sama* is believed to capture a lovers' suffering for the Beloved, emanating from the material and the spiritual realms. Thus it is ironic that in such an assembly Sufis would search for physical comfort while striving for union with the Beloved.[109]

Sufis like Zain al-Din made occasional exemptions when he advised that light food in the form of rice or soup may be taken before coming into the assembly of *sama*. According to Zain al-Din, those with an empty stomach feel a greater degree of intoxication from *sama*. After *sama* there is no harm in consuming a full meal of bread, meat, and sweets. Zain al-Din further remarked that nourishment can be of two types: one for the body (*jismani*) and the other for the soul (*ruhani*). Bodily nourishment consists of eating, drinking, and sleeping. Nourishment for the soul is derived from hunger, sleeplessness, remembering and contemplating the Divine. *Sama* is a passion for the soul, the taste of which cannot be savoured by a listener who is keen only for physical nourishment.[110]

---

[105] Ernst, *Eternal Garden*, 153.
[106] Ibid.
[107] *Ahsan al-aqwal*, 128–134.
[108] Ibid.
[109] Ibid.
[110] Mir Hasan, *Hidayatul Qulub*, Urdu trans. Nisar Ahmed Faruqi (Aurangabad: Unique Publications, 2013), 65.

Both in north India and the Deccan, Chishti Sufis were responsible for closely regulating assemblies of *sama*. The rule of thumb for the exercise was centred on maintaining an intense concentration on the thought of the Divine Beloved. For Chishti Sufis, *sama* reflected the culmination of their spiritual efforts in establishing an attachment to the Divine through external and internal adherence to *adab*.

One of the last major Chishti Sufis to migrate from Delhi to the Deccan was Sayyid Muhammad Husayni Gisu Daraz, the disciple of Nasir al-Din Mahmud Chiragh-e Dehli. A strong advocate of *sama*, Gisu Daraz put forth an elaborate set of rules, which, in his opinion should regulate an assembly of *sama*. Gisu Daraz carried a major branch of the spiritual legacy of north Indian Chishtis into the Deccan at a time when the *silsila* was facing a crisis in leadership after Zain al-Din passed away in Khuldabad without appointing a spiritual successor. At this crucial juncture, Gisu Daraz retrieved the mantle of Chishti spirituality not only as a shaykh who could train generations of disciples in the spiritual path, but as a scholar of repute, well versed in traditions of the *shariah*, *fiqh*, *tasawwuf*, and Hadith. Thus it is of little surprise that *sama* became the core ritual at the *khanqah* of Gisu Daraz.

Gisu Daraz was of the opinion that participants in *sama* must free themselves from activities like eating, drinking, prayer, and religious duty, and disengage from all worldly bonds. For those who could not withstand limb movements in *sama*, it was advised that they should move into a retreat. Their absence from the assembly is for their own good, so that they may not be destroyed by the intoxicated state of their companions.[111]

Drawing on the classical tenets of Sufism, Gisu Daraz based his instructions on *sama* on the tradition of Junaid of Baghdad. It was Junaid's insistence on the three essential elements of time (*zaman*), place (*makan*), and brethren (*ikhwan*) that inspired Gisu Daraz to formulate his instructions along similar lines. With regard to time, Gisu Daraz insisted that *sama* should be performed at night, and in a well illuminated place. During the night it is easier for one to hide his actual spiritual state (*hal*). However, if a Sufi expects visitors in his *khanqah*, it is advised that he should organize *sama* during the daytime for the convenience of his visitors, so

---

[111] Gisu Daraz, *Khatima Sharif*, 62.

that the latter can attend the assembly as well before taking leave from the *khanqah,* probably around sunset.[112]

Even in the midst of noise and din the participant should strive to focus his attention on the affairs of the assembly for securing the desired spiritual benefit.[113] Hence it was suggested that *sama* should ideally be performed only after the completion of all religious and social duties, so that there remains no distraction for the Sufi saint in *sama.* In the light of the above preferences, it is understandable why *sama* was prescribed at night, after the day's religious and social obligations had been dispensed with.[114]

According to Gisu Daraz the place for the performance of *sama* needs to be carefully chosen.[115] It should be an enclosed and secured (*mahfuz*) space with walls on all sides and a roof. Open spaces must be avoided, since the presence of strong winds can cause the voice of the *qawwal* to echo and be carried away rather than reaching the desired destination (*mahal*), the ears of the listener.[116] Gisu Daraz was perhaps wary of commoners being attracted to the assembly of *sama* due to a high pitched voice, carried by strong winds. Together with being well lit, the place should be well fragranced (*murawwah*) and free (*khali*) from all disturbances. Places where Gisu Daraz attended *sama* used to be well lit and filled with the fragrance of aloes wood and ambergris, together with flowers of various kinds, incense, and sandalwood, whose fragrance enlivened the spirit (*ruh*).[117] Thus the spirit when it receives nourishment from various sources becomes strengthened, which in turn increases the refined taste (*zawq*) for *sama.* Gisu Daraz was careful not to compromise on the sanctity of the ritual, hence he forbade holding *sama* in general public spaces, including wedding ceremonies and mosques.[118] When attending the assembly members should ensure that they do not face the Mecca, nor should their back be towards it.[119]

---

[112] *Khatima,* 34.
[113] Ibid.
[114] *Siyar i-Muhammadi,* 155.
[115] Ibid.
[116] *Khatima,* 46.
[117] Sayyid Muhammad HussainiGisu Daraz, *Sharh i Adab al Muridin: Intikhab,* ed. and trans. Khusro Hussaini (Gulbarga: All India Sayyid Muhammad Gisu Daraz Research Academy, 2014), 23, 34.
[118] *Khatima,* 34.
[119] Ibid., 46.

With regard to the participants in *sama* Gisu Daraz advised that the members in the assembly be of the same spiritual preceptor and belong to similar spiritual dispositions (*yak khanawadah*).[120] Regulations were also imposed as to who should not be allowed in *sama*. Such individuals included the condemner (*munkir*), unaffected disciples (*muta'allimi bi suz*), prosaic jurists (*matafaqqihi bi saz*), masters without passion (*ustadi bi dard*), impure scholars (*danishmandi bi safa*), vagabonds (*gumrah*), members of royalty (*abnai-mulk*), and worldly beings (*arbabi-dunya*). Apart from these, women (*awrat*) were not to be allowed even to peep from doors and windows.[121] Even if the above-mentioned individuals did not show behaviour of discord, their presence was believed to bring stinginess and misfortune. Thus a wide section of the population was not allowed to participate in *sama*. This was done with the primary intention of ensuring that the Divine grace gained from such an intense spiritual exercise is not ruined by the presence of frivolous and unworthy participants.

Instructions left behind by Gisu Daraz reflect the concept of union (*jam*) which the shaykh was attempting to uphold through the ritual of *sama*, both in external and internal aspects.[122] Participants in the assembly of *sama* need to be careful in performing proper ablutions, and should wear white clothes.[123] Since the ritual of *sama* requires purity of the heart, it is in a way symbolic that participants should wear white clothes, which in the spiritual parlance symbolize purity (*safa*).

Gesudraz, taking a cue from his Suhrawardi counterpart, Abu Najib Suhrawardi, stated that assemblies of *sama* should begin and end with a recitation of the Holy Quran.[124] This became mandatory to the extent that if a reciter was unavailable one had to at least try and read the opening verse or *fatiha* from the Holy Book.[125] The explanation forwarded in support for such a practice is that the first part of what is being recited in between the Quranic recitations (*tilawat*) connects to the beginning of *sama*. Similarly, the second half of what is being recited in the

---

[120] Ibid., 21.
[121] Ibid.; Gisu Daraz, *Khatima Sharif*, 6.
[122] *Khatima*, 139.
[123] Ibid.
[124] Hussaini, *Gisudaraz On Sufism*, 132.
[125] *Khatima*, 21.

assembly of *sama* connects to the concluding part of the session. Now, according to Sufi masters if the session begins and ends with the recitation of the Quran then the portion being read in between gets connected to the Quranic recitations, making the entire exercise an audition of the Quran (*sama-i Quran*).[126] Gisu Daraz argued that this is primarily the reason why the Prophet of Islam instructed his companion Mimshad al-Dinawari in a dream that there is no harm in people gathering to listen to *sama*, but it should begin and end with recitation of the Quran. When *sama* begins and ends with the Quran, then the exercise of *sama* in its entirety will be part of the Quranic recitation.[127]

The concentration of the listener in an assembly of *sama* must be fixed on the *qawwal*.[128] If this is not the case then the listener should fix his vision on the front and refrain from looking around towards others.[129]

The central function of the ritual of *sama* remains the practice of meditation and contemplation (*muraqaba*).[130] In this, the Sufi listener should set his goal before him, and concentrate completely on achieving that goal (*maqsud*). Meditation is seen as the primary and most important means of elevating the spirit and moving towards one's goal of Divine witnessing (*shahada*).[131] It is recommended that the mystic should practice silent remembrance (*zikr-i khafi*) of the Divine and should contemplate Him within his heart, so that the desired effect of manifestation is achieved.[132] This combination of *sama* and the *zikr-i khafi* leads to an effective outcome through the ascension of the soul. Though it is recommended that in the assembly of *sama* Sufis should practice silent recollection from the heart, it is also warned that the listener must never practice loud recollection or *zikr-i jali* in an assembly of *sama* through the invocation of *la ilaha ila 'llah* along the beat of the tabla and the duff, as this would be against the spirit of the assembly, transforming its nature into a gathering for *zikr*.[133] Thus although strict remembrance of the Divine is prescribed

---

[126] Ibid.
[127] Ibid.; Gisu Daraz, *Sharh i Adab al Muridin*, 34.
[128] *Khatima*, 34.
[129] Ibid.
[130] Ibid., 24.
[131] Ibid.
[132] Ibid.
[133] Ibid., 41; Gisu Daraz, *Khatima Sharif*, 4–5.

as an essential practice for the Sufi, care must be taken so that the ritual of *sama* does not transform into a practice of *zikr*.

Any sort of bodily movement is discouraged in an assembly of *sama*. Even if such movements arise from physical discomfort, the listener is not permitted to complain or divert his attention away from the proceedings of the assembly.[134] On occasions when the listener is overcome by exhaustion and laxity, he should not drink water or search for refreshments.[135] At the same time, if a sense of intense spiritual energy agitates the Sufi in the course of the proceedings of *sama*, he should refrain from making erratic movements (*jumbishi*) and should rather concentrate on his mentor (*pir*) and try and relate the verses recited in the assembly to the qualities of his *pir*.[136] This is because it is the *pir* who is in charge of the assembly and it is through him that the beneficence of the Divine descends on all participants.[137]

Similar to his predecessors in Khuldabad, Gisu Daraz too recognized the importance of the *qawwal* in *sama*.[138] Hence he vociferously prohibited against any sort of disrespect towards the *qawwal* in course of the assembly. In another context he instructed that the singer should never be questioned with regard to the quality of the verses. The suitability and non-suitability of the verses read out in the assembly of *sama* should be left to the decision of the *qawwal*.[139] Participants of the assembly will have no say in it. At the same time a participant should never request the *qawwal* to recite a particular verse or sing a special *raag* in accordance with his preference and spiritual state.[140] Gisu Daraz stated that the choice of verses is from the Unseen, and whatever the *qawwal* recites in an assembly of *sama*, the inspiration for it arrives from the Divine.[141] Therefore, as the content of the assembly emanates from the Unseen (*ghayb*), it is to be considered as faultless.[142]

---

[134] *Khatima*, 42.
[135] Ibid., 21.
[136] Ibid.
[137] Ibid.
[138] Hussaini, *Gisudaraz On Sufism*, 132.
[139] *Khatima*, 20.
[140] Ibid., 43.
[141] Gisu Daraz, *Khatima Sharif*, 6.
[142] *Khatima*, 43.

It is advised that, if possible, the *qawwal* may be chosen from within the community (*qaum*) of Sufis, so that he is in tune with the mood and sanctity of the assembly.[143] If the *qawwal* is not one from the community, then at least he should be a person of knowledge (*ilm*) and dignity so that he can command respect from the participants of the assembly.[144] The *qawwal* should be absolutely clean (*ba-taharat*) at the time of conducting the affairs of the assembly, or else he should be barred from participating in the exercise.[145] The *qawwal* is also prohibited from actively participating in the affairs of Sufi saints. He is specifically not permitted to rise up and do *raqs* in the course of *sama*.[146] During the proceedings of the assembly, if any participant gets agitated by feelings of ecstasy and thus tears his clothes, then the pieces should be given only to the *qawwal* and no one else.[147]

Sama affects different individuals differently. It may so happen that one participant may be drawn into a sense of ecstasy sooner than his companions. On such an occasion it is incumbent on the part of fellow mystics to conform (*muwafaqat*) to that feeling of ecstasy and thus stand up in support of the agitated Sufi, so that he is not left alone in his state of rapture.[148] But at the same time it is also warned that if a Sufi finds himself regularly in rapture manifested through an agitation in his limbs, it is unwise for him to indulge in *sama* on a regular basis.[149] Under such circumstances the sanctity of the ritual is compromised, and *sama* turns into a frivolous pastime. This would lead to hypocrisy (*nifaq*) within the participant, rather than aid his spiritual elevation.[150]

Such strict guidelines as those enumerated above, in the spirit of the great Sufi masters from earlier generations, helped regulate the practice of *sama* by upholding its sanctity in the face of strong opposition from the state, legists, and religious scholars, thereby preventing its degeneration into an everyday musical performance. Sufi shrines which preserve the exalted spiritual tradition of these bygone Sufi saints for lay devotees,

---

[143] Ibid., 34.
[144] *Khatima*, 47.
[145] Ibid.
[146] Ibid., 43.
[147] Ibid.
[148] Ibid., 42.
[149] Ibid., 41.
[150] Ibid.

who offer their respect at the grave of the deceased saint, organize *sama* after completing the last prayer, accompanied by the recitation of the Holy Quran.[151] Music is strictly forbidden on such occasions, and it is known as *shar-i urs*, meaning the celebration of *urs* where music is not allowed. Such is the practice of *sama* at the shrine of Usman al- Hujwiri in Lahore, where music is not allowed, and participants spend the night engaging themselves in prayers and recitation of the Quran.[152]

What emerges from the above discussion is the fact that for the Sufi saint to benefit from the exercise of *sama*, it is necessary that his heart is free from worldly distractions, and remains orientated strictly towards the ultimate goal (*maqsud-i- tamam*) of spiritual union with God. It is only through a proper adherence to this path of spiritual progress that the Sufi can hope to achieve spiritual triumph (*fatah*), taking him closer to- wards the experience of the Divine.

Adab in *Sama* among Suhrawardi Sufis

On many occasions Suhrawardi participation in *sama* resulted from companionship with shaykhs of other orders who were inclined towards the exercise. An exception in this regard is Qazi Hamid al-Din Nagauri, whose elaborate *sama* parties at his *khanqah* were comparable to *sama* in the Chishti *khanqahs*.[153] However it is interesting to note that Suhrawardi Sufis emphasized proper conduct in *sama*, together with the ways in which the assembly can be organized. An analysis of this throws much light on the Suhrawardi approach to *sama*.

The most important issue for Suhrawardi Sufis concerned the necessity of *sama* as a spiritual exercise, along with the exercise of remembrance (*zikr*).[154] In any assembly of *sama*, if participants show sincere intention and seek the spiritual path then first and foremost all lustful desires need to be shunned. Participants in the assembly should be united (*jam*) in

---

[151] John A. Subhan, *Sufism: Its Saints and Shrines, An Introduction to the Study of Sufism with Special Reference to India* (Lucknow: Lucknow Publishing House, 1938), 114.
[152] *Khatima*, 41.
[153] Subhan, *Sufism*, 120.
[154] *Awarif al Maarif*, 57.

their spiritual quest, setting aside worldly thoughts that may disrupt the benefits desired from such an exercise.[155]

In many instances it may be such that individuals participating in *sama* demonstrate a superficial spiritual sense, only to gain access to the assembly where they ultimately indulge in frivolity. It is then necessary to purify the ambience of such an assembly through invoking the blessings of the Divine through supererogatory prayers and special recitations.[156]

Sama being an intensely spiritual exercise, it is possible that an individual who enters such an assembly with an impure heart may, under Divine grace, undergo a change within his self, as a result of the spiritual and sacred ambience of the gathering. Under such circumstances, what should be the response of other attendants? It is suggested that even under changed conditions of the heart it is incumbent upon participants to shun such an assembly at the first instance.[157] This is because it is the initial condition of the heart that matters, rather than the transformed state of the individual, and thus the assembly will remain polluted in its essence. Thus it can be deduced that purity of the self was considered a primary prerequisite for participation in *sama,* and such a state should prevail among all the participants of the assembly from the beginning until the end.

Certain things are absolutely prohibited in *sama,* including the elaborate spread of food, especially from non-permissible and illegal sources, and if donated by corrupt individuals. Women should also be kept away from the vicinity of such an assembly.[158] In Chishti accounts, the details of which have been elaborated, it is prohibited to hold *sama* in open spaces, lest womenfolk witness it from the balconies and windows of surrounding houses.[159] Suhrawardi Sufis, though not explicit to that extent, are equally conservative on the issue of women participating in any type of spiritual exercise, not to mention *sama.* In the same breath, the presence of beardless youths is forbidden in *sama.*[160]

---

[155] Ibid.
[156] Ibid.
[157] Ibid.
[158] Ibid.
[159] *Kashf al Mahjub,* 420.
[160] *Awarif al Maarif,* 57.

Certain kinds of individuals are also unwelcome in an assembly of *sama* as they tend to pollute the ambience of the gathering rather than add to its purity. First are those who though apparently religious in their demeanour have no attachment to the assembly, and do not emotionally connect to other participants.[161] Such individuals if present in the gathering do not take any delight in the proceedings of *sama*, and as a result hinder the smooth flow of blessings from the Unseen, therefore harming the spiritual progress of the gathering so that other participants, though concentrated on the remembrance of God, do not feel the refined taste (*zawq*) of *sama*, and are bereft of the desired blessings from God. Under such circumstances it is obligatory on the master of the assembly to throw out the person from the gathering, even if it requires the application of force.[162]

In an assembly of *sama* the intention is to gain maximum spiritual benefit, where Sufi saints are engaged in the contemplation of the Divine. In such an assembly, relations of hierarchy are dissolved in the spiritual path, and participants in *sama* are equal in the eyes of the Lord. When an individual with a sense of superiority enters such an assembly, he disrupts the calmness of the spiritual gathering. The assembly is diverted from its aim of seeking the Divine Beloved.[163] Therefore one who demonstrates any sense of superiority in an assembly of *sama* must not be allowed in such gatherings.

The last regulation concerns the effect of *sama* as it descends on the participant with a pure heart. As elaborated earlier, it is known that *sama* affects each individual differently, in tune with his spiritual maturity. However, individuals who do not experience ecstasy (*wajd*) are often tempted to exhibit false emotions. It is warned that such individuals dilute the spirit of the assembly.[164] Since Suhrawardi Sufis did not encourage empathetic ecstasy (*tawajud*), it was strictly forbidden to take recourse to such emotions. If any individual present in the assembly demonstrates such feelings, it is the duty of the master of the assembly to stop such participants, or else the spiritually minded should leave the assembly at the earliest opportunity.[165]

---

[161] Ibid.
[162] Ibid., 58.
[163] Ibid.
[164] Ibid.
[165] Ibid.

What, then, is the ideal conduct in *sama*? Elaborating on this aspect, Shihab al-Din Suhrawardi states that those present in *sama* should behave with proper manners (*adab*) and dignity. The person should not be of a frivolous nature. His intent and manner of participation is crucial to his experience of the spiritual truth. On such occasions he should not be overcome with feelings of agitation at the slightest indication of Divine favour.[166] Rather it is proper for him to remain restrained in the assembly, especially in the presence of the master. His remaining under the control of his emotions is central to attracting Divine beneficence that may be bestowed upon him. Under such circumstances he should not voluntarily express either a murmur (*shahqat*) or any sort of loud calling (*za'q*) so as to shatter the calmness of the assembly.[167]

Suhrawardi Sufis were strong advocates of sobriety in *sama*. Our earlier discussion on participation of Suhrawardi saints in *sama*, and what can be preferably called their measured proximity to elaborate *sama* assemblies with music and dance, is illustrative of this approach. It was on a rare occasion when Baha al-Din participated in *sama* and his peers remembered him as someone not bestowed with the taste for music. This approach to *sama* is reinforced through an incident recorded in the life of a Suhrawardi Sufi from Ucch, Jalal al-Din Bukhari Makhdum-i Jahaniyan (d. 1384). As mentioned earlier, itinerant *qawwals* and musicians would often pass through Suhrawardi territories in western Punjab, at times performing *sama* in their *khanqahs*. One such group visited Jalal al-Din from Shiraz, and performed in his presence. After recitation from the Quran, and some verses of poetry, when the performers played the flute the assembly went into a rapture. A certain Maulana Taj al-Din Muhammad was so overcome with ecstasy that he began to weep, fell on the ground, and started to crawl while foaming from the mouth. The loud noise and chaos affected the deep meditation (*muraqaba*) of Jalal al-Din, who enquired on the matter from his attendants. When he heard about the Maulana, he prayed to God to provide the Maulana with strength to recover from his state.[168]

[166] Ibid.
[167] Ibid.
[168] Amina M. Steinfels, *Knowledge Before Action: Islamic Learning and Sufi Practice in the Life of Sayyid Jalal al-Din Bukhari Makhdum-I Jahaniyan* (Columbia: University of South Carolina Press, 2012), 84.

Suhrawardi Sufis recommend severe admonishment for individuals who exhibit false emotions in *sama*. If an individual who is yet to experience ecstasy (*wajd*) does limb movements, that person is the most despicable one in the assembly. By taking recourse to falsehood, they ruin the spirit of the ritual.[169] At the same time they deceive other participants in *sama,* through their false spiritual state (*hal*). Deceit in spiritual matters is considered to be a foul act that amounts to treachery and is therefore the source of repulsion for any state (*hal*) in an individual—particularly spiritual. When an individual through such disgraceful acts in the name of spiritual pursuit leads astray his fellow mystics, he in turn deprives himself of the beneficial effects that descend from the Unseen.[170]

Rather it is the characteristic of individuals who experience ecstasy (*wajd*) that they retain their calmness and posture during *sama* until they are completely overtaken by their emotional turmoil so that they are no longer able to control their outward self, just as the person who, no matter how hard he tries to control himself, cannot help but sneeze. It is then considered to be the mercy of the Divine, since experiencing true ecstasy in *sama* is a gift from the Divine bestowed only on loved ones.

Such uncontrolled expressions of ecstasy arise from novices who are new to the practice of *sama*.[171] When a novice utters a loud cry while in the assembly of *sama*, he actually enjoys a portion of the Divine beneficence that descends on the assembly of which he is a recipient, through the situation of his *hal*. Such an action is permitted for the novice, keeping in mind his lack of spiritual maturity.[172] But for the adept it is a reprehensible act. This is because for them, their entire entity is witness to the Divine truth, and their spiritual state (*hal*) is in a constant state of purity—inwardly and outwardly.[173]

Thus one can argue in the words of the famous mystic Abu Abd Allah Rudhabari that *sama* is realized in its entirety, and in turn benefitted from, by those individuals who are truthful in their intention and possess three things at the time of participation. Firstly, the knowledge of God—which is imperative for any individual who intends to heighten his

---

[169] *Awarif al Maarif,* 58.
[170] Ibid. 59.
[171] Ibid.
[172] Ibid.
[173] *Kitab Adab al-Muridin,* 33.

spiritual gains in *sama*. Secondly, fulfilment of what is required by his spiritual state (*hal*)—when the heart of the mystic yearns for beneficence of the Divine it is blessed by the Almighty. And finally, the concentration of his religious ambition (*jam al- himma*)—where he completely immerses himself in contemplation of his Beloved so that nothing material stops him from achieving his spiritual goal.

Regarding the basic etiquette of holding the assembly of *sama*, Shihab al-Din Suhrawardi refers to the Sufi master from Baghdad, Junaid, who, when asked as to why he was not in favour of holding *sama*, replied 'With whom may I hold *sama*?' And when people further stated to Junaid that in an assembly of *sama* one ought to hear with his own heart, Junaid retorted back in a mode of enquiry, 'From whom may I hear?'.[174] It is with regard to such a spiritual disposition of one of the greatest mystics of his times that Shihab al-Din argued that one should participate in an assembly of *sama* with individuals who empathize, both spiritually and morally, with each other. Only then will he be able to rise above his material trappings and strive towards a common spiritual goal, in the path of the Divine. In an assembly of *sama*, spiritual elevation should be such that the mystic resides in the glory of the Almighty, and thus hears from His essence. Such heights of spiritual maturity make the mystic realize his love for the Beloved, which rises above and goes beyond the confines of the material world, towards the next. Only in such circumstances does the sweetness of the *qawwals*' voice truly touch the realm of divinity.

[174] Ibid.

Conclusion

Research on Sufism in South Asia during its formative period, which is also the focus of this book, has evolved continuously, allowing us valuable insight on the history of Sufi orders (*silsila*), the role of charismatic Sufi masters negotiating social, political and the spiritual worlds, their decisive roles as shaykhs and world-renouncing ascetics, the contribution of Sufi masters and their disciples towards the formation of Indo-Muslim culture, the internal spiritual strategies of early orders like the Chishti and Suhrawardi, and, most importantly, the individual lives of the early masters, among other things. Complementing such a range of Sufi experiences, this book explores the aspect of Sufi rituals and spiritual practices. The work rests on an analytical framework which studies the latter as an essential element of institutional Sufism in South Asia, as well as an integral religious practice which Sufi masters engaged with in varying degrees. In the period that is surveyed, the formalization of core Sufi rituals like *sama* and *zikr* takes place in South Asia, seen through the teaching and practice of individual Sufi masters. An understanding of this process underlines the narrative of this work.

Certain major issues are explored and analysed in this study. The first concerns the question of what is a Sufi ritual, for example *sama*, and why is it important as a religious practice among Sufis. Sufi rituals can be understood as facilitating a spiritual experience that Sufis seek in their endless quest for the Divine. It is also an exercise of remembering God, driven by deep emotions of love and devotion, to the extent where one can lose his *self* in the essence of the Lord.

Sama as a Sufi practice has been long prevalent in Iran and Iraq, from the earliest times when Sufism was more a spiritual idea than an institutionalized practice. Arab texts from the tenth century speak of the practice of listening to poetry and music for spiritual benefit. With passing time, however, it became important to distinguish between music and poetry

Sufi Rituals and Practices. Kashshaf Ghani, Oxford University Press. © Kashshaf Ghani 2024.
DOI: 10.1093/oso/9780192889225.003.0007

as a lay practice, and the same for spiritual succour. The controversial status of music in the eyes of Islamic law started a strong debate around the practice of music in Sufism. Permissibility of such a practice required elaborate conditions as advised by Sufi masters, who saw great spiritual merit in *sama* when organized under strict regulations. It is with regard to implementing the latter that *sama* does not remain simply as a spiritual experience. The intellectual ability of the listener, which allowed him to interpret verses of poetry along the attributes of the Divine, became an important precondition for participation in *sama*. Hence the context of the ritual, a religious activity undertaken for spiritual experience, together with the people involved in it determined the permissibility of the practice. Circumstances in which *sama* was organized thus came to be accepted as a determinant of its legality. In many instances Sufis stressed the rigorous conditioning of the heart before participating in *sama*, so that ecstatic behaviour could be controlled. By the twelfth century, Sufi masters who left behind treatises that captured their spiritual knowledge as well as their experience of training disciples, and scholars who wrote on Sufism, were commonly in agreement that *sama* is not a ritual for the masses. Its permissibility and legality were contingent on proper training of the listener, reciting poetry which did not include descriptions of physical sensuality, avoiding the use of musical instruments of the stringed variety which produced sharp sounds, correct interpretation of the verses recited, recitation of the Quran at the beginning and the end—but most importantly the common desire of the assembly to seek Divine grace.

The second issue concerns the importance of *sama* as a Sufi practice in a specific regional context—that of South Asia. Beginning from the thirteenth century, Sufi saints trained under eminent shaykhs in Iran, Iraq, and Central Asia began to establish their spiritual domain in India; complementing the process of state formation by the Turkish military elite in and around Delhi. While carving out domains of territorial authority (*wilayat*) in India—the Suhrawardis in Multan, Ucch, Punjab, and Bengal; and the Chishtis in Ajmer, Delhi, Punjab, Deccan, and Bengal—the early Sufis were instrumental in establishing Sufism as an institutionalized religious practice in South Asia, evident through the spiritual orders, and formalized through initiatic genealogies which connected the living shaykh to his master and eminent Sufis of earlier generations, upholding *sama* and *zikr* as core practices of their orders, and a strong emphasis on teaching and training disciples.

The Chishti order defended *sama* as their core spiritual practice. The role of individual Chishti Sufis in formalizing this ritual is comprehensible through first-hand accounts, particularly from the time of Nizam al-Din. It is through his oral discourses compiled in the *Fawaid al Fuad* that we get an insight into Baba Farid al-Din and Qutb al-Din Bakhtiyar Kaki's participation in *sama*. Thus, in the period that we cover, the approach of the 'Chishti order' towards *sama* can be understood not as a set of codified rules, guidelines, and spiritual experiences handed down in an unaltered form from Muin al-Din Chishti onwards to successive Chishti masters. In fact, we hardly learn anything on Muin al-Din Chishti and his spiritual experiences and teachings from contemporary accounts, not to mention that the saint and his immediate successors did not leave behind any writings. A similar dearth of written sources characterizes Chishti historiography until the time of Nizam al-Din. Rather it is helpful for our purpose to analyse the engagement of individual Chishti masters with *sama* in varying capacities, as disciples, and thereafter as Sufi shaykhs, thereby allowing us a historical understanding of the ritual as it evolved as the core practice of the Chishti order.

Such understandings are made possible through the study of oral discourses of Sufi masters compiled by their elite disciples, over a period of time, and how these constituted an inseparable component of spiritual training offered by the shaykh. Together with the spiritual disposition of individual Chishti shaykhs with regard to *sama*, which is understandably not uniform as we proceed from one generation to the next—like Nizam al-Din Awliya to Burhan al-Din Gharib, and Nasir al-Din Mahmud to Gisu Daraz—Chishti *malfuzat* and biographical literature also capture the socio-political tensions around *sama* as a controversial practice in the shifting religious climate of the Delhi Sultanate around the age-old debate on listening to music in the eye of Islamic law, brought into focus through the strong criticism advanced by Ibn Taimiyya.

Third is the importance of the historical context when analysing *sama* as a Sufi ritual. Nizam al-Din's elaborate discourses on *sama*, building on the works of earlier Sufi masters, are the most comprehensive we can get from the first cycle of Chishti Sufis. The saint touches upon the preconditions for organizing the assembly, categorizes the kinds of listeners as well as the nature of participants in *sama*, emphasizes upon maintaining the integrity of the *shariah* when organizing *sama*, categorizes *sama*, sets out the ideal conditions for organizing *sama* including the behaviour of participants, and attributes the success of *sama* to Divine grace on the assembly. These guidelines need to be understood against the background of the tensions pervading this Sufi practice within the Tughluq Empire. That Chishti Sufis made extensive references to Hadith traditions and Islamic law in defence of *sama* is strongly proven through the *Usul al Sama* of Maulana Fakhr al-Din Zarradi. It provides us a valuable insight into the intellectual climate of Delhi, and the approach undertaken by Nizam al-Din when defending *sama* in the court of Sultan Ghiyas al-Din Tughluq, and points towards the diverse backgrounds from which individuals, such as a reputed scholar of Islamic sciences like Fakhr al-Din Zarradi, invested themselves in the Chishti spiritual tradition to the extent of defending a debated spiritual practice.

Sama as a core practice was also integral to the creation of a Chishti sacred geography through a network of centres where disciples of eminent Chishti saints like Baba Farid al-Din and Nizam al-Din continued their practice of teaching and spiritual pursuit. Deccan constituted an important territory to the south of Delhi, where Khuldabad and Gulbarga emerged as major centres of Chishti Sufism. Burhan al-Din Gharib, being well aware of the controversies around *sama* during the lifetime of his master, Nizam al-Din, and together with his own ecstatic behaviour during *sama*, which at times attracted critical attention, laid down strict rules with regard to participation in the exercise. The recommendations of the saint categorized *sama* depending on the psychological inclination of the participant, which included novices as well as adepts, stressed on the proper interpretation of poetry, and allowed novices to practice empathetic ecstasy, but included a reminder that for adepts *sama* often loses usefulness. Though Burhan al-Din was more of a lover and dervish at heart, focused on spiritual contemplation and emotions of the heart, his legalistic approach towards the practice of *sama* is understandable from his experiences at the *khanqah* of Nizam al-Din, along with the responsibility of single-handedly heading the Chishti order in the Deccan.

Later, when Gisu Daraz arrived in the Deccan and settled in Gulbarga, he carried with him the experience of his confrontation with the *ulama* in Delhi, who had accused the saint of indulging in the un-Islamic and frivolous practice of *sama*. Even though Gisu Daraz was attached to *sama*, he was also a reputed scholar in the various branches of Islamic knowledge, trained under the austere Nasir al-Din Mahmud Chiragh e Dehli. Through a combination of legal and spiritual approaches, Gisu Daraz strongly advocated an elaborate set of rules for *sama*, starting with recitation of the Quran at the beginning and the end of *sama*, types of *sama*, the quality of the participant, need for restrained behaviour, allowing *sama* according to the level of spiritual training of the participant, it being non-permissible for the masses, and advice for controlling one's emotions during the assembly.

The fourth issue is to understand practices like *sama* and *zikr* as spiritual experiences which are integral to a particular order, but are not unacceptable to other orders. As a core spiritual practice, *zikr* epitomized the quest of the Suhrawardi Sufis for the Divine, combining within itself an interiorization of the Quran with specialized litanies. Like *sama*, the exercise of *zikr* too was organized at specific hours, through a careful selection of the place, the participants, and the content. Though it is popularly accepted that preferences for *sama* and *zikr* constituted a major distinction between Chishti and Suhrawardi orders, the assumption is often that of disrespect towards *sama* by Suhrawardi Sufis. Such a position is conveniently reinforced through the fact that the Suhrawardi order is legalistic in its orientation, along with references to Baha al-Din Zakariya's lack of inclination for music and poetry, as with his Suhrawardi contemporaries and disciples. Such a spiritual preference is taken to be a normative position—fixed and unchanging. While we have the example of the Suhrawardi saint of Delhi, Qazi Hamid al-Din Nagauri, being an ardent lover of *sama*, the practice also came to be defended in the arbitration council called by Sultan Ghiyas al-Din Tughluq, as an acceptable religious activity by the descendants of Baha al-Din Zakariya. Shihab al-Din Suhrawardi's *Awarif ul Maarif* carries a detailed discussion on *sama*, including its manners and etiquette. In a similar manner Chishti treatises emphasize the importance of *zikr* as a spiritual practice, to the extent that Nizam al-Din once remarked that under no circumstances can the goals for *sama* and *zikr* be considered separate.

Finally, *adab* as moral conduct is emphasized as necessary criteria for the spiritual path, and constitutes an inalienable aspect as far as spiritual practices like *sama* and *zikr* are concerned. *Adab* came to be seen as integral to spiritual training, a prerequisite for maintaining external and internal conduct, and adherence to it ensured an uninterrupted flow of knowledge and grace from the master to the disciple. In Sufi rituals like *sama* and *zikr*, the practice of *adab* came to be stressed as an important requirement which not only controlled the external behaviour of the participant, but helped in maintaining internal composure in the face of ecstatic experiences. For Sufis, across orders, the perfection of the spiritual state was contingent upon proper training under the master, where etiquette needed to be adhered to not only during external conduct in the presence of the shaykh; rather *adab* became important as a quality the awareness of which helped in the perfection of a disciple's spiritual state. The latter thus became an important qualifier for any spiritual seeker.

Sufi rituals like *sama* are multilayered, while at the same time carrying a rich historical legacy which allows us to understand its development through subtle adjustments, changes in approach, and innovations under generations of Sufi shaykhs. While spiritual experiences are beyond expression through written words, the contribution of religious practices like *sama* and *zikr* towards realizing the essence of God through seeking spiritual union is recognized by Sufi saints across generations and regions.

The current work is an attempt to study the layers of this history, and the practice of these rituals from medieval South Asia, arguing that there is much more to Sufi spiritual practices than simply being signs of morbid inwardness among those who practice it. If readers find this idea clearly expressed and cogently argued, the work has been worth undertaking.

Spiritual Genealogy of Chishti and Suhrawardi Silsilas

Chishti Order in South Asia

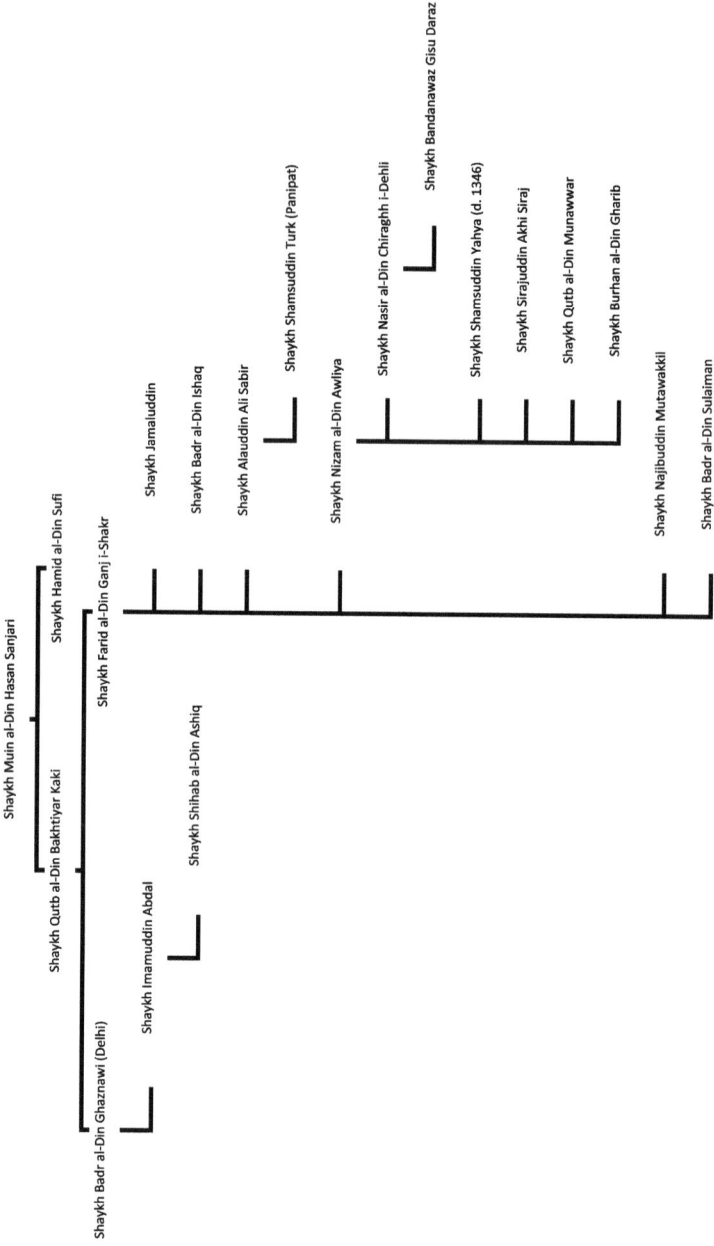

Shaykh Muin al-Din Hasan Sanjari

Shaykh Qutb al-Din Bakhtiyar Kaki

Shaykh Hamid al-Din Sufi

Shaykh Farid al-Din Ganj i-Shakr

Shaykh Badr al-Din Ghaznawi (Delhi)

Shaykh Imamuddin Abdal

Shaykh Shihab al-Din Ashiq

Shaykh Jamaluddin

Shaykh Badr al-Din Ishaq

Shaykh Alauddin Ali Sabir

Shaykh Shamsuddin Turk (Panipat)

Shaykh Nizam al-Din Awliya

Shaykh Nasir al-Din Chiragh i-Dehli

Shaykh Bandanawaz Gisu Daraz

Shaykh Shamsuddin Yahya (d. 1346)

Shaykh Sirajuddin Akhi Siraj

Shaykh Qutb al-Din Munawwar

Shaykh Burhan al-Din Gharib

Shaykh Najibuddin Mutawakkil

Shaykh Badr al-Din Sulaiman

Suhrawardi Order in South Asia

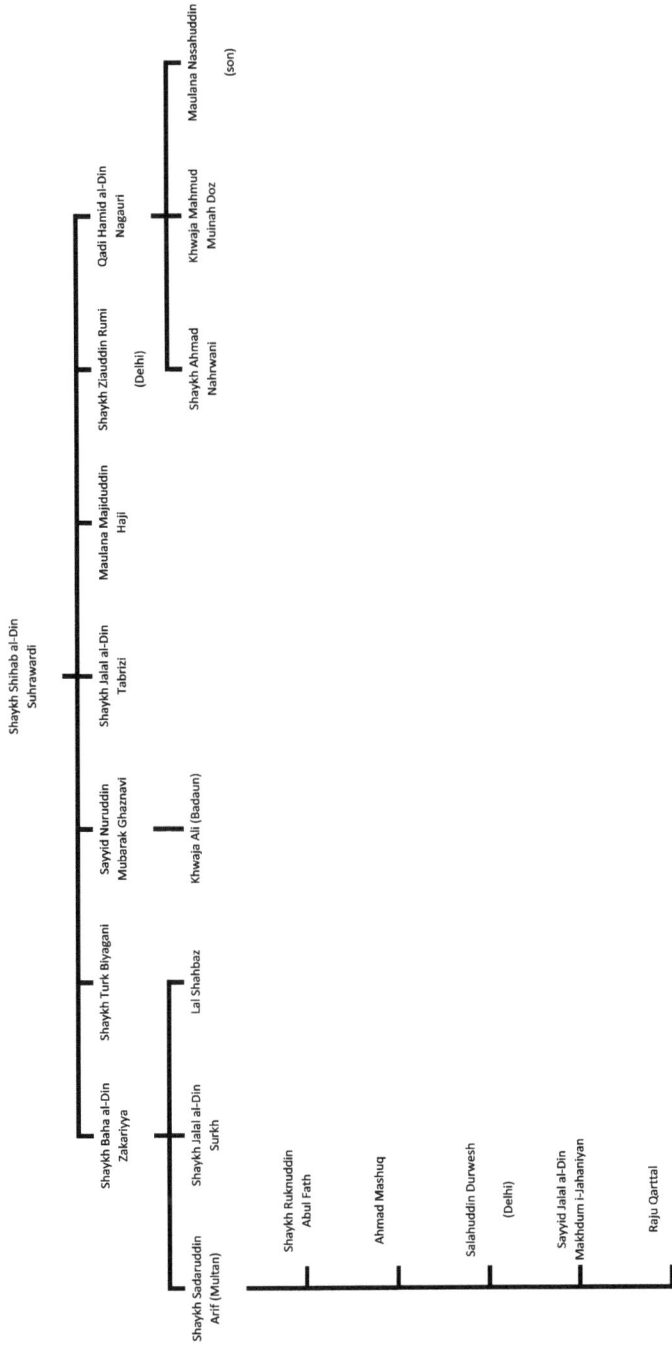

Shaykh Shihab al-Din
Suhrawardi

- Shaykh Baha al-Din Zakariyya
  - Shaykh Turk Biyagani
    - Sayyid Nuruddin Mubarak Ghaznavi
    - Shaykh Jalal al-Din Tabrizi
    - Maulana Majiduddin Haji
    - Shaykh Ziauddin Rumi (Delhi)
    - Qadi Hamid al-Din Nagauri

- Shaykh Sadruddin Arif (Multan)
  - Shaykh Jalal al-Din Surkh
  - Lal Shahbaz
    - Khwaja Ali (Badaun)

- Shaykh Rukmuddin Abul Fath

- Ahmad Mashuq

- Salahuddin Durwesh (Delhi)

- Sayyid Jalal al-Din Makhdum i-Jahaniyan

- Raju Qarttal

- Shaykh Ahmad Nahrwani
- Khwaja Mahmud Mulnah Doz
  - Maulana Nasahuddin (son)

Glossary

Abna-i mulk	Royalty
Abhava	(Sanskrit) Non-Existence
Adab	Manners and Etiquette
Azan	Call for prayer
Ahwal	(sing. Hal) Spiritual state
Ajab	Strange
Ajami	Persian
Anbiya	(sing. Nabi) Prophet
Andih	Grief
Anwar	Illumination
Aql	Mind
Ashiq	Lover
Arbab-i dunya	Worldly individual
Arif	Gnostic
Asir ullah	Captive of God
Assar	Impression
Athar	Sublime Impression
Awliya	(sing. Wali) (literally 'friend')—used to denote Sufis as friends of God.
Award	Invocatory
Ba-Haq	With truth
Ba-Nafs	Sensually
Baqa	Permanence
Basher	Glad tidings
Ba-Taharat	Absolutely clean
Batin	Inner
Bhava	(Sanskrit) Existence

Buka	Lamentation
Chang	Harp
Danishmand	A wise man
Danishmandi bi safa	Impure scholar
Darb	Beat
Dard	Pain
Dargah	Sufi shrine built around the tomb of a saint.
Dholak	Barrel shaped double headed wooden drum.
Duff	Handheld drum made of a circular wooden frame.
Duwidani	Running
Eitmenan	Calmness
Fanaa	Annihilation
Fatah	Triumph
Fatwa	An Islamic religious ruling, a scholarly opinion on a matter of Islamic law.
Fiqh	(literally 'understanding)—the science of law; jurisprudence
Firaaq	Separation
Flute	Wind instrument
Gaddi	(literally 'sitting cushion')—sitting place of a Sufi master.
Gashtami	Circling
Ghair Hajim	Non-Invasive
Ghayb	Unseen
Ghaybat	Absent
Ghazal	Light classical vocal genre based on poetry.
Ghina	Song
Giryah	Crying
Gulistan	Rose garden
Gumrah	Vagabond
Hadith	Saying of the Prophet
Hadith-i Qudsi	Sayings of Prophet Muhammad as revealed to him by Almighty Allah.
Hajim	Invasive
Hajj	Pilgrimage to Mecca

Hal	State
Halal	Permitted
Haqaiq	Truth
Haram	Forbidden
Hawa	Pleasure
Hifz	Memorizing the Quran
Hijab	Veil
Hujra	Meditation cell
Hulul	Encounter
Huzn	Sorrow
Ibadat	(literally 'divine worship')—taken to mean the worship of Allah.
Idtirab	Agitation
Ikhwan	Brethren
Ilahi	Divine
Ilhan	Lilt
Ilm-i tasawwuf	Spiritual Knowledge
Insan-i Kamil	Perfect man
Isharat	Signs
Jabarut	Transconscience
Jadhbah	Attraction
Jam	Union
Jamaat Khana	Home of Sufi master where teaching takes place.
Jannat	Paradise
Jayez	Lawful
Jazb	Rapture
Jumbish	Erratic movement
Kamil	Adept
Karamat	Miracle of a saint
Karishma	Coquetry
Kashf	To 'unveil'
Khad	Cheek

Khal	Mole
Khali	Free
Khalifa	Deputy of a Sufi
Khanah	House
Khanqah	A Sufi hospice
Khatib	Preacher
Khilafatnama	Document of sucessorship
Khudi	Self
Khawf	Fear
Khwass	Select
Kibryayi	Magnificence
Kuffar	Unbeliever
Lahi	Frivolous
Lahut	Divine
Lataif	(sing. Latifat) Elegance
Layla't ul Qadr	(literally 'night of power')—Muslims believe the first verses of the Quran were revealed to Prophet Muhammad (SAW) on this night. It could be one of the odd-numbered days in the last days of the month of Ramadan.
Magaz	Intellect
Mahall	Destination
Mahbub-i Ilahi	Beloved of God
Mahfuz	Enclosed
Mahzar	Council
Majhdhab	Schools of Islamic jurisprudence
Majlis	Assembly
Makan	Place
Makruh	Disapproved
Malaqut	Spiritual
Malfuzat	(sing. Malfuz) (literally 'words')—the sayings of a Sufi collected and recorded by one of his disciples.
Maqam	Spiritual station
Maqsud	Goal

Mashuq	Beloved
Matafaqqihi bi saz	Prosaic jurist
Mazamir	Instruments
Mazhar	Manifestation
Maujud	Material existence
Mehfil	Assembly
Mubah	Allowable
Mubtadi	Beginner
Muhibb	Friend
Mulki	Resident
Munkir	Condemner
Muqayyad	Accompanied by music
Muraqaba	Meditation
Murawwah	Perfumed
Murid	Disciple
Murshid	Spiritual master
Mushahada	Manifestation
Mustami	Listener
Muta'allimi bi suz	Unaffected disciple
Mutawassit	Advanced
Mutlaq	Soundless
Mutmaina	Cleansing
Muwafeqat	Conformity
Nadhir	Warner
Nafs	The lower self
Naz	Pride
Nifaq	Hypocrisy
Nur-i ilahi	Divine light
Nur ul Haqq	Light of truth
Paidani	To and fro
Pidar	Father
Pir	Spiritual master

Qubul	Accepted
Qazi	Jurist
Qalb	Heart
Qaum	Community
Qawwal	Performer of Sufi music
Qiraat	Quranic cantillation
Qul	To 'say'
Quwwat	Power
Qutub	Pole
Rabab	Bowed instrument
Rah	Path
Rahman	Beneficent
Rahmat	Kindness
Rahim	Merciful
Raji	Hope
Rakat	A unit of prostration, genuflexion, and prescribed prayer formulae in Muslim ritual prayer.
Raqs	Ecstatic dance
Ruhani	Spiritual
Safa	Purity
Sahib	Master
Sajadah	Prostration
Salaat	Prayer
Salaat al asr	Afternoon daily prayer recited by practicing Muslims.
Salaat al maghrib	Evening prayer recited by practicing Muslims.
Sama	(literally 'audition')—musical session held by Sufis to induce spiritual ecstasy.
Sama bi'l Mazamir	Listening to music accompanied by instruments.
Samakhana	Place where *sama* is performed.
Sawm	Fasting
Shahada	Witness
Shariah	Islamic law
Shaykh ul Islam	Leader of Islam

Siddiq	Purist
Silsila	(literally 'chain')—a term for Sufi order.
Sura	Chapter of the Quran
Suzi	Burning
Tab'	Instinct
Tabii	Sensual
Tahaqqaqa	Attaining truth
Taharat	Purity
Tahmil	Correlation
Takalluf	Forced behaviour
Tajalli	Flashes
Takhti	Writing slate
Talabi	Seeking
Tasawwuf	Mysticism
Tarawih	A prayer offered in congregation after the night prayer in the month of Ramadan.
Tardid	Repitition
Tariqat	Way
Tartil	Rhythmic tone
Tauba	Repentance
Tauhid	Unity of God
Tawakkul	Dependence
Tawajjuh	Contemplation
Tawajud	Empathetic ecstasy
Tazandaqa	Heresy
Tawafuq	Imitation
Tilawat	Recitation of the Quran
Ulama	(sing. Alim) A man trained in the Islamic religious sciences; class of theologians supported by the state to uphold Islamic orthodoxy in the kingdom.
Urs	(literally 'wedding')—celebration of a saint's final union with God on his death anniversary.
Ustadi bi dard	Merciless master

Wad	Rule
Wahadat ul Wujud	Unity of being
Wajd	Ecstasy
Warid	Visitation
Wazn	Rhythmic
Wifaq	Conformity
Wudu	Ablution
Wujud	Existence
Wisal	Union
Yak khanawadah	Same faith
Zahir	Outer
Zakat	Donation
Zaq	Loud cry
Zaman	Time
Zamin	Earth
Zauq	Taste
Zikr	The repetition/recollection of God or His attributes with the aim of bringing the Sufi closer to God.

Bibliography

Works in Persian, Arabic, and Urdu

Attar, Farid al-din, *Tazkirat ul-Awliya* (Tehran: Intisharat-i Zavvar, 1987).

Bakk, Masud, *Mirat al-arifin* (Hyderabad: Mufid-i Dakan, 1891).

Barani, Ziyauddin, *Tarikh-i Firuz Shahi*, ed. Sayyid Ahmad Khan (Calcutta: The Asiatic Society of Bengal, 1862).

Bilgrami, Ghulam Azad, *Rawzat al-awliya al-maruf bi-nafahat al-asfiya*, Urdu trans. Muhammad Abd al-Majid (Hyderabad: Matba-i Karimi, 1926–1927).

Biruni, Abu Rayhan al-, *Kitab ul-Hind*, Eng. trans. Edward Sachau, *Alberuni's India* (Delhi: S. Chand, 1964).

Chishti, Abdur Rahman, *Mirat ul-Asrar*, Urdu trans. Wahid Baksh Siyal (Lahore: Sufi Foundation, 1982).

Chishtı, Alı Asghar, *Jawahir-i farıdı* (Lahore: Punjab Press, 1884).

Dehlawi, Abd al-Haqq Muhaddis, *Akhbar al-akhyar fi asrar al-abrar* (Delhi: Matba-i Mujtabai, 1913–1914).

Dunya, Ibn Abi al-, *Dhamm i-Malahi*, trans. James Robson, *Tracts on Listening to Music* (London: Royal Asiatic Society, 1938).

Firishta, Muhammad Qasim, *Gulshan-i Ibrahimi* (Lucknow: Nawal Kishore, 1865), Eng. trans. J. Briggs, *History of the Rise of the Mahomedan Power in India* (Calcutta: Editions Indian, 1966).

Gesudaraz, Husayni, *Asmar al-Asrar*, ed. Ata Hosayn (Hyderabad: Azam Press, 1931).

Gesudaraz, Husayni, *Khatima: Tarjuma adab al muridin*, Urdu trans. Sayyid Yasin Ali Nizami (Delhi: Adabi Dunya, 2007).

Ghazali, Abu Hamid al-, *Ihya ulum al-din*, Eng. trans Duncan MacDonald, 'Emotional Religion in Islam as Affected by Music and Singing', *Journal of the Royal Asiatic Society of Great Britain and Ireland* (Apr. 1901), 195–252, (Oct. 1901), 705–748, (Jan. 1902), 1–28.

Ghazali, Abu Hamid al-, *Mishkat al-Anwar*, Eng. trans. W. H. T. Gairdner (Lahore: Shaykh Muhammad Ashraf, 1952).

Ghazali, Majiduddin al-Tusi al-, *Bawariq ul-Ilma*, trans. James Robson, *Tracts on Listening to Music* (London: Royal Asiatic Society, 1938).

Hujwıri, Uthman al-, *Kashf al-Mahjub*, trans. R. A. Nicholson, *The Kashf al Mahjub: The Oldest Persian Treatise on Sufism* (Leyden: E. J. Brill, 1911).

Husayni, Akbar, *Jawami al-Kalim* (Hyderabad: Intizami Press, 1937–1938).

Ibn, Battuta, *Rehla*, Eng. trans. Mahdi Husain (Baroda: Oriental Institute, 1953).

Isami, Maulana, *Futuh al-Salatin ya shahnama-i Hind*, ed. Mahdi Husain (Educational Press, Agra, 1938).

Jamali, Maulana Fazlullah, *Siyar al-arifin* (Delhi: Rizvi Press, 1893).

Jami, Abd al-Rahman, *Lawaih*, trans. H. Whinfield and Mirza Muhammad Kazvini, *Lawaih: A Treatise on Sufism* (London: Royal Asiatic Society, 1906).

Jami, Abd al-Rahman, *Nafahat al-uns min hazarat al-quds*, ed. Mahdi Tawhidipur (Tehran: Kitabfurushi Mahmudi, 1959).

Juzjani, Minhaj al-Siraj, *Tabaqat-i Nasiri*, Eng. trans. Major H. G. Raverty, 2 vols. (Calcutta, 1881).

Kalabadhi, Abu Bakr al-, *Kitab al-Tarruf li-Madhhab ahl al-Tasawwuf*, Eng. trans. A. J. Arberry, *The Doctrine of the Sufis* (Cambridge: Cambridge University Press, 1935).

Kashani, Hammaduddin, *Ahsan al-Aqwal* (Khuldabad, 1718), Urdu trans. Farheen Banu (Aurangabad: Welldone Graphics, 2013).

Kashani, Rukn al-Din, *Shamail al-atqiya* (Hyderabad: Matbua Ashraf Press, 1929).

Kirmani, Sayyid Muhammad Mubarak al-, 'Mir Khwurd', in Chiranji Lal, ed., *Siyar al-awliya* (Delhi: Matba-i Muhibb-i Hind, 1885).

Mandavi, Muhammad Ghaus Shattari, *Gulzar i-Abrar*, trans. Fazl Ahmad Jewari, *Adhkar-i abrar* (Agra: Matba-i Mufid-i Amm, 1908).

Maneri, Sharaf al-din Ahmad Yahya, *Maktubat-i Sadi*, Eng. trans. Paul Jackson, *The Hundred Letters* (New York: Newman Press, 1980).

Nizami, K. A., *Tarikh-i Mashaikh-i Chisht* (Delhi, 1953).

Qalandar, Hamid, *Khair-al-Majalis, Conversations of Shaikh Nasiruddin Chiraghh-i-Dihli*, ed. K. A. Nizami (Aligarh: Aligarh Muslim University, 1959).

Qushayri, Abul Qasim al-, *Al Risala al qushayriyya fi ilm al-tasawwuf*, Eng. trans. Alexander Knysh, *Al Qushayri's Epistle on Sufism* (Reading: Garnet Publishing Limited, 2007).

Samani, Ali, *Siyar-i Muhammadi*, ed. and trans. S. S. N. Ahmad Qadiri (Hyderabad: Matbuah Ijaz Printing Press, 1969).

Sarraj, Abu Nasr al-, *Kitab al Luma fi'l Tasawwuf*, ed. R. A. Nicholson (Leyden: E. J. Brill, 1914).

Sarwar, Ghulam, *Khazinat al-Asfiya* (Lucknow: Nawal Kishore, 1914).

Sijzi, Amir Hasan, *Fawaid al-fuad*, ed. Latif Malik (Lahore: Malik Siraj al-din and Sons Publishers, 1966), Eng. trans. Bruce Lawrence, Nizam ad-din Awliya. Morals for the Heart: Conversations of Shaykh Nizam ad-din Awliya recorded by Amir Hasan Sijzi (New York: Paulist Press, 1992).

Suhrawardi, Abu al-Najib al-, *Kitab Adab al-Muridin*, Eng. trans. Menahem Milson, *A Sufi Rule for Novices: Kitab Adab al-Muridin* (Cambridge: Harvard University Press, 1975).

Suhrawardi, Shihabuddin, *Awarif ul Maarif*, Urdu trans. Shams Barelwi (Lahore: Progressive Books, 1998), Eng. trans. Wilberforce Clarke, The Awarif ul Maarif (Delhi: Taj Company, 1984).

Yamani, Nizam Gharib, *Lataif-i Ashrafi* (Delhi: Nusrat al Matabi, 1878).

Works in European Languages

Abbas, Shemeem Burney, *The Female Voice in Sufi Ritual: Devotional Practices of Pakistan and India* (Austin: University of Texas Press, 2002).

Ahmad, Aziz, *An Intellectual History of Islam in India* (Edinburgh: Edinburgh University Press, 1969).

Ahmad, Aziz, *Studies in Islamic Culture in the Indian Environment* (Oxford: Clarendon Press, 1964).

Ajwani, L. H., *History of Sindhi Literature* (New Delhi: Sahitya Akademi, 1977).

Akhtar, Mohd. Saleem, 'A Critical Appraisal of the Sufi Hagiographical Corpus of Medieval India', *Islamic Culture*, 52 (1978), 139–150.

Anand, B. S., *Baba Farid* (New Delhi: Sahitya Akademi, 1975).

Ansari, Z., *Life, Times and Works of Amir Khusrau Dehlavi, Seventh Centenary* (New Delhi: National Amir Khusrau Society, 1976).

Aquil, Raziuddin, 'Chishti Sufi Order in the Indian Subcontinent and Beyond', *Studies in History* 21/1 (2005), 99–111.

Aquil, Raziuddin, 'Hazrat-i-Dehli: The Making of the Chishti Sufi Centre and the Stronghold of Islam', *South Asia Research*, 28/1 (2008), 23–48.

Arberry, A. H., *Sufism: An Account of the Mystics of Islam* (London: George Allen and Unwin, 1956).

Ardalan, Nader and Bakhtiar, Laleh, *The Sense of Unity: The Sufi Tradition in Persian Architecture* (Chicago: Chicago University Press, 1973).

Arnold, Thomas, *The Caliphate* (London: Oxford University Press, 1965).

Arnold, Thomas, *The Preaching of Islam: A History of the Propagation of the Muslim Faith* (London: Constable, 1913).

Asani, Ali S., 'Sufi Poetry in the Folk Tradition of Indo-Pakistan', *Religion and Literature* 20/1 (1988), 15–28.

Bahadur, Krishna, *Sufi Mysticism* (New Delhi: Ess Ess Publications, 1999).

Bakhtiar, Laleh, Sufi *Expression of the Mystic Quest* (London: Thames and Hudson, 1976).

Baksh, Khuda, *Essays: Indian and Islamic* (London: Probsthain and Co., 1912)

Banerji, S. K., 'Shaikh Salim Chishti, the Shaikh-ul-Islam of Fathpur Sikri', in N. K. Siddhanta et al., eds., *Bharata-Kaumudi. Studies in Indology in Honour of Dr. Radha Kumud Mookerji*, Part 1 (Allahabad: The Indian Press Ltd., 1945), 69–76.

Begg, W. D., *The Big Five of India in Sufism* (Ajmer: W. D. Begg, 1972).

Begg, W. D., *The Holy Biography of Hazrat Khwaja Muinuddin Chishti* (Ajmer: W. D. Begg, 1960).

Bhatnagar, R. S., *Dimensions of Classical Sufi Thought* (Delhi: Motilal Banarsidass, 1984).

Bihari, Bankey, Sufis, *Mystics and Yogis of India* (Bombay: Bharatiya Vidya Bhavan, 1971).

Bowering, Gerhard, 'The Light Verse: Quranic Text and Sufi Interpretation', *Oriens*, 36 (2001), 113–144.

Chaghatai, Abdullah, *Pakpattan and Baba Farid* (Lahore: Kitab Khana Nauras, 1968).

Chand, Tara, *Influence of Islam on Indian Culture* (Allahabad: The Indian Press, 1946).

Chopra, R. M., *Great Sufi Poets of the Punjab* (Calcutta: Iran Society, 1999).

Choudhury, M. L. Roy, 'Music in Islam', *Journal of Royal Asiatic Society: Letters*, 23/2 (1957), 43–102.

Crooke, W., *An Introduction to Popular Religion and Folklore of Northern India*, 2 vols (Delhi: Munshiram Manoharlal, 1968).

Currie, P. M., *The Shrine and Cult of Mu'in al-din Chishti of Ajmer* (New Delhi: Oxford University Press, 1989).

Dehlvi, Saadia, *Sufism: The Heart of Islam* (New Delhi: Harper Collins, 2009).

Delvoye, F., 'Nalini 'Indo-Persian Literature on Art Music: Some Historical and Technical Aspects', in F. N. Delvoye, ed., *Confluence of Cultures: French Contributions to Indo-Persian Studies* (New Delhi: Manohar, 1994), 93–130.

Desai, Ziyauddin, *Mosques in India* (New Delhi: Ministry of Information and Broadcasting, Government of India, 1971).

de Tassy, Garcin, *Muslim Festivals in India and Other Essays* (New Delhi: Oxford University Press, 1995)

Dey, Amit, 'Mystical and Eclectic Traditions as Reflected in Persian Sources of Medieval India', in Chhanda Chatterjee, ed., *Literature as History: From Early to Contemporary Times* (New Delhi: Primus Books, 2014), 27–48.

Dey, Amit, 'Muslim Mystics of South Asia in Historical Perspective', *Indo Iranica*, 69/1–4 (2016), 113–136.

Dey, Amit, 'Role of Sufi Silsilahs in South Asian Society', *Journal of Islamic History and Culture of India*, 4 (2015), 1–19.

Dey, Amit, 'Sufis and Sufi Silsilahs in South Asia', *The Calcutta Historical Journal New Series* 31/1 (2015), 45–65.

Dey, Amit, *Sufism in India* (Kolkata: Ratna Prakashan, 1996).

Dey, Amit, 'Sufism and Society in Medieval India', in Suparna Gooptu, ed., *Themes and Individuals in History* (Kolkata: K. P. Bagchi & Co., 2019), 3–32.

Digby, Simon, 'Early Pilgrimages to the Graves of Muin ad-din Sijzi and Other Indian Chishti Shaykhs', in M. Israel and N. K. Wagle, eds., *Islamic Society and Culture* (New Delhi: Manohar, 1983), 95–100.

Digby, Simon, 'Qalandars and Related Groups (Elements of Social Deviance in the Religious Life of the Delhi Sultanate of the 13th and 14th Centuries)', in Y. Friedman, ed., *Islam in Asia*, vol. 1 (Jerusalem: The Magnes Press, 1984), 87–98.

Digby, Simon, 'The Sufi Shaykh and the Sultan: A Conflict of Claims to Authority in Medieval Islam', *Iran*, 28 (1990), 71–81.

Digby, Simon, 'Sufis and Travellers in the Early Delhi Sultanate: The Evidence of the Fawaid al Fuad', in Attar Singh, ed., *Socio-cultural Impact of Islam on India* (Chandigarh: University of the Panjab, 1976), 171–179.

Digby, Simon, '*Tabarrukat* and Succession among the Great Chishti Shaykhs', in R. E. Frykenberg, ed., *Delhi through the Ages: Essays in Urban History, Culture and Society* (New Delhi: Oxford University Press, 1986), 63–103.

Eaton, Richard M., 'Approaches to the Study of Conversion to Islam in India', in Richard C. Martin, ed., *Approaches to Islam in Religious Studies* (Tucson: University of Arizona Press, 1985), 106–123.

Eaton, Richard M., 'The Political and Religious Authority of the Shrine of Baba Farid in Pakpattan, Punjab', in Barbara Metcalf, ed., *Moral Conduct and Authority: The Place of Adab in South Asian Islam* (Berkeley: University of California Press, 1984), 333–356.

Eaton, Richard M., 'Sufi Folk Literature and the Expansion of Indian Islam', *History of Religions*, 14/2 (Nov. 1974), 117–127.

Eaton, Richard M., *Sufis of Bijapur: 1300–1700. Social Roles of Sufis in Medieval India* (Princeton: Princeton University Press, 1978).

Embree, Ainslie, ed., *Muslim Civilisation in India* (New York: Columbia University Press, 1964).

Engineer, Asghar Ali, *Sufism and Communal Harmony* (Jaipur: Printwell, 1991).

Entwystle, Alan W., and Mallison, Francoise, eds., *Studies in South Asian Devotional Literature* (New Delhi: Manohar, 1994).

Ernst, Carl W., 'Conversations of Sufi Saints', in Donald S. Lopez Jr., ed., *The Religions of South Asia* (Princeton: Princeton University Press, 1995), 513–517.

Ernst, Carl W., *Eternal Garden: Mysticism, History, and Politics at a South Asian Sufi Center* (New Delhi: Oxford University Press, 2004).

Ernst, Carl W., 'From Hagiography to Martyrology: Conflicting Testimonies to a Martyr of the Delhi Sultanate', *History of Religions*, 24/4 (May 1985), 308–327.

Ernst, Carl W., 'An Indo-Persian Guide to Sufi Shrine Pilgrimage', in Grace Martin Smith and Carl W. Ernst, eds., *Manifestations of Sainthood in Islam* (Istanbul: The Isis Press, 1994), 43–68.

Ernst, Carl W., 'Lives of Sufi Saints', in Donald S. Lopez Jr., ed., *The Religions of South Asia* (Princeton: Princeton University Press, 1995), 495–506.

Ernst, Carl W., *Ruzbihan Baqli: Mystical Experience and the Rhetoric of Sainthood in Persian Sufism* (London: Curzon Press, 1996).

Ernst, Carl W., *The Shambhala Guide to Sufism* (Boston: Shambhala, 1997).

Ernst, Carl W., and Lawrence, Bruce B., *Sufi Martyrs of Love: The Chishti Order in South Asia and Beyond* (London: Palgrave Macmillan, 2002).

Farmer, Henry George, 'The Religious Music of Islam', *The Journal of the Royal Asiatic Society of Great Britain and Ireland*, 1/2 (Apr. 1952), 60–65.

Faruqi, Nisar Ahmed, 'Ameer Khusro in the Presence of His Mentor Hazrat Nizamuddin Aulia', in Syeda Saiyidain Hameed, ed., *Contemporary Relevance of Sufism* (New Delhi: Indian Council for Cultural Relations, 1993), 59–81.

Foster, W. ed., *The Embassy of Sir Thomas Roe to India* (London: Hakluyt Society, 1965).

Friedmann, Yohanan, *Islam in Asia. Vol. 1, South Asia* (Boulder: Westview Press, 1984).

Frishkopf, Michael, 'Authorship in Sufi Poetry', *Alif: Journal of Comparative Poetics* 23 (2003), 78–108.

Frykenberg, R. E., ed., *Delhi through the Ages: Essays in Urban History, Culture and Society* (New Delhi: Oxford University Press, 1986).

Geyoushi, M. al-, 'Al-Tirmidhi's Theory of Saints and Sainthood', *Islamic Quarterly*, 15/1 (1971), 23–36.

Ghani, Kashshaf, 'The Mughals and Sufism', in Lloyd Ridgeon, ed., *Routledge Handbook on Sufism* (London: Routledge, 2020), 387–398.

Ghani, Kashshaf, 'In Quest for the Unbound: Sufi Ritual as Sacred and Secular', in Kurian Kachappilly, ed., *Mystic Musings in Religions* (New Delhi: Christian World Imprints, 2013), 153–170.

Ghani, Kashshaf, 'Seeking a Sufi Heritage in the Deccan: Shrines, *Sama* and Succession', in Anjana Sharma, ed., *Records, Recoveries, Remnants and Inter-Asian Interconnections: Decoding Cultural Heritage* (Singapore: ISEAS Publications, 2018), 222–238.

Ghani, Kashshaf, 'Sound of Sama: The Use of Poetical Imagery in South Asian Sufi Music', *Comparative Islamic Studies*, 5/2 (2009), 273–296.

Ghani, Kashshaf, 'Succeeding the Master: Locating Chishtia Sufis in the Political and Social Environs of Peninsular India', in N. Chandramouli, ed., *Religion and Society in Peninsular India (6th–16th Centuries CE)* (New Delhi: Aryan Books International, 2015), 216–230.

Gibb, H. A. R. *Studies on the Civilisation of Islam* (Boston: Beacon Press, 1962).

Gilmartin, David, 'Shrines, Succession and Sources of Moral Authority in the Punjab', in Akbar S. Ahmed, ed., *Pakistan: The Social Sciences' Perspective* (Karachi: Oxford University Press, 1990), 146–164.

Gilmartin, D., and Lawrence, B. eds., *Beyond Turk and Hindu: Rethinking Religious Identities in Islamic South Asia* (Gainesville: University Press of Florida, 2000).

Gol Muhammadi, Firuzeh, *The Blood Bathed Pigeons of the Harem* (Tehran: Ministry of Culture and Islamic Guidance, 1988).

Goldziher, I. *Muslim Studies*, 2 vols, ed. S. M. Stern (London: George Allen & Unwin, 1967–1971).

Goulding, H. R. *Old Lahore* (Lahore: Universal Books, 1925).

Green, Nile, 'Emerging Approaches to the Sufi Traditions of South Asia: Between Texts, Territories and the Transcendent', *South Asia Research*, 24/2 (2004), 123–148.

Gribetz, Arthur, 'The Sama Controversy: Sufi vs. Legalist', *Studia Islamica*, 74 (1991), 43–62.

Gulraj, J. P., *Sind and its Sufis* (Lahore: Sang-e-Meel Publications, 1979).

Habib, *Hazrat Nizam al-din Awliya* (Lahore: Progressive Books, 1974).

Habib, *Shaikh Nasiruddin Chiragh of Delhi* (Aligarh: Aligarh Muslim University, 1950).

Habib, Muhammad, *Hazrat Amir Khusrau of Dehli* (Bombay: Taraporevala Sons & Co., 1937).

Habib, Muhammad, and Nizami, K. A., *A Comprehensive History of India* (New Delhi: People's Publishing House, 1970).

Habibullah, A. B. M., *The Foundation of Muslim Rule in India* (Lahore: Muhammad Asraf Bookseller and Publisher, 1945).

Halim, A., 'Mystics and Mystical Movements of the Saiyyad-Lodi Period: 1414 A.D. to 1526 A.D', *Journal of the Asiatic Society of Pakistan*, 8 (1963), 71–108.

Haq, Moinul, 'Rise and Expansion of the Chishtis in the Subcontinent', *Journal of Pakistan Historical Society*, 21 (1974), 157–181; 23 (1974), 207–248.

Haq, Moinul, 'Sufi Shaykhs and Sufi Poets in the 17th, 18th, and 19th Centuries', *Journal of the Pakistan Historical Society*, 25/2 (1977), 77–124.

Hardy, Peter, *Historians of India: Studies in Indo-Muslim Historical Writing* (London: Luzac & Company Ltd., 1960).

Hassett, Philip, 'Open *Sama*: Public and Popular *Qawwali* at Yusufain *Dargah*', *The Bulletin of the Henry Martin Institute of Islamic Studies, Hyderabad*, 14/ 3–4 (1995), 29–63.

Hodgson, Marshall, *Venture of Islam* (Chicago: University of Chicago Press, 1974).

Hoffman, Valerie J., 'Annihilation in the Messenger of God: The Development of a Sufi Practice', *International Journal of Middle East Studies*, 31/3 (Aug. 1999), 351–369.

Hoffman, Valerie J., 'Eating and Fasting for God in Sufi Tradition', *Journal of the American Academy of Religion*, 63/3 (1995), 465–484.

Huda, Qamar ul, 'Memory, Performance, and Poetic Peacemaking in *Qawwali*', *Muslim World* 97 (Oct. 2007), 678–700.

Huda, Qamar ul, *Striving for Divine Union: Spiritual Exercises for Suhrawardi Sufis* (London: RoutledgeCurzon, 2003).

Husain, Mahdi, *Tughluq Dynasty* (Calcutta: Thacker Spink, 1963).

Husain, Yusuf, *Glimpses of Medieval Indian Culture* (London: Asia Publishing House, 1959).

Hussaini, Khusro, 'Bund Sama (or Closed Audition)', *Islamic Culture*, 44 (Jul. 1970), 177–185.

Hussaini, Khusro, *The Life, Works and Teachings of Khwajah Bandahnawaz Gisudiraz* (Gulbarga: Sayyid Muhammad Gisudiraz Research Academy, 1986).

Hussaini, Khusro, *Sayyid Muhammad al-Husayni-i Gisudiraz (721/1321-825/ 1422): On Sufism* (Delhi: Idarah-i Adabiyat-i Delli, 1983).

Iraqi, Shahabuddin, *Medieval India 2: Essays In Medieval Indian History And Culture* (New Delhi: Manohar, 2008).

Islam, Riazul, 'A Comparative Study of the Treatment of *Futuh* in the Principal Chishti Records', *Journal of the Pakistan Historical Society*, 40 (1992), 91–96.

Islam, Riazul, 'Ideas on *Kasb* in South Asian Sufism', *Indian Historical Review*, 17 (1991), 90–121.

Islam, Riazul, 'A Note on Zanbil: The Practice of Begging among the Sufis in South Asia (Mainly 14th Century)', *Journal of the Pakistan Historical Society*, 44/1 (1996), 5–11.

Islam, Riazul, 'South Asian Sufis and their Social Linkage (Mainly 14th Century)', in S. A. I. Tirmizi, ed., *Cultural Interaction in South Asia* (New Delhi: Hamdard Institute of Historical Research, 1993), 90–99.

Islam, Riazul, 'Sufism and Economy: A Study in Interrelationship (A Study of the *Futuh* System in South Asia Mainly during the Fourteenth Century)', *Indian Historical Review*, 18 (1992), 31–58.

Islam, Riazul, *Sufism in South Asia: Impact on Fourteenth Century Muslim Society* (Oxford: Oxford University Press, 2002).

Israel, M., and Wagle, N. K., eds, *Islamic Society and Culture: Essays in the Honour of Professor Aziz Ahmad* (New Delhi: Manohar, 1983).

Jackson, Paul, 'A History of the Chishti Shaikhs', in Christian W. Troll, ed., *Islam in India: Studies and Commentaries*, Vol. 2, *Religion and Religious Education* (New Delhi: Vikas Publishing House Pvt. Ltd., 1985), 250–260.

Jackson, Paul, 'Khair Al-Majalis: An Examination', in Christian W. Troll, ed., *Islam in India: Studies and Commentaries*, Vol. 2, *Religion and Religious Education* (New Delhi: Vikas Publishing House Pvt. Ltd., 1985), 34–57.

Jackson, Paul, *The Way of a Sufi: Sharafuddin Maneri* (Delhi: Idarah-I Adabiyat-i Delli, 1987).

Knysh, Alexander, *Islamic Mysticism: A Short History* (Leiden: E. J. Brill, 2000).

Kugle, Scott, '*Qawwali* between Written Poem and Sung Lyric, Or … How a *Ghazal* Lives', *Muslim World*, 97 (Oct. 2007), 571–610.

Lal, K. S., *Growth of Muslim Population in Medieval India (A.D. 1000–1800)* (Delhi: Research Publications, 1973).

Lane-Poole, Stanley, *Medieval India under Mohammedan Rule (A.D. 712–1764)* (London: T. F. Unwin, 1926).

Latif, Abdul, *Muslim Mystic Movement in Bengal, 1301–1550* (Calcutta: K. P. Bagchi, 1993).

Lawrence, B., 'Afzal al-fawaid—A Reassessment', in Z. Ansari, ed., *Life, Times and Works of Amir Khusrau Dehlawi* (New Delhi: National Amir Khusrau Society, 1976), 119–131.

Lawrence, B., 'The Chishtiya of Sultanate India: A Case Study of Biographical Complexities in South Asian Islam', in Michael A. Williams, ed., *Charisma and Sacred Biography* (Chico: Scholars Press, 1981), 47–67.

Lawrence, B., 'The Diffusion of Hindu/Muslim Boundaries in South Asia: Contrasting Evidence from the Literature and the Tomb Cults of Selected Indo-Muslim Sayings', in Peter Gaeffke and David A. Utz, eds., *Identity and Division in Cults and Sects in South Asia*, *Proceedings of the South Asia Seminar* (Philadelphia: University of Pennsylvania, 1984), 125–132.

Lawrence, B., 'The Early Chishti Approach to Sama', in M. Israel and N. K. Wagle, eds., *Islamic Society and Culture* (New Delhi: Manohar, 1983), 69–94.

Lawrence, B., 'An Indo-Persian Account of the Formation and Organization of the Early Persian Sufi Orders', in Leonard Lewisohn, ed., *Classical Persian Sufism: from its Origins to Rumi* (London: Khaniqahi Nimatullahi, 1994), 19–32.

Lawrence, B., *Notes from a Distant Flute: The Extant Literature of Pre-Mughal Indian Sufism* (Tehran: Imperial Iranian Academy of Philosophy, 1978).

Lawrence, B., 'Thematic Antecedents for the Urdu Ghazal in the Sufi Poetry of the Sultanate Period', in Muhammad Umar Memon, ed., *Studies in the Urdu Ghazal and Prose Fiction* (Madison: University of Wisconsin, 1979), 61–100.

Levtzion, Nehemia, ed., *Conversion to Islam* (New York: Holmes & Mier Publishers, 1979).

Lewis, Jerome, 'Music and Rituals', *Anthropology Today*, 15/1 (Feb. 1999), 20–21.

Lewisohn, Leonard, 'The Sacred Music of Islam: Sama' in the Persian Islam Tradition', *British Journal of Ethnomusicology*, 6 (1997), 1–33.

Lopez, Donald S. Jr. ed., *The Religions of South Asia* (Princeton: Princeton University Press, 1995).

Majumdar, R. C., ed., *The Delhi Sultanate* (Bombay: Bharatiya Vidya Bhavan, 1960).

Malamud, M., 'Sufism in Twelfth-Century Baghdad: The Sufi Practices and Ribat of Abu Najib al-Suhrawardi', *Bulletin of the Henry Martin Institute of Islamic Studies Hyderabad*, 13/1–2 (1994), 6–18.

Martin, Richard C., 'Understanding the Quran in Text and Context', *History of Religions*, 21/4 (May 1982), 361–384.

Masoodul, Hasan, *Data Ganj Bakhsh* (Lahore: Ferozsons, 1972).

Matthews, D. J. and Shackle, C., *An Anthology of Classical Urdu Love Lyrics, Text and Translations* (London: Oxford University Press, 1972).

Mayne, Peter, *Saints of Sind* (London: Murray, 1956).

McLeod, W. H., *Early Sikh Tradition: A Study of the Janam-Sakhis* (New York: Oxford University Press, 1980).

Mirza, Wahid, *Life and Works of Amir Khusrau* (Calcutta: Baptist Mission Press, 1935).

Mujeeb, Muhammad, *The Indian Muslims* (London: Allen & Unwin, 1967).

Nabi, Mohammad Noor, *Development of Muslim Religious Thought in India from 1200 A.D. to 1450 A.D.* (Aligarh: Aligarh Muslim University Press, 1962).

Netton, Ian Richard, *Sufi Ritual: The Parallel Universe* (Richmond: Curzon, 2000).

Newell, James R. 'Unseen Power: Aesthetic Dimensions of Symbolic Healing in Qawwali', *Muslim World*, 97 (Oct. 2007), 640–656.

Nicholson, R. A., *Studies in Islamic Mysticism* (Cambridge: Cambridge University Press, 1967).

Nizami, K. A., 'Durrar-i-Nizami: A Unique but less-known Malfuz of Shaikh Nizam ud-din Auliya', in Hilal Ahmad Zubairi, ed., *Dr. Ishtiaq Husain Qureshi Memorial Volume II* (Karachi: Dr. Ishtiaq Husain Qureshi Academy, 1994), 231–248.

Nizami, K. A., 'Early Indo-Muslim Mystics and their Attitude towards the State', *Islamic Culture*, 22 (1948), 387–398.

Nizami, K. A., 'Historical Significance of the Malfuz Literature of Medieval India', in K. A. Nizami, ed., *On History and Historians of Medieval India* (New Delhi: Munshiram Manoharlal Publishers, 1982), 163–197.

Nizami, K. A., *On History and Historians of Medieval India* (New Delhi: Munshiram Manoharlal Publishers Pvt. Ltd., 1982).

Nizami, K. A., *The Life and Times of Shaikh Farid-u'd-din Ganj-i-Shakar* (Delhi: Idarah-i Adabiyat-i Delli, 1955).

Nizami, K. A., *The Life and Times of Shaikh Nasir-u'd-din Chiraghh-i-Dehli* (Delhi: Idarah-i Adabiyat-i Delli, 1991).

Nizami, K. A., *The Life and Times of Shaikh Nizamuddin Auliya* (New Delhi: Oxford University Press, 2007 reprint).

Nizami, K. A., 'Some Aspects of Khanqah Life in Medieval India', *Studia Islamica*, 8 (1957), 51–69.

Nizami, K. A., *Some Aspects of Religion and Politics in India during the 13th Century* (Delhi: Idarah-i Adabiyat-i Delli, 1961).

Nizami, K. A., *Studies in Medieval Indian History and Culture* (Allahabad: Kitab Mahal, 1966).

Nizami, K. A., 'Sufis and Natha Yogis in Mediaeval Northern India (XII to XVI Centuries)', *Journal of the Oriental Society of Australia*, 7/1–2 (1970), 119–133.

Nizami, K. A., ed., *Politics and Society in India During the Early Medieval Period: Collected Works of Professor Muhammad Habib* (New Delhi: People's Publishing House, 1974).

Oman, J. C., *The Mystics, Ascetics and Saints of India* (London: T. F. Unwin, 1905).

Qureshi, Regula Burckhardt, 'Exploring Time Cross-Culturally: Ideology and Performance of Time in the Qawwali', *The Journal of Musicology*, 12/4 (Autumn 1994), 491–528.

Qureshi, Regula Burckhardt, 'His Master's Voice? Exploring Qawwali and 'Gramophone Culture' in South Asia', *Popular Music*, 18/1 (Jan. 1999), 63–98.

Qureshi, Regula Burckhardt, 'Indo-Islam Religious Music, an Overview', *Islam Music* 3/2 (1972), 15–22.

Qureshi, Regula Burckhardt, 'Islamic Music in an Indian Environment: The Shi'a Majlis', *Ethnomusicology*, 25/1 (Jan. 1981), 41–71.

Qureshi, Regula Burckhardt, 'Musical Gesture and Extra-Musical Meaning: Words and Music in the Urdu Ghazal', *Journal of the American Musicological Society*, 43/3 (Autumn 1990), 457–497.

Qureshi, Regula Burckhardt, 'Sama in the Royal Court of Saints: The Chishtiyya of South Asia', in Grace Martin Smith and Carl W. Ernst, eds., *Manifestations of Sainthood in Islam* (Istanbul: The Isis Press, 1994), 111–127.

Qureshi, Regula Burckhardt, *Sufi Music of India and Pakistan: Sound, Context and Meaning of Qawwali* (Cambridge: Cambridge University Press, 1986).

Rahim, Abdal, 'Two Saints of Bengal—Shaikh Jalal ad-din Tabrezi and Shah Jalal', *Journal of the Pakistan Historical Society*, 7 (1960), 206–226.

Ramakrishna, Lajwanti, *Punjabi Sufi Poets: AD 1460–1900* (New Delhi: Ashajanak Publications, 1973).

Richards, J. F. *Kingship and Authority in South Asia* (Madison: University of Wisconsin, 1978).

Rizvi, S. A. A., *A History of Sufism in India*, vols. 1 & 2 (New Delhi: Munshiram Manoharlal Publishers Pvt. Ltd., 1978).

Rosehnal, Robert, 'A "Proving Ground" for Spiritual Mastery: The Chishti Sabiri Musical Assembly', *Muslim World*, 97 (Oct. 2007), 657–677.

Salim, Muhammad, *The Holy Saint of Ajmer* (Bombay, 1949).

Salim, Mohammad, 'Jama`at-Khana of Shaikh Nizamuddin Auliya of Delhi', *Proceedings of the Pakistan Historical Conference*, 3 (1953), 183–189.

Schimmel, A., *Islam in the Indian Subcontinent* (Leiden: E. J. Brill, 1980).

Schimmel, A., 'Islamic Literatures of India', in J. Gonda, ed., *A History of Indian Literature*, vol. 7 (Wiesbaden: Otto Harrassowitz, 1973), 1–60.

Schimmel, A., *Mystical Dimensions of Islam* (Chapell Hill: University of North Carolina Press, 1975).

Schimmel, A., *As Through a Veil: Mystical Poetry in Islam* (New York: Columbia University Press, 1982).

Schimmel, A., and Awde, N., eds., *Treasury of Indian Love* (New York: Hippocrene Books, 1999).

Schwerin, Kerrin Graefin, 'Saint Worship in Indian Islam: The Legend of the Martyr Salar Masud Ghazi', in Imtiaz Ahmad, ed., *Ritual and Religion among Muslims in India* (New Delhi: Manohar, 1984), 143–161.

Sharab, A. H., *The Life and Teachings of Khawaja Moinud-din Hasan Chishti* (Ajmer: Khawaja Publications, 1959).

Sherwani, H. K., *The Bahmanis of Deccan: An Objective Study* (Hyderabad: Saood Manzil Himayatnagar, 1953).

Sherwani, H. K., and Joshi, P. M., eds., *History of Medieval Deccan (1295–1724)*, 2 vols (Hyderabad: Publication Bureau, Govt. of Andhra Pradesh, 1974).

Shiloah, Amnon, 'Music and Religion in Islam', *Acta Musicologica*, 69/fasc. 2 (Jul.–Dec. 1997), 143–155.

Shiloah, Amnon, *Music in the World of Islam: A Socio-Cultural Study* (Detroit: Wayne State University Press, 1995).

Siddiqui, Iqtidar Husain, 'Resurgence of Chishti Silsila in the Sultanate of Delhi during the Lodi Period (A.D. 1451–1526)', in Christian W. Troll, ed., *Islam in India: Studies and Commentaries*, Vol. 2, *Religion and Religious Education* (New Delhi Vikas Publishing House Pvt. Ltd., 1985), 58–72.

Siddiqui, M., ed., *The Life and Teachings of Hazrat Data Ganj Bakhsh* (Lahore: Shahzad Publishers, 1977).

Siddiqui, Suleman, *The Bahamani Sufis* (Delhi: Idarah-i Adabiyat-i Delli, 1989).

Singh, Attar, 'Sheikh Farid and the Punjabi Poetic Tradition', in Gurbachan Singh Talib, ed., *Perspectives on Sheikh Farid* (Patiala: Baba Farid Memorial Society, 1975), 225–233.

Smith, Bardwell, ed., *Religion and Legitimation of Power in South Asia* (Leiden: E. J. Brill, 1978).

Steinfels, Amina, 'His Master's Voice: The Genre of Malfuzat in South Asian Sufism', *History of Religions*, 44 (2004), 56–69.

Steinfels, Amina, *Knowledge Before Action: Islamic Learning and Sufi Practice in the Life of Sayyid Jalal al-din Bukhari Makhdum-i Jahaniyan* (Columbia: University of South Carolina Press, 2012).

Subhan, John, *Sufism: Its Saints and Shrines* (Lucknow: Lucknow Publishing House, 1938).

Suvorova, Anna, *Masnavi: A Study of Urdu Romance* (Karachi: Oxford University Press, 2000).

Talib, Gurbachan Singh, *Baba Sheikh Farid: His Life and Teaching* (Patiala: Punjabi University, 1973).

Talib, Gurbachan Singh, *Perspectives on Sheikh Farid* (Patiala: Baba Farid Memorial Society, 1975).

Tamizi, Mohammad Yahya, *Sufi Movement in Eastern India* (Delhi: Idarah-i Adabiyat-i Delli, 1992).

Taneja, Anup, ed., *Sufi Cults and the Evolution of Medieval Indian Culture* (New Delhi: Indian Council for Historical Research, 2003).

Trimingham, J. S., *The Sufi Orders in Islam* (London: Oxford University Press, 1971).

Troll, C. W., ed. *Islam in India: Studies and Commentaries*, Vol. 2, *Religion and Religious Education* (New Delhi: Vikas Publishing House Pvt Ltd., 1985).

Troll, C. W., ed., *Muslim Shrines in India: Their Character, History and Significance* (New Delhi: Oxford University Press, 1989).

Valiuddin, Mir, *The Quranic Sufism* (Delhi: Motilal Banarasidass, 2002).

Vassie, Roderic, 'Abd al-Rahman Chishti & the Bhagavadgita: Unity of Religion Theory in Practice', in Leonard Lewisohn, ed., *The Legacy of Mediaeval Persian Sufism* (London: Khaniqahi Nimatullahi, 1992), 367–378.

Westrup, J. A., 'Mysticism in Music', *The Musical Times*, 65/979 (Sept. 1924), 804–805.

Zilli, I. A., 'Precepts and Paradox: The Chishti Attitude towards Social Labour', *Proceedings of the Indian History Congress*, 47 (1986), 281–289.

About the Author

KASHSHAF GHANI specializes in pre-modern South Asia covering the period 1000–1800, focusing on the history of Sufism, its practices, interactions, networks, and regional experiences. He is also interested in Indo-Persian histories, interreligious interactions, the history and culture of the Persianate world, and Asian interconnections.

Kashshaf studied History at Presidency College, Calcutta, and at the University of Calcutta, where he completed his PhD. He has held teaching positions at Aliah University, Kolkata, and the University of Calcutta.

He has held research positions as Sir Amir Ali Research Fellow in Islamic History and Culture at the Asiatic Society, Kolkata, Perso-Indica Visiting Fellow at the Sorbonne-Nouvelle, Paris, Visiting Fellow at the Leibniz-Zentrum Moderner Orient, Berlin, and Fellow at the Maulana Abul Kalam Azad Institute of Asian Studies, Kolkata.

In 2018, Kashshaf was the US State Department Academic Visitor at Temple University, and received a further US State Department follow-on grant in 2020. He was carrying out research on religious pluralism in the United States, with a focus on modern-day Sufi networks in the United States.

His publications include *Exploring the Global South: Voices, Ideas, Histories* (2013) and *Imagining Asia(s): Networks, Actors, Sites* (2019), along with several articles and essays. He has delivered lectures throughout India and in Singapore, Europe, and the United States.

Kashshaf teaches History at Nalanda University, India.

Index

Milton Keynes UK
Ingram Content Group UK Ltd.
UKHW020804081223
433944UK00003B/17

9 780192 889225